Mark Twain in the Company of Women

Mark Twain in the Company of Women

Laura E. Skandera-Trombley

University of Pennsylvania Press

Philadelphia

Library of Congress Cataloging-in-Publication Data
Skandera-Trombley, Laura E.
   Mark Twain in the company of women / Laura E. Skandera-Trombley.
      p.   cm.
   Includes bibliographical references and index.
   ISBN 0-8122-3218-6
   1. Twain, Mark, 1835–1910 — Relations with women.   2. Twain, Mark,
1835–1910 — Political and social views.   3. Women and literature —
United States — History — 19th century.   4. Women and literature —
United States — History — 20th century.   5. Feminism and literature —
United States — History.   6. Authors, American — 19th century —
Biography.   7. Women — New York (State) — Elmira — History.
8. Clemens, Olivia Langdon, 1845–1904.   9. Elmira (N.Y.) —
Intellectual life.   10. Men authors — Psychology.   I. Title.
PS1332.S88   1994
818'.409 — dc20
   [B]   94-19712
                                                       CIP

For My Darling Nelson

Contents

Illustrations

Acknowledgments

I would like to express my deep gratitude to Mrs. Irene Finkelstein for her support of higher education and for selecting me as the Lester and Irene Finkelstein Fellow for 1988–89. I want to thank the Center for Mark Twain Studies at Quarry Farm for choosing me as their 1989 Fellow-in-Residence; Gretchen Sharlow, Director of the Center, for her many kindnesses; and the University of Southern California for awarding me the Graduate English Student Scholarship and the Virginia Barbara Middleton Scholarship. In addition, I appreciate the opportunity afforded by the National Endowment for the Humanities to study with Kathryn Kish Sklar and Thomas Dublin in their 1990 summer seminar program on "The History of American Women Through Social Movements." And I thank Potsdam College of the State University of New York, for supporting my work with two Faculty-Undergraduate Research Grants, which provided me with fine research assistants, Deborah O'Connell-Brown and Russell Swanker III, and a 1992 Research and Endeavors Grant.

My deepest thanks go also to Alan Gribben for welcoming me to his field and for his excellent counsel, and to Jay Martin, who provided me with the opportunity to become involved in Mark Twain scholarship, lent support regardless of the country I happened to be living in, and guided me through the maze of doctoral and postdoctoral studies. Not to be forgotten is Michael Kiskis for his willingness to share ideas and for his invaluable sense of humor. I also would like to express my appreciation to the Mark Twain Project at the University of California at Berkeley and to Project Editor Kenneth Sanderson.

The following people provided me with invaluable reference assistance in researching my topic: Sunny Gottberg, Beth Bernstein, Jane Murray, and Shawna Fleming of the Mark Twain Project; Mary Anne Curling of the Stowe-Day Library; Mark Woodhouse of the Center for Mark Twain Studies; and Diana Royce and Suzanne Zack of the Stowe-Day Foundation.

And, finally, I would like to express my heartfelt gratitude to those closest to me: my dear Diane Schwartz for trespassing with me into Twain scholarship; Ernst Endt for his love and Ernst tapes; Elaine Boel for always rescuing me; Linda Carr for cheerfully allowing me to rattle on; the Malibu "Pranksters"; Randoll Huff for his cagey advice; and my students, past and present, for their insights and excitement. Above all, I would like to thank my husband, Nelson Trombley, for his sound advice, and my parents, Mary and John, for their love and support and for their respect for my work.

*   *   *

All Mark Twain's previously unpublished words quoted herein are copyright © 1994 by Edward J. Willi and Manufacturers Hanover Trust Company as Trustees of the Mark Twain Foundation, which reserves all reproduction or dramatization rights in every medium. Quotation is made with the permission of the University of California Press and Robert H. Hirst, General Editor, Mark Twain Project at Berkeley. Each quotation is identified by an asterisk (*).

The previously unpublished writings of Olivia Louise Langdon Clemens, Susan Olivia Clemens, and Jean Clemens are copyright © 1994 by Chemical Bank and Richard A. Watson as trustees of the Mark Twain Foundation.

Jean Clemens's Diaries are reproduced by permission of The Huntington Library, San Marino, California.

Isabel Van Kleek Lyon's daily reminders, notebook, and journal are reproduced by permission of the Isabel Lyon Heirs.

A letter from Mary Ann Lewis to Olivia L. Langdon dated August 23, 1841, and information regarding the Gleason Water Cure are reproduced by permission of the Chemung County Historical Society, Elmira, New York.

A letter from Samuel Langhorne Clemens to Joseph Twichell dated January 1, 1869, is reproduced by permission of the Yale Collection of American Literature, Beinecke Rare Book and Manuscript Library, Yale University.

A letter from Samuel Langhorne Clemens to Elizabeth Jordan dated March 10, 1905, is reproduced by permission of the Elizabeth Jordan Papers, Rare Books and Manuscripts Division, The New York Public Library, Astor, Lenox and Tilden Foundations.

Three letters from *The Love Letters of Mark Twain*, edited by Dixon Wecter (copyright © 1947, 1949 by the Mark Twain Company) are reprinted by permission of HarperCollins Publishers, Inc.

Abbreviations

Many citations refer to previously unpublished archive documents. Below is a comprehensive list of abbreviations used in the text.

CCHS   Chemung County Historical Society. Elmira, New York.

HL   The Huntington Library. San Marino, California.

MHS   Missouri Historical Society. St. Louis, Missouri.

MTM   Mark Twain Memorial. Hartford, Connecticut.

MTP   The Mark Twain Papers. University of California, Berkeley.

SDF   The Stowe-Day Foundation. Hartford, Connecticut.

Preface

I became involved with Mark Twain scholarship entirely by chance. In 1986, while I was in the midst of pursuing my doctorate at the University of Southern California, Dr. Jay Martin asked if I would be interested in investigating a claim made by a retired businessman that he had purchased one hundred original letters written by Mark Twain for the sum of one hundred dollars. Naturally, I was intrigued and agreed to follow up on the lead, yet I remained skeptical. It was some weeks before I could arrange a meeting with this individual. As it turned out, the letters he had purchased proved to be authentic, and the ensuing research and literary detective work were wonderfully exciting. I will not go into the details here, as my story of the search and recovery of the lost "Clara letters" was published in the February 1987 issue of the *Mark Twain Circular* and I was the subject of a featured article entitled "The Lost Legacy of Mark Twain" that appeared in the May 10, 1987, edition of the *Los Angeles Times Magazine* (Swanbrow); suffice it to say that in the end my efforts to protect the letters and to bring them to the attention of Twain scholars proved successful. Five out of the one hundred letters were previously unknown to the Mark Twain Project, and two others had been partially transcribed by them at an earlier date; the Project obtained complete transcriptions of those seven letters and was also allowed to correct prior transcriptions of the other ninety-three. The lucky businessman sold his find in two lots at Christie's for approximately a quarter of a million dollars.

While researching the "Clara letters," I developed an interest in Twain's relationships with the women in his life and how these relationships may have influenced his writing. This was a timely subject, relatively untouched by other scholars working in the field. I then began reading Twain biographies, commencing with Albert Bigelow Paine's three-volume set, to determine how past biographers had dealt with women in their studies of Twain. It quickly became evident that little had been written on the women in Twain's life; moreover, as historian Gerda Lerner points out, women had not received extensive attention by historians or biographers, not because of . . . evil conspiracies of men in general or male [biographers] in particular, but because we have considered [biography] only in male-centered terms. We have missed women and their activities. . . . To rectify this, and to light up areas of historical darkness we must, for a time, focus on a *woman-centered* inquiry. (178)

Since becoming active in Twain scholarship, I have explored the interrelated areas of women in Twain biography and Elmira's cultural environment. For the past few years, I have presented my work at American Literature Association and Modern Language Association conferences. The papers given at these meetings focused on reinterpreting the character of Samuel Langhorne Clemens. In presenting on this topic my goal was twofold: first, to encourage a critical reappraisal of scholarship regarding Twain biography; second, to encourage research in areas of Twain biography traditionally left unexplored.

The central question I posit in my work is that of what happens to Twain biography when viewed through the women in Clemens's life and ordered by the values these women define (Lerner 178). Past criticism by both men and women has wrongly dismissed Twain as being anti-female and has come to portray Twain almost as a caricature of the "man's man," far removed from the realm of women. I find this view fallacious.

Some feminist critics have responded to this conception of Twain by repeatedly attacking and finally dismissing him, yet it is questionable whether critics have been responding to the man or to an invention of past biographers. Thus, central to my work is the challenge of distinguishing the person from the plethora of published opinion. My intention is to dynamite this hollow creation and reveal Twain as he really was, an author so dependent upon female interaction and influence that without it the sublimity of his novels would have been lost.

Mark Twain in the Company of Women

1. Olivia Langdon's miniature, circa 1867–68. (Courtesy of The Mark Twain Project, The Bancroft Library)

Introduction

The miniature. Photographed against a white background, Olivia Louise Langdon is dressed to an austere extreme. No ringlets or frills are present as in the portraits of her friends; she is simply clad in a formal, front-button-down, black silk dress with a high white collar. Devoid of jewelry, she is photographed in profile with her head turned to the right, exposing her left side. Her plain appearance and comfortable attire would have found favor with Victorian dress reform advocates. Her skin is pale, her features regular and even, with a high forehead, Roman nose, and a jutting ear. Her long black hair is parted down the middle, drawn severely back and gathered into a large snood with the bottom just touching her collar. Her expression is serious, yet amiable. She is approximately twenty-two years old.

The miniature is a porcelaintype, possibly done in 1867, by Wm. E. Wilbur & A.P. Hart Photographers, No. 22 Lake St., Elmira, New York. The portrait was originally set in an ornate frame resting in a case of purple velvet given by Olivia to her eighteen-year-old brother, Charles Jervis Langdon, as a remembrance. He carried the portrait on board the ship *Quaker City* on what was advertised as the first Mediterranean luxury cruise with a pilgrimage to the Holy Land included in the fare.

The popular mythos surrounding the miniature follows along these lines: Samuel Langhorne Clemens, after glimpsing Olivia's face, immediately and eternally fell in love with her, laid siege to her parents until they surrendered her, and, after marrying her, lived rapturously ever after. This version has been maintained and fortified for more than eighty years by the couple's relatives and Twain biographers.[1] However, the time has come to examine the circumstances surrounding the miniature and the myth. Time, in fact, plays an important role in this investigation. The *Quaker City* embarked on June 8, 1867, and was at sea five months; it returned to its home port in New York Harbor on November 19. It was on Saturday, September 7, 1867, while anchored in the Bay of Smyrna, that Charles showed the thirty-two-year-old Clemens the portrait of his sister (Ganzel 215).

Clemens spent the period after the cruise traveling between New York and Washington, D.C., working briefly as a private secretary and then as a journalist for assorted newspapers. Clemens and Olivia Langdon met for the first time on December 31, 1867, in New York City, where, accompanied by her father, Jervis Langdon, her mother, Olivia Lewis Langdon, and her brother, Charles, they attended a performance by Charles Dickens, who read excerpts from *David Copperfield* (Baetzhold 5).[2] The day after the reading (not five days later, as Clemens would remember), Clemens visited Olivia at the home of Mr. Thomas S. and Mrs. Anna E. Berry, friends of the Langdon family. A third meeting took place on January 18, 1868. Alice Hooker, daughter of Isabella Beecher Hooker and close friend of Olivia, wrote to her mother in Hartford that "Mr. Clemens called yesterday took dinner with us — and informed me that he was going to Hartford on Monday for a few hours business there" (Jan. 19, 1868, SDF). In addition to Clemens, Alice, and Olivia, Mr. and Mrs. Langdon were also present at the meal. The next meeting between Clemens and Olivia was not until six months later, on August 24, 1868, in Elmira, where he stayed with the Langdon family until September 8. (On September 4, Clemens signed Charles Langdon's autograph book.) They saw each other again at the end of September 1868, and it was during this second visit to Elmira that Clemens's now well-known accident with a carriage occurred. As Olivia explained to Alice, the incident was more dramatic than serious:

> Mr. Clemens spent two days here on his way back to Hartford from St. Louis, he intended only to remain one day, but as he and Charlie started for the Depot, they were thrown out of the back of the waggon (it was a democrat waggon and the seat was not fastened) both striking on their heads. Charlie's head was quite badly cut, Mr. Clemens was stunned — It did not prove to be serious in either case — We all enjoyed Mr. Clemens [sic] stay with us very much indeed. (Sep. 29, 1868, SDF)

Clemens's wooing of Olivia lasted a year and a half, and their marriage took place on February 2, 1870.

Turning back to the beginning, however, we can find Clemens's own account of his reaction upon seeing the miniature. It is decidedly different in tone from the accounts of subsequent chroniclers. Dictating his autobiography almost two years after Olivia's death, Clemens is uncharacteristically reticent about his first glimpse: "I saw her first in the form of an ivory miniature in her brother Charley's stateroom in the steamer *Quaker City* in the Bay of Smyrna, in the summer of 1867, when she was in her twenty-second year" (Feb. 1, 1906, Autobiographical Dictation, No. 64, MTP*).[3]

Obviously, it was the portrait that caught Clemens's eye, but Charles Langdon's upbringing and social status must have served as a strong reinforcement of its subject's charms. And just what did Clemens see when he looked at Olivia's photograph? A woman of spotless reputation, far removed from the dance-hall women Clemens disparaged in essays and letters; a woman simply clad (Clemens had a life-long distaste for women whom he considered overdressed); a woman who possessed considerable intelligence and an independent spirit; and a woman who was the daughter of wealthy, respected, iconoclastic Easterners.[4]

Clemens wanted this way of life as well as this woman who typified it. He was, however, deliberate in his courting. He did not hurl himself at her in the throes of passion; instead, he made cautious overtures that culminated in prolonged negotiations by which he managed to assure her father that he would maintain Olivia's way of life. Coming from a background of financial hardship, a single-parent home (his father died when he was twelve), and a family that had fallen from its former social status (his father, an unsuccessful lawyer, had been reared as a gentleman in Virginia, and family legend held that the Clemenses were related to English aristocracy), Clemens must have found the entire picture, and not just the visual image produced photomechanically by Wm. E. Wilbur & A.P. Hart, extremely appealing.

And just what did Olivia Langdon bring to Samuel Clemens? Everything. In addition to social position and respectability, Olivia was able to bestow a more important personal gift: a stable center. Olivia gave order to the creative chaos of this man of contradictions and expressed as well as repressed fury. Clemens described his relationship with Olivia in a letter to Joseph Twichell written January 1, 1869: "My letters are an ocean of love in a storm — hers an ocean of love in the majestic repose of a great calm. But the waters are the same — just the same, my boy" (*Mark Twain's Letters, 1869*, vol. 3: 1).

When Clemens met Olivia he was a newspaper correspondent with aspirations to become an editor, perhaps ultimately a publisher.[5] After Olivia's death he came full circle and returned to writing letters, editorials, and essays. But what is crucial to note here, and what cannot be refuted, is that it was only while Olivia was alive that Clemens wrote his greatest works, and only while paired with Olivia that Samuel Clemens achieved the fictional mastery of Mark Twain.

Notes

1. Albert Bigelow Paine was the first to present this reverential version, in *Mark Twain: A Biography:*

> He [Clemens] looked at it with long admiration, and spoke of it reverently, for the delicate face seemed to him to be something more than a mere human likeness. . . . [Clemens resolved] that some day he would meet the owner of that lovely face — a purpose for once in accord with that which the fates had arranged for him, in the day when all things were arranged, the day of the first beginning. (Vol. 1: 339)

Samuel Charles Webster, son of Annie Moffett Webster, Samuel Clemens's niece, recalled that "he had . . . fallen in love with a picture of Livy" (Webster 98); and Ida Langdon, Olivia's niece, reported: "Mr. Clemens could not put the little portrait down. His reaction to it has often been described as 'love at first sight.' . . . it is certain that the beauty of the head and face haunted him from the moment that he saw it" (Jerome and Wisbey 51).

2. There is some debate regarding Clemens and Olivia's first meeting. Clemens recalled in an autobiographical dictation four years before his death that their first meeting occurred on December 27 (Feb. 13, 1906, Autobiographical Dictation, No. 64, MTP*); a year later, in another dictation, Clemens stated that he met Olivia the same day they had attended a Dickens reading. The only evening performance Dickens gave was on the 31st. Additional information about the initial and second, subsequent meetings can be found in *Mark Twain's Letters, 1867–1868,* vol. 2: 145–46.

3. In his book *Mr. Clemens and Mark Twain,* Justin Kaplan contends that Clemens was fond of dramatizing incidents like the miniature and later making them into what he terms "turning points." Kaplan claims that it was common for Clemens to connect what was initially an innocuous incident to a subsequent major event in his life. Clemens related the ivory miniature, Kaplan asserts, to a publisher's inviting him two months later to begin *The Innocents Abroad,* thus launching him on his literary career (52–53). Clemens probably did consider the miniature a turning point in his life, and justifiably so, but Kaplan's contention that Clemens viewed the occurrence as the impetus for his first book contract ignores what undoubtedly Clemens always felt to be the most important result of this first sighting — his marriage to Olivia. In Clemens's 1909 essay, "The Turning Point of My Life," which Kaplan draws upon, Clemens says that his desire to travel resulted in the genesis of *The Innocents Abroad;* nowhere in the essay is the miniature mentioned.

4. Concerning Clemens's views on women's dress see *Mark Twain: Early Tales and Sketches (1851–1864),* vol. 1, eds. Edgar Branch and Robert Hirst (Berkeley: University of California Press, 1979): 308–19; Harold Aspiz, "Mark Twain's Jen-

kins," *Mark Twain Journal* 21 (Spring 1983): 7–8; Letter to "Susy" Clemens from Samuel Clemens, Dec. 27, 1893, MTP*; Bernard DeVoto, ed., *Mark Twain in Eruption* (New York: Harper, 1940): 325. On Olivia's plain dress see Mary Lawton, *A Lifetime with Mark Twain* (New York: Haskell House, 1972): 239–40.

5. Hamlin Hill, in *Mark Twain: God's Fool* (New York: Harper and Row, 1973), suggests that "before *Innocents Abroad* [his first travelogue] was published, Twain was a newspaperman, and after *Roughing It* was published, he was on a more 'literary' path" (22–23). Hill attributes this change to Elisha Bliss and the American Publishing Company and calls their influence "tremendous." Hill briefly acknowledges that during this same period Clemens met, wooed, and married Olivia, but he claims that Clemens's "courting" interfered with the writing of the book and that this created a "nightmare" situation. A recent work portraying the Clemenses as a literary pair wherein Olivia functioned as a central, calming partner comes from Jeffrey Steinbrink in *Getting To Be Mark Twain* (Berkeley: University of California Press, 1991).

1. Polishing Off a Genius

> In reviewing the [Brooks/DeVoto] controversy, the person of informed humility will remind himself that what he is reading is the story of how men's [sic] minds have reacted to Mark Twain, his achievements and his limitations, and that it is not really about Mark Twain at all. That is another subject, which will be longer with us, and more absorbing.
>
> — Lewis Leary, *A Casebook on Mark Twain's Wound*

With the sheer mass of criticism published concerning Mark Twain, it appears that writing about Samuel Langhorne Clemens has become a rite of passage for many distinguished scholar-biographers specializing in American literature. Such luminaries as Van Wyck Brooks, Bernard DeVoto, Everett Emerson, and Hamlin Hill have commented on Clemens; Justin Kaplan's *Mr. Clemens and Mark Twain* was awarded the Pulitzer Prize. Although there is a spread of sixty years among these biographical scholars, they share two common denominators: their gender and their critical approach. The field of Twain biography has remained an area of American literature peopled principally by men, and to date two main paths of biographical discourse have emerged (with various offshoots): that of Brooks's division of the self, and, in direct opposition, that of DeVoto's integration of the self.

In what has become an obligatory act, biographers must now choose which side of the Brooks-DeVoto court to play. The Brooks side maintains that Clemens had a "divided self" and that this division became so pronounced that his capacity for fiction writing was irreparably damaged. On the DeVoto side, critics undertook to prove that Clemens's later fiction was intact — and so was his personality. Yet both sides are limited severely by a dearth of discussion concerning the impact female family members and colleagues had on Clemens.

Indeed, Samuel Clemens's biographers have identified a dichotomy in his relationships with women, but they have failed to find the explanation for this dichotomy or to consider the possibility that it may not exist outside of their own constructions. For example, why did Mark Twain, the archetypal "American Adam" (riverboat pilot, Western correspondent, silver prospector, world traveler) ask women such as Mary Fairbanks, Olivia Langdon Clemens, and Isabel Lyon to edit his writing? Was this an aberration or error in judgment—as it has been treated in the past—or a calculated move on his part? While there is a critical consensus that women were a factor in Clemens's life, biographers' interpretations of the role they played run the negative gamut: women were the psychological ruin of Clemens; women were the monetary ruin of Clemens; women had little effect on Clemens; Clemens managed to survive the effect women had on him. Critics from Brooks to Hill have recognized that Clemens was surrounded by women, virtually presenting Clemens in that way—surrounded—as though no productive interaction consequently took place.

But what biographers have not recognized is that Clemens's interactions with women helped define his boundaries. In both the personal and literary realms, he was a man voluntarily controlled and influenced by women. Women shaped his life, edited his books, provided models for his fictional characters, and, through their correspondence, heavily influenced his fiction and literary works.

Another tendency of past scholarship has been to view the women in Clemens's personal life as an undifferentiated whole. An Olivia Langdon Clemens could be substituted for a Mary Fairbanks, a Mary Ann Cord for a Katy Leary, a Susan Crane for a Mary Rogers, and each Clemens daughter for either of the others. Because no individual differentiations are made and thus simplistic conclusions are reached, women are seen either as having a debilitating effect or as being nullities. But in reality each woman played a different and key role in Clemens's personal and artistic life, with Olivia functioning as the central figure. While Clemens and Olivia maintained a relationship based on mutual respect, Clemens nonetheless at times played the dependent child, relying on her for social instruction, criticism, and intense devotion. (It is telling that Olivia's lifelong endearment for Clemens was "Youth.")[1]

An opposite strategy has been used by critics in exploring the interchange between Clemens and women writers of his time. In the rare instance when an article on this topic has appeared, the focus has been on the individual female writer. No comprehensive study of the relationship between Clemens and these writers has been done. Alan Gribben's massive work, *Mark Twain's Library: A Reconstruction* (1980), challenges the long-held misconception of Clemens as unread man. Now Gribben's findings must be extended further, and Clemens must be reinterpreted as knowledgeable not only about male writers but about female writers as well. As Gribben reveals, Clemens's library was filled with texts by women writers. Clemens used these works for their factual content and background information in his travelogues and historical novels; he also utilized female writers' fiction, alluding to their works, paraphrasing them, or employing them as inspiration for his own fiction.

Clemens also maintained a voluminous correspondence with more than one hundred female writers from five different countries. Along with such well-known American women novelists as Elizabeth Akers Allen, Sarah K. Bolton, Virginia F. Boyle, Rose Terry Cooke, Mary Mapes Dodge, Mary E. Wilkins Freeman, and Ellen Louise Moulton, Clemens also corresponded with feminists Anna Dickinson and Alexandra Gripenberg, social reformers Diana Belais and Lady Jane Grey Swisshelm, educators Jane Louise Brownell and Mary A. Jordan, and journalists Jennie O. Starkey and Ada Patterson. It is significant that Clemens did more than simply encourage women writers — he also published them. Clemens's Charles L. Webster Publishing Company printed Civil War memoirs by Elizabeth Bacon Custer, Madeleine Vinton Dahlgren, and Almira Russell Hancock; novels by Martha Jane Crim, Mary Russell Mitford, and Annie E. Holdsworth; and biographies by Annie E. Ireland and Mary Young Ridenbaugh. Of the nearly sixty authors published by the Webster Company, twelve writers, with a total of sixteen titles, were women.[2] (Clemens's relationships with these women writers, via correspondence and publishing, is itself a subject for further critical attention.)

Departing from the Brooksian-based critical position of dual selves, I contend that Clemens was indeed an integrated personality, and that the dichotomous type of biography that has been employed to date has failed to recognize the major wellspring of Clemens's inspiration. I would argue that it is due to the exclusionary methodology used to examine Clemens's final years that critics such as DeVoto and Hill have been unable to account satisfactorily for the waning of Clemens's fiction writing and the rise of his pronounced cynicism. To examine this problem, and to give a more credible reading of Clemens's final years, I propose an alternative to the critical paths established by previous biographers. This text will have as its focus Clemens's female community, as represented by his immediate family members: his wife Olivia and their three daughters Susy, Clara, and Jean.

Clemens was clearly interested in the events shaping the latter half of the nineteenth century, and upon joining the Langdon family he was exposed to and eventually evolved into a defender of reformist, liberal, feminist interests. Clemens's wife and in-laws were well-educated, autonomous, iconoclastic individuals who interacted with Clemens intellectually, creatively, and philosophically. Centering my attention on the family enabled me to investigate several crucial areas: the nature of Clemens's family's participation in his writing process, the degree to which their experiences as females during the mid- and late nineteenth century affected his writing, and the extent to which the loss of his family may have impeded and ultimately ended Clemens's ability to write lengthy narratives. In short, Clemens's capacity to produce extended fictions had almost as much to do with the environment shaped by his wife and his daughters as with his abilities as a writer.

Considerable space will be devoted here to portraying Olivia Langdon Clemens as an individual possessing a distinct personality and history apart from her famous husband's, and to exploring the gender politics of her upbringing and social milieu. Instead of considering only the influence Clemens had on Olivia, I ask exactly the reverse: How did Olivia influence Clemens? When Olivia consented to marry Clemens, what beliefs and political views did she bring with her? Who and what were Olivia's friends and influences, and how might they have helped determine the kind of relationship she would have with Clemens?

It can no longer be taken as a given that Olivia's intellect was the product of a sheltered upbringing and conventional education. Moreover, Olivia's influence worked on Clemens's imagination in ways not previously detailed by earlier scholars. In Olivia's immediate family and in the general ambiance of abolitionist and pro-women's-rights thinking that infused her upbringing and her Elmira surroundings, Clemens encountered an atmosphere in which his highly traditional attitude toward women gradually but definitively changed. Clemens came to embrace many of the Langdons' beliefs and periodically returned to Olivia's birthplace, Elmira, over the course of more than thirty years. After his marriage, Clemens's views on such issues as women's rights underwent distinct revision; an important issue to be explored here is whether Olivia provided the motivation behind this change.

The valuable insights Clemens gained from his female community were reinforced by his writing techniques and surfaced in his realist novels. Women in effect functioned collectively as Clemens's personal and creative touchstone. Clemens was surely "one of the boys," but whereas he could abandon the men in his life, he never could do the same to the women. Instead of envisioning Clemens as continually turning away from a harmful

"Other," it would be more accurate to view him as allying himself with the female. Indeed, Clemens particularly viewed himself and his art as inseparable from his life with Olivia.

Shortly after Clemens's death, two works on Twain were published: William Dean Howells's memoir, *My Mark Twain* (1910), and Albert Bigelow Paine's *Mark Twain: A Biography* (1912). Both authors proclaimed that Clemens embodied his persona, Mark Twain, inextricably interweaving fact and fiction to form a beloved character whom Howells called the "Lincoln of our Literature" (101). This "integrated" image would be carefully preserved by Clemens's daughter Clara up to her death in 1962.

The age of critical Twain biography began in 1920 with Brooks's *The Ordeal of Mark Twain*. His work marked the beginning of what has become a continuing dispute. Writing in reaction to Paine's and Howells's sympathetic biographies of Clemens, Brooks claimed that, instead of rustic, charming storyteller, a more accurate description of Clemens would be that of tortured, embittered, artistic failure. To examine the question of Clemens's selfhood, Brooks applied psychoanalytic theory, in what became one of the earliest such investigations of an author (Fraiberg). Brooks asserted that there was a split in Clemens's personality and that the women in Clemens's life were firmly entrenched within the realm of a hostile "Other." Brooks's views regarding Clemens's psychological make-up continue to reverberate in contemporary scholarship (the most recent entry is Guy Cardwell's psychoanalytic biography, *The Man Who Was Mark Twain* [1991]), and the debate continues over the origin of the supposed split and its manifestations.

In what Brooks labels Clemens's "ordeal," Clemens obliterated any possibility of becoming a fully realized writer of fiction upon his marriage to Olivia Langdon: "From the moment of his marriage his artistic integrity ... had ... been irreparably destroyed" (115). Brooks argues that the only time Clemens functioned at the height of his creative powers was when he composed *Life on the Mississippi*. Clemens, Brooks claims, succeeded because the subject matter dealt with the happiest time of Clemens's life, the four years he spent piloting on the Mississippi. (An obvious inconsistency Brooks chooses not to address comes some pages later, when Brooks quotes Clemens as saying that the happiest time in his life was the ten-year period during which his daughters were young.) Brooks concluded by naming Olivia — the censorious wife superseding Jane Clemens, the castrating mother — as a "blight" upon Clemens's art. Brooks's study was based on his contention that Clemens suffered an "arrested development" as the result of a struggle between his need to remain true to his artistic intentions and his desire for wealth and popularity. In Clemens's later years, Brooks claimed, a "pessimistic cynicism" surfaced due to his attempts to rationalize his guilt over his unrealized talent (6).

In *Mark Twain's America* (1932), DeVoto responded vehemently to Brooks's assertions. Among other issues, DeVoto challenged Brooks's interpretation of the supposed lovelessness of Clemens's childhood, the assertion that Jane Clemens quashed her son's artistic nature, and the notion that the severity of Olivia's editing detracted from Clemens's fiction. DeVoto refutes Brooks masterfully. On the negative influence of Jane Clemens, DeVoto claims quite rightly that the "coffin-side" scene that supposedly led to Clemens's apprenticeship—on which Brooks based so much of his analysis—very likely never occurred, but was actually one of two versions Clemens gave in his autobiography (*Mark Twain's America* 80–85). (Clemens provided yet another version of his apprenticeship in an essay of 1910, "The Turning Point of My Life.") And DeVoto steadfastly dismisses the matter of Olivia's injurious editing: "If she had wholly withheld her hand, propriety would still have done its surgery on Mark Twain. He came and accepted tuition" (210).

Still, DeVoto also contributed to the critical neglect of the women in Clemens's life. Indeed, in one curious passage, DeVoto attempts to discuss what precipitated Olivia's two-year collapse at age sixteen. Using ludicrously allusive language, he refers the reader to several sources concerning her affliction, then states that he has "no time" to elaborate further. He finally, gratefully, exits the topic by stating: "At any rate, Olivia was neurasthenic and was completely drilled in the gentilities of her sex and era" (208). The meeting and wooing of Olivia is given exactly one sentence: "In February, 1870, he married Olivia Langdon of Elmira" (180). This courtship was marked by the one hundred and eighty-four letters that Clemens sent to Olivia and was clearly a major event in Clemens's personal and creative growth, but DeVoto ignores it. (Olivia at least receives better treatment than Mary Fairbanks, Clemens's *Quaker City* fellow passenger, who goes unmentioned.)

DeVoto devotes most of his text to contesting Brooks's central thesis that the pessimism that emerged in Clemens's later years was due to an unconscious conflict whose origin was in his childhood. Whereas DeVoto notes that for Brooks this pessimism was "a symptom that Mark Twain was a divided soul" (229), he argues that the pronounced pessimism of the later works is traceable to Clemens's earliest efforts. His final proclamation on

Mark Twain is that Clemens's pessimism requires no explanation: it is representative of the literature of reality. Moreover, in *Mark Twain at Work* (1942), DeVoto claims that Clemens was not creatively incapacitated at the end of his life; rather, he points to *The Mysterious Stranger* as proof that Clemens's creative vision remained intact. (DeVoto undermines his argument, however, when he reasons that Clemens should be lauded because the work was completed, not because of its merit.)

It is crucial to note here how DeVoto creates his own dichotomy. He asserts that Brooks was wrong in his critique of the women in Clemens's life, but once he makes the point that they had no ill effect, he concludes that they had no effect at all. They are dropped from further discussion. DeVoto also declines to address the embittered shift in tone in Clemens's later work. While the seeds of pessimism may have always been inherent in Clemens's fiction, his post-1900 works display a new bitterness so sharp that at times they fall far short of satire. Yet DeVoto asserts that the unlearned, flamboyant, self-reliant Clemens continued to reside resolutely within a world of men where women were only fringe dwellers.

Once the Brooks-DeVoto battle lines drawn, so too were the divergent paths that subsequent Twain biographers would follow. Justin Kaplan tiptoes on both sides of the great divide in *Mr. Clemens and Mark Twain* (1966), where he is largely in agreement with DeVoto's view of Clemens's later years, although he retreats from DeVoto's hyperbolic claim that Clemens ultimately "brought his talent into fruition and made it whole again" (130). Instead, Kaplan contents himself with noting that Clemens "survived" his last years and that considering his travails this must be interpreted as "something of a triumph" (348). Brooks's influence emerges when Kaplan propounds the idea of Clemens's "dualistic" self, reporting that as early as 1866, he was "already a double creature" (18). In substantiating this statement, Kaplan asserts that Clemens "wanted to belong, but he also wanted to laugh from the outside" (18), a statement, surely, which could be made of many "nondualistic" authors who write satire. Susan Gillman, who subscribes to Kaplan's views, sums up his thesis: "The whole issue of duality is represented as Clemens 'wrestling' with the enigma of dual personality . . . [the] personal, psychological problems often worked out in, or placed in parallel relationship to, Twain's writing" (2). The Kaplan biography, finally, appears to fall within a Brooksian paradigm with a subtle shift: the division of thwarted artistic intention and the remaining commercial pretension have been converted into the dilemma of who Clemens was and when he became Mark Twain.

For examples of this personality confusion, Kaplan brings Clemens's *faux pas* under examination. Regarding Clemens's infamous speech at the Whittier birthday dinner on December 17, 1877, Kaplan concludes that "after wrestling long with the enigma of dual personality, Clemens might have recognized that his speech . . . was the kind of speech his 'dream self' . . . would give" (211). In his monologue, Clemens told the story of stopping in at a miner's log cabin only to find the resident had already been visited by three other writers: namely, Emerson, whom Clemens described as "a seedy little bit of a chap"; Holmes, who "was as fat as a balloon"; and Longfellow, who "was built like a prize-fighter." All three of these "littery" men arrived drunk, cheated at cards, and made the miner sing "When Johnny Comes Marching Home" (*The Complete Humorous Sketches and Tales of Mark Twain* 345–48). It is striking how differently DeVoto viewed the Whittier speech, which he saw in terms of a forceful, unapologetic Clemens telling Brahmin New England that its literary tenure was *am Ende*. Another opinion about the dinner comes from one in attendance — William Dean Howells. He recalls Clemens's mortification when, at the close of his speech, "there fell a silence, weighing many tons to the square inch, which deepened from moment to moment, and was broken only by the hysterical and bloodcurdling laughter of a single guest, whose name shall not be handed down to infamy" (60).

Howells viewed the incident as a humorist executing a pratfall that no one found funny. Simply put, Clemens told a bad joke to the wrong crowd. This explains, in part, why Clemens saw the Whittier banquet as so devastating. After having come so far, he had been humiliated in front of the society he wanted to join, and for Clemens the most crushing blow of all was that the injury was by his own hand.[3] Clemens read and reread the speech he gave that night up until he neared the end of his life, when he announced defiantly (and safely, thirty years after its occurrence) that if the scene were to be repeated, he would have done the same:

> If I had those beloved and revered old literary immortals back here now on the platform at Carnegie Hall I would take that same old speech, deliver it, word for word, and melt them till they'd run all over that stage. (180, Jan. 11, 1906, Autobiographical Dictation, No. 64, MTP*)

Despite his private hubris, this public embarrassment so haunted Clemens that he included in his autobiography manuscript a letter written to him by an admirer which complimented him on his speech. The letter, sent by Laura K. Hudson, is a glowing account of how she had read a transcript of his speech twenty years ago in a New York paper, had never forgotten it, and wished to know if she could obtain a copy. Clemens was overjoyed by her request. In his reply, also included in his autobiography, Clemens admitted his feeling of failure: "the first year or two after it happened, I could not bear to think of it. My pain and shame were so intense, and my sense of having been an imbecile so settled, established and confirmed, that I drove the episode entirely from my mind" (179, Jan. 11, 1906, Autobiographical Dictation, No. 64, MTP*).

Clemens was not at all defiant in a second autobiographical dictation, where he admitted, "I have examined that speech a couple of times since, and have changed my notion about it—changed it entirely. I find it gross, coarse—well, I needn't go on with particulars. I didn't like any part of it, from the beginning to the end" (Paine, ed., *Autobiography,* vol. 2: 5). In Isabel Lyon's annotated copy of the *Autobiography,* she wrote in the margin beside this excerpt: "He [Clemens] did not like the speech when he made it in 1877, & he condemned it now [in] 1906, for he felt it would involve criticism of his taste, & he could not stand criticism. To him there was no humor in it" (MTP).

Kaplan holds the women in Clemens's family partly accountable for the personal problems that resulted in Clemens's "duality." The Clemens women are, for the most part, portrayed as financial burdens. Kaplan characterizes Clemens as, as early as 1856, "whipped by guilt about his family and by an oppressive sense of obligation to them" (15). Kaplan's discussion of the relationship between Clemens and his mother, for example, is largely restricted to excerpts from Jane Clemens's letters which portray her as a complaining, socially ambitious woman whose concern for Clemens was apparently focused on his wallet. But anyone who has read much of the correspondence between Clemens and his mother is aware that concerns for her financial welfare comprised only one facet of their relationship. Jane Clemens's sense of humor and iron resolve helped prepare her son for his own personal and artistic triumphs and crises.

Jane Lampton Clemens: The Roots of a Storyteller

Jane Clemens was widowed in 1847 after twenty-four years of marriage. At the time of her husband's death she was forty-four years old and had borne seven children. John Marshall Clemens's demise was the fourth in a series of family tragedies: just five years earlier, their son Benjamin had died, following the deaths of children Pleasant and Margaret. Jane's youngest — and favorite — son, Henry, would outlive his father by barely a decade, dying in a riverboat accident at age nineteen. Samuel was eleven years old at the time of his father's death.

Over the years, John Clemens had suffered a series of economic reversals from which he could not recover, and he died in relative poverty. It became Jane's responsibility to keep the family together and to provide for her two young sons, Samuel and Henry. Jane's older surviving children both worked — twenty-two-year-old Orion as a printer and twenty-year-old Pamela as a music teacher — and their slender earnings helped to support the family. Poverty remained a constant threat; not until many years later, after her son Samuel's success, would Jane finally come to know economic security.

The letters Kaplan uses to indict Jane Clemens of scheming self-interest actually illuminate the dire dilemma women of her generation faced when the primary wage earner of a family died. Between 1820 and 1870 there were virtually no well-paying occupations for women (Baym 30). If Jane did not rely on her children for financial help, what then was she to do? Married at age nineteen, possessing no formal education, no vocational training, and sightless in one eye, Jane Clemens had no alternatives. And yet, despite the hardships of her life, Jane Clemens was a strong woman who refused to succumb to personal difficulties and sorrows. In a laudatory essay, "Jane Lampton Clemens," Clemens remembered his mother as possessing a vibrant personality, an inextinguishable sense of humor, and an iron-clad will — all traits that would serve her well and would later surface in her youngest surviving son.

In her youth, Jane Lampton had been an excellent horsewoman and dancer (she continued dancing into her seventies). Well-known for her red-haired beauty and spirited nature, she married the somber and unaffectionate John Clemens at age nineteen reportedly "to spite another man" (Wecter 125). Notwithstanding her difficult economic circumstances and her husband's dour personality, Jane enjoyed social occasions, for they provided her with an opportunity to dress up and display her ample wit among friends and relatives. Jane was a talented storyteller and would freely sacrifice accuracy in favor of effect. Both Charles Webster and Dixon Wecter, in their accounts of Jane Clemens, refer to her intense love of pageantry: no matter the event, be it a parade or funeral procession, Jane would be an excited on-looker. In a 1906 autobiographical dictation, Clemens remembered his mother as a connoisseur of public gatherings:

My mother [was] very much alive; [her] age counted for nothing; . . . fond of excitement, fond of novelties, fond of anything going that was of a sort proper for members of the church to indulge in. . . . Always ready for Fourth of July processions, Sunday-school processions, lectures, conventions, camp-meetings, revivals in the church — in fact, for any and every kind of dissipation that could not be proven to have anything irreligious about it — and [she] never missed a funeral. (*Mark Twain's Letters, 1853–1866*, vol. 1: 94)

Clemens shared his mother's love of spectacle. He gloried in the pageantry surrounding the conferral of his Oxford degree in 1907 and was inordinately fond of his doctoral garb, even wearing the ruby-red gown (his mother's favorite color) at his daughter Clara's wedding in 1909.

Indisputably, Jane Clemens had an enormous influence on her son. Early on she inculcated Samuel with a love of animals. Jane was a cat fancier — the more cats the better — and Clemens recalled that in 1845, when the family was living in Hannibal, nineteen felines were in residence (Wecter 92). (Apparently, John Clemens did not share his wife's affection for these creatures, telling daughter Pamela that when she married she should ensure her husband's comfort and "not have too many cats in the house" [Wecter 92]). As a child, Clemens often used his pets in his practical jokes. Puss Quarles, Jane Clemens's niece, recalled that when the Clemenses would visit the Quarles's farm, Clemens would leave garter snakes in his Aunt Patsy's sewing basket and hide bats in his mother's coat pockets (Wecter 93). Cats came to occupy a privileged place in the Clemens household after his marriage to Olivia, and they would of course make their way into Clemens's fiction.

In addition to their mutual love of excitement and animals, Clemens and his mother also exhibited similar personality quirks. Clemens's niece, Annie Moffett Webster, recalled that Jane kept a personal dislike list of people who had fallen out of her favor, "and it was amazing to see the names of the candidates." According to Charles Webster, Clemens too maintained a blacklist as an adult, and, as in his mother's system, once a name appeared, it was seldom removed (Webster 41–42). Mother and son also shared an interest in spiritualism.[4]

Annie Webster remembered her grandmother's personality as unpredictable. Sometimes, despite promises to the contrary, Jane Clemens would act with a startling lack of consideration:

My grandmother was always doing the unexpected. Once Uncle Sam brought home an atrocious spider made out of wire as a present for me. He showed it

first to my mother and grandmother while I was away at school, and my
mother warned my grandmother, "Don't frighten Annie. Be careful how you
give it to her." . . . When I came back from school . . . Grandma walked over to
the mantelpiece and brushed the spider into my lap. It took the entire family to
calm me. My mother was furious with my grandmother. . . . My grandmother
was astonished. "I thought it was all right," she said. She had only been anxious
to give me my present. (Webster 46–47)

This incident provides a foretaste of Clemens's own irrepressible behavior
when his children were concerned. In 1891, Clemens accepted an invitation
from the president of Bryn Mawr College to speak at the school. Eldest
daughter Susy, a Bryn Mawr student, begged her father not to tell his ghost
story, "The Golden Arm." Clemens duly promised, and then nonetheless
proceeded to end his performance with the frightening tale. Susy was
inconsolable and fled the hall in tears. Clemens, in futile attempts to
comfort her, claimed he had been unable to stop himself.

Clemens's early letters to his mother reveal a writer honing his craft in
front of a particularly creative audience. Clemens, a writer of tall tales, was
writing to a well-established teller of tall tales. In a letter to Jane written
from Carson City, California, in 1861 Clemens describes a tremendous fire
in vivid prose:

The level ranks of flame were relieved at intervals by . . . the tall dead trees,
wrapped in fire, and waving their blazing banners a hundred feet in the air.
Then we could turn from this scene to the Lake, and see every branch, and leaf,
and cataract of flame upon its bank perfectly reflected as in a gleaming, fiery
mirror. (*Mark Twain's Letters, 1853–1866*, vol. 1: 124)

This conflagration would later resurface in chapter 23 of *Roughing It*
(1872):

[The fire] went surging up adjacent ridges — surmounted them and disappeared in the canyons beyond — burst into view upon higher and farther
ridges . . . threw out skirmishing parties of fire here and there, and sent them
trailing their crimson spirals away among remote ramparts. . . . Away across
the water the crags and domes were lit with a ruddy glare, and the firmament
above was a reflected hell! Every feature of the spectacle was repeated in the
glowing mirror of the lake! Both pictures were sublime, both were beautiful.
(170)

This letter written to his mother served as an initial draft of the story
Clemens would complete and publish more than ten years later.

Significant, Yet Peripheral

A second woman Kaplan identifies as having a significant role in Clemens's life is Mary Fairbanks. Here Kaplan performs a Brooksian turnabout with Fairbanks, in place of Olivia, serving as the adverse influence on Clemens and his fiction. Kaplan asserts that the result of the Fairbanks and Clemens exchange was for Clemens "a certain willing suspension of identity—the price of which . . . was anger and a divided heart" (Kaplan 45). Was Clemens really this pliable? Kaplan apparently thinks so, and he falls back on familiar ground when he charges that "in his apparent submission to her [Mary Fairbanks's] literary standards, were foreshadowed some of the scenes of his life with Olivia Langdon and their children: a writer surrounded by women and seeking their approval" (45).

In Kaplan's view, Clemens's tendency to seek approval was so intertwined with the pressure to perform and to support his family that the influence of Clemens's wife and daughters, Fairbanks, and Jane Clemens could only be construed as a negative one. Kaplan argues that the family's overwhelming demands for financial security were ultimately manifested in Clemens's fiction; the story he selects to underscore this point is Clemens's perverse impulse to retell "The Golden Arm." Kaplan suggests that in this story "in Mark Twain's pattern of associations the relation with a woman has turned into money" (310). But Kaplan again vacillates between critical camps when he discusses the extent of Olivia's editing of Clemens's work. Here he sides with DeVoto and states that her "standards of decorum were scarcely more rigorous than [Howells's]" and more liberal than Gilder's (263).

All told, Kaplan's biography promotes the impression that women were on the periphery of Clemens's life. Apart from reiterating issues that by 1966 had been previously mined and that constituted routine biographical data, the new scholarship having to do with women is directed toward the psychological difficulties Clemens suffered due in part to his sense of familial responsibility, and, as a by-product of that duty, the fragmentation of his personality.

Isabel Van Kleek Lyon, Clemens's personal secretary, for instance, goes largely unmentioned in Kaplan's work. This can be only partially attributed to the fact that certain materials about her were not yet available for examination at the time of his book's publication. Just seven years later, Lyon would appear as one of the principal figures in Hamlin Hill's biography *Mark Twain: God's Fool* (1973). Hill addresses his work to the last decade of Clemens's life and provides the reader with an often sordid, behind-the-scenes look at the workings of Clemens's household. The centerpiece of the sources Hill used were the daily reminders, journal, and notebooks of Isabel Lyon. Lyon joined the family in November 1902, and lasted until April 1909, when she left under a cloud of ignominy and emotional trauma. Albert Paine and Clara Clemens, according to Hill, apparently agreed that Lyon detracted from the Mark Twain persona they wished to present to the public, so they excluded mention of her in Paine's *Biography,* a banishment that lasted for sixty years. Scholars were previously unable to explore Lyon's role within the family due to a stipulation in Lyon's will that prohibited access to her writings until after Clara's death.

Hill's chronicling of the downward spiral of Clemens's last years begins on New Year's Day, 1900. In fact, however, the descent had begun more than three years earlier, on August 18, 1896, with the death of his oldest daughter, Susan Olivia Clemens. Hill does not provide an extended discussion of Susy, but does include a telling reference about her critical role within the family unit. Hill describes a visit Olivia and Clemens made to a spiritualist in 1901, then states that "the spiritualist's failure to reach Susy was emblematic of the family's failure to recover the equilibrium and security of the years she symbolized" (34). This statement is too true. While Hill notes the ghoulish observances by the family on Susy's birthday and the anniversary of her death, the "equilibrium" Susy provided the family, and more importantly Clemens, deserves further attention. Hill contends that Clemens treated his family with a marked degree of insensitivity and that this "had also been an undercurrent in his domestic life during the halcyon years of his marriage" (270). Hill cites Clemens's insensitivity in his laconic recording of Susy Clemens's last words in his notebook: "Up go the trolley cars for Mark Twain's daughter. Down go the trolley cars for Mark Twain's daughter" (*Mark Twain's Notebook* 319). Hill claims that this jotting was purely an act of egotism, that Clemens comforted himself with the thought of Susy thinking solely of him upon her deathbed. But instead of Hill's egocentric version, these lines can be viewed as particularly emblematic of Susy's concern that her father would be known by the public merely as Mark Twain and not as Samuel Clemens, a concern she had earlier voiced in her biography of her father. Clemens's copying of Susy's words also can be interpreted as a hysterical regression in grief to childhood nonsense, as if Clemens, not Susy, were the child. Unquestionably, Susy was an important measure of Clemens's sense of identity.

Although Clemens was prone to act rashly (with results often detrimental to his family), his personality could be more accurately characterized by his oversensitivity. Whenever disaster, either personal or financial, struck, Clemens always claimed responsibility, and would browbeat himself for allowing it to happen. Jay Martin, in a 1985 essay, "The Genie in the Bottle: Huckleberry Finn in Mark Twain's Life," effectively counters Hill's charge:

> Twain's superego was sensitive and hyperactive. Between legitimate guilt, which he usually embraced (though sometimes warding it off angrily), and unwarranted guilt, which he also accepted eagerly, was a large shifting pool of uneasy, uncertain, troubled self-accusation. (59)

Hill develops a particularly unflattering picture of Clemens, who emerges as a soured, aging widower condemned in his last years to being surrounded by sycophants; to dictating his autobiography to an audience of three (Lyon, Paine, and Josephine Hobby); to grimly setting off on round after round of laudatory luncheons and dinners; to shooting endless games of billiards to pass the time; to cajoling little girls to be his playmates; and, between fleeting entertainments and distractions, cursing the damned human race with his every breath.

Hill's stated intention in his book is to reveal Samuel Clemens as he really was—no whitewashing here. Yet at certain junctures Hill becomes too caught up in writing exposé and loses sight of his original goal. One of Hill's most egregious attacks comes in his discussion of Clemens's grief upon the death of Olivia in 1904. Paine portrayed Clemens's reaction as one of overstated eloquence. But Hill, fully armed with documentary evidence, charges, contending that Clemens's grief, as expressed in letters to his friends Howells, Henry Huttleson Rogers, and Richard Watson Gilder "are examples of . . . false and inflated rhetoric"; that a telegram Clemens composed to Olivia's brother Charles was "contrived, too polished, too ceremonial"; and that Clemens "confused his sincere grief by expressing it in contrived literary modes" (85). Hill summarizes his critique of Clemens's sorrow by noting, "it is distressing that he declaimed his grief in such platitudinous forms of expression" (86).

Two observations must be made before the record is set straight: First, grief, during its early stages, frequently is characterized by a sense of unreality and detachment (the letters Hill quotes from were written in the two weeks immediately after Olivia's death); second, the recipients of the letters from which Hill quotes were all male (see Kubler-Ross), all the more reason for Clemens to adopt the stoicism that may have resulted in the awkwardness of his language.

A previously unpublished letter discovered in 1986 attests to Clemens's grief. The letter is addressed to Susan Crane, Olivia's adopted sister and a favorite of Clemens. Clemens's eloquence speaks for itself:

> Lee, July 25/[19]04
>> Dear Susy —
>> Yes, she did love me; & nothing that I did, no hurt that I inflicted upon her, no tears that I caused those dear eyes to shed, could break it down, or even chill it. It always rose again, it always burned again, as warm & bright as ever. Nothing could wreck it, nothing could extinguish it. . . . I know one thing, & I get some poor small comfort out of it: that what little good was in me I gave to her to the utmost — full measure, the last grain & the last ounce — & poor as it was it was my very best, & far beyond anything I could have given to any other person that ever lived. It was poverty, but it was all I had; & so it stood for wealth, & she so accounted it. I try not to think of the hurts I gave her, but oh, there are so many, so many! (MTP*)

Enough time had passed for Clemens to gather himself from his shock. Moreover, his correspondent was a woman, one with whom Clemens could drop his guard and reveal himself. This letter is a clear expression of just how deeply grief-stricken Clemens was, and indicates the sort of person with whom he felt most emotionally and profoundly allied.

With Olivia's death, Hill asserts, the last pacifying influence on Clemens was removed. His moodiness proceeded to rage unchecked, and Clemens grew increasingly estranged from his two remaining daughters. The youngest, Jean, was a particularly tragic figure. Immediately after her mother's death, her epileptic seizures recurred, and her worsened condition culminated in a violent attack on Katy Leary (a beloved family employee). Clemens was unable to deal with the enormity of Jean's affliction and, inappropriately, thrust the responsibility on Isabel Lyon. Jean remained at home for approximately two years after Olivia's death; she entered a sanatorium on October 25, 1906. She would not return home to live until April 26, 1909, a scant eight months before her death.

Clemens's other surviving daughter, Clara, is portrayed in Hill's book as a villainness. Admittedly, Clara does appear to have been uncaring at times, but one must take into account that much of what we know about Clara is revealed through Isabel Lyon's accounts, and that the two had a stormy relationship. One particularly telling clue comes from Lyon's

1906–8 notebook where she quotes Clemens as saying that Clara was in the same predicament he was when he was young and directionless: "What's the use, I'm 20 & haven't got a start in life yet—" (Notebook No. 3, MTP*). In order to treat Clara and the obvious alienation between her and Clemens fairly, one must examine the role Clara was reduced to playing in the family drama. At the age of thirty, with her mother and sister dead, Clara was the designated caretaker. Dealing with Clemens had never been easy for her mother, a woman Clemens idolized, and now Clara had the task of trying to fulfill her mother's role while her father still grieved his favorite daughter's loss and openly claimed to hate the human race after the loss of his wife. It must have been painfully clear to Clara that her father's fondest thoughts of her were limited to her childhood. He had no place for her as an adult.

Indeed, for most of her adult life, Clemens refused to recognize Clara as a grown woman. In two well-known incidents, male attention to the attractive Clara incurred Clemens's anger. The first occurred when Clara attended a social gathering in Berlin and was momentarily the only woman in a room full of German military officers, and the second in Florence when Clemens and Clara were in a tearoom and Clara was stared at by Italian officers. On both occasions Clemens became furious. After the latter incident he decided that the artificial fruit on Clara's hat had incited the men and he promptly snipped off the offending ornaments. Try as he might, though, Clemens could not halt his daughter's growing maturity. As a final measure of control, Clemens insisted that Clara be chaperoned until the age of thirty, an action Clara understandably must have resented. Clara's life became a struggle to develop her own identity in the present with a father who only wanted to remember the past. Declaring her intention never to marry, she embarked on an abortive singing career, financed by her largely unenthusiastic father. It was not until she was thirty-five years old that she married classical pianist and conductor Ossip Gabrilowitsch. Immediately following her wedding, she left her ailing father and epileptic sister and went to live in Europe.

After reading Hill's account of this family's interaction, one is struck by the chaos that appeared to reign in the household. Family members appear to career about in self-destructive, frenetic activity. Jean and Clara go on hysterical rampages, are in and out of sanatoriums, and struggle with the love they have for their father and with their loathing for the way they are treated. Isabel Lyon also does battle with her demons and periodically retreats on rest cures ordered by her doctor. (Throughout her tenure she was subject to violent headaches and anxiety attacks, and, in one documented instance, she reportedly drank whiskey to fortify herself).[5]

What could have been the cause of this collective hysteria? An answer can be found in the plight of Isabel Lyon. With Clara deliberately absent, Lyon was increasingly obliged to take on Olivia's duties. As Hill recognizes, Lyon's role "far transcended the purely secretarial" (94). What Lyon became was Clemens's new companion, his "Olivia-player." She was his uncomplaining audience for his tirades and manuscript readings; she attempted to act as editor, controlled the household accounts, and managed his two increasingly unmanageable daughters. And what did Isabel receive? Fifty dollars a month with no overtime and the lasting enmity of Clemens and Clara. In her life with Clemens she was called on to perform the duties of a wife — with none of the benefits. Lyon assumed Olivia's role, and it should not be surprising that Clemens would eventually grow to hate his creation. She was Isabel, not Olivia, and she had her own needs and desires. Indeed, there are hints in her journals that she would not have been adverse to the prospect of marriage. On April 23, 1905, after noting that a certain John Kendrick had remarried after the death of his first wife, Isabel remarked, "But that's no harm. I've known of several men who have married several times — they couldn't live without the companionship and sympathy of a woman, and I like the thought of it" (Daily Reminder, vol. 2, MTP). Remarriage was not without ample precedent within Clemens's social circle.[6] As Isabel was rehearsing the role of wife, perhaps she should not be castigated for desiring the security of one as well. Ultimately, she was censured, although the blame cannot all be placed on the querulousness of Clemens and the machinations of Clara. For this situation to evolve, Lyon had to be a willing participant. She agreed to take on the additional responsibility and enjoyed her periodically powerful position.

A crucial element for understanding the relationship between the secretary and her employer is Lyon's idolization of Clemens. Olivia clearly adored her husband but — and here the differentiation is important — she had known him before he evolved into "Mark Twain, American Spokesman," whereas Isabel had not. Isabel was dealing with a personage instead of a person. For Clemens, this idol worship would prove to be particularly harmful.

The pet names Olivia and Lyon gave to Clemens aptly reflect their individual perceptions of him. For Olivia, her "Youth" would always remain the adoring young man who courted her in her father's parlor. But Lyon's nickname for Clemens was "the King."[7] For her, the "King" was a grandiose figure far removed from the realm of ordinary people; in one breathless entry in her daily reminder, Lyon rhapsodized: "He is the King — the King — & you [Paine] and I are lifted into a paradise of flashing wonderful colors & perfumes & songs by his personality. . . . How have we deserved it?" (Daily Reminder, Jan. 25, 1907, MTP).

Isabel Lyon was assigned a role that would eventually be revoked; and what Clemens requested of his daughters was an impossible task: that they become his little girls again. Clemens, at age seventy, did not want to contend with two grown daughters, one seriously ill and the other latently rebellious. He longed for a return to simpler times when they were young and carefree. And Clemens raged at the universe as he realized the fruitlessness of his longing. As adult women his daughters served as constant reminders of the unrepeatable past, and Clara and Jean must have sensed this. Isabel was reduced to enacting an artificial part, and Clara and Jean were faced with their father's rejection. Is it any wonder, then, that the three women suffered breakdowns? As Jean plaintively wrote in her diary: "Father can't possibly find any entertainment or interest in me" (Jan. 14, 1907, 1906–1907 Diary, HL).

What was it within Clemens that caused the deterioration of his family and his literature? Fear, Hill maintains, was the controlling emotion of Clemens's life: fear of being poor, of losing his family and friends, of losing his audience, and of the type of writing he was producing. Hill asks, "Was he a journalist or a writer of books?" (271) Hill attributed the events of the last ten years of Clemens's life to the fact that "[Clemens] moved insecurely in all the worlds he inhabited" (269). According to Hill, Clemens, although a man of contradictory impulses all his life, managed to maintain control over himself and his world through his "artistic capacities" until what Hill holds to be the watershed year of 1900 (273). After 1900, and increasingly so until his death, "his despair, pessimism, frustration, and insensitivity" compounded, and his creative skills were lost (273). Hill concludes his study by observing: "Something occurred which made the adversity and the conflicts no longer convertible into finished art" (273). But just what was that "something"? This question must be answered if we are to make sense of the events of Clemens's last years.

To understand Clemens's bitterness and the silencing of his fiction, we must explore the relationship between the two. I propose that what fed Clemens's propensity for pessimism (evident to a lesser degree throughout his life) and robbed him of his creative voice was the demise of what I call his "charmed circle." In order for Clemens to create and complete novel-length fictions, several essential elements needed to coalesce: a female audience, sufficient time, and an environment conducive to writing. Clemens was constantly conceiving ideas for stories — his notebooks and journals testify to that — yet carrying these story germs to fruition proved difficult, and after 1897, impossible. Clemens needed a female audience to whom he could read drafts and receive feedback, and a particular writing environment where he could be alone and unhurried. At the same time, he also needed to feel his family's immediate presence.

"Are not we Twain one flesh?"

Clemens insisted from the outset of his relationship with Olivia that theirs was a merging of two persons into one. Writing to Olivia shortly before their marriage, Clemens told her:

> What we want is a *home* — we are done with the shows & vanities of life & are ready to enter upon its realities — we are tired of chasing its phantoms & shadows, & are ready to grasp its substance. At least *I* am — & "I" means both of us, & "both of us" means I of course — for are not we Twain one flesh? (*Mark Twain's Letters, 1869,* vol. 3: 103)

He believed Olivia was his other self, with which he would finally be united.

Before 1869, Clemens had achieved a small measure of celebrity out West as a journalist and correspondent, and he was known in the East as the author of "The Jumping Frog of Calaveras County." After 1897, he stopped writing novels, and after 1904 he produced mainly polemical writing. (He attempted to write extended works of fiction many times, but the manuscripts were left largely unfinished.) These three dates coincide with Clemens's first literary collaboration with Olivia, the year after the death of his daughter Susy, and the year of Olivia's death.

A major problem with past scholarship is that critics have been unable to account for Clemens's ceasing to write fiction. The Brooks camp intimates that the split in Clemens's personality eventually became so pronounced that his capacity for fiction-writing was irreparably damaged. Brooks pinpointed the split as occurring during boyhood, where Clemens was the victim of a "castrating" mother; Kaplan theorized that the split hapened later, but before middle age, in approximately 1866. The other Twain camp, headed by DeVoto, undertook to prove that Clemens's later ficion was of a piece with his earlier work — that Clemens remained an integrated man. Obviously, both views have their merits and their limitations, yet each neglects to explore the impact of female family members and colleagues on Clemens.

This absence of women is not restricted only to Twain scholarship; American male writers historically have been portrayed as being "immune" or "beyond" the influence of women. In this androcentric scholarship, the male author operates within an asocial context. Closeted away from the tainting influence of those "damned scribblers" (interestingly, Clemens paraphrased Hawthorne, calling himself "a scribbler of books"), men supposedly relied on their one true source of inspiration — themselves. Joyce Warren, in *The American Narcissus,* addresses the critics' rejection of outside influences in her discussion of American characters in fiction and legend:

> When the image of the individual is disproportionately large, there is no room for the individuality of other people. . . . [These] characters were all solitary male figures, without wife, family, or any other human relationships. . . . The "American Narcissus" . . . looked at himself in this unreal, inflated, isolated figure and saw what he wanted to see — an ideal picture of himself. (13)[8]

Like the autonomous fictional male characters Warren analyzes, Clemens, too, has been portrayed by past biographers *as a fiction.* They have variously described him as a King Lear, an American Adam, or a fallen angel. Such labels have placed Clemens, the man, into the realm of Mark Twain, the fiction, and in so doing they have perhaps rejected the ambiguity of human nature — the complex interactions that make up a life story. Indeed, biographers from Paine to Hill have treated Clemens as a larger-than-life figure, although it is important to note that in Clemens they found a more than willing subject. Clemens, particularly toward the end of his life, actively engaged in self-mythologizing.

Cynthia Fuchs Epstein's *Deceptive Distinctions: Sex, Gender and the Social Order* (1989) suggests a connection between the critical avoidance of ambiguity and the tendency toward creating dichotomous categorizations: "It is no surprise that dichotomous models as an ideological weapon survive challenge because it is easier to propose a dichotomy than to explicate the complexities that make it invalid" (15). Epstein goes on to explain:

> It may be that such thinking is more economical, rewarding, seductive, or just easier in that mutually exclusive categories are parsimonious and even aesthetic. Of course, ambiguities may capture the imagination of poets and create literature, but the ambiguity . . . is difficult to tolerate for most people, who find comfort in consistency and punish those who deviate from its practice. (12)

Previous Twain scholars have fallen into the trap of avoiding "ambiguity." But Twain's life and work require a foray into ambiguous territory. And, truly, a complex reading of Twain necessitates analysis of the female component of Twain's life.

The time has thus arrived to examine the critical function of women in Clemens's life and literature, as well as the elements of gender, politics, environment, culture, and time — all of which are contained within his "charmed circle."

Notes

1. Brooks claimed that Olivia's power lay in keeping him a child; certainly, Clemens insisted on retaining his childlike qualities (115). Jay Martin discusses the transference of Clemens's childlike qualities into his fiction and argues that Clemens consistently portrayed his adult characters as oversized children, "in a way that would seem intolerably restrictive — Twain virtually confined his work to the representation of children or childlike behavior" (77).

2. Information about women writers published by the Webster Publishing Company is derived from an unpublished manuscript by Kenneth Sanderson, Editor, Mark Twain Project.

3. See Henry Nash Smith's article, "'That Hideous Mistake of Poor Clemens's,'" *Harvard Library Bulletin,* 9 (Spring 1955): 145–80.

4. Jane Clemens's interest in psychic phenomena is mentioned in Dixon Wecter's *Sam Clemens of Hannibal* (126) and Charles Webster's *Mark Twain, Business Man* (41); Clemens's fascination with the occult is discussed at length in Alan Gribben's "'When Other Amusements Fail': Mark Twain and the Occult" in *The Haunted Dusk: American Supernatural Fiction, 1820–1920,* ed. Howard Kerr (Athens: University of Georgia Press, 1983), 171–89.

5. An admittedly cursory reading of Lyon's 1905, 1906, and 1907 daily reminders suggests that her attacks of poor health occurred with a certain monthly regularity:

1905	Feb. 10	Headache.
	May 22	Headache.
1906	Jan. 12	Headache.
	May 6	I have taken two heavy drugs, but they don't effect. . . .
	June 10	but I felt pretty ill when Mr. Clemens was reading aloud to me. . . .
	July 8	It is only by means of fertilization that any best in us can be brought to full flower and fruit; and unlike the growing plants we can partake of the fertilization of many minds.
1907	Apr. 13	my outlet for superfluous emotions just now is my Boyagians and their "something junk." . . . Mr. and Mrs. Twichell arrived and I'm so tired — so tired.

May 1   All day in bed.

June 7   Today I'm ill, ill all day. . . .

July 9   Headache.

Aug. 13   Headache.

Aug. 14   Been very ill all day.

Aug. 30   Savagely ill all day.

Sep. 9   Dorothy [Quick] was here and made an interruption to everything it seemed to me, who am now little tired.

Oct. 10   all day I was so ill, but I wouldn't give in. . . . I played Hearts for an hour, just as I was going up to lie down for that hour. I never slipped a cog all day long, with that supreme pain in my head and careening down my spine. (MTP)

6. Some of Clemens's closest friends had been married twice: Abel Fairbanks married Mary Mason after his first wife died; Thomas Beecher remarried after the death of his first wife; Calvin Stowe married Harriet Beecher after his first wife's demise; Henry H. Rogers remarried after his wife's death; and Clemens's official biographer, Albert Bigelow Paine, had been married twice, his first marriage ending in divorce. Clemens's father-in-law's mother, Eunice Ford, was married three times.

7. When Isabel Lyon first came to work for Clemens, she commonly referred to him as "Marse Clemens." This moniker was later dropped in favor of "the King."

8. Warren uses as the basis for her argument Constance Rourke's landmark work, *American Humor: A Study of the National Character* (1931; reprint, Tallahassee: Florida State University Press, 1959).

2. The Charmed Circle

> The whole tenor of this new life was to feminize Mark Twain, to make him feel that no loyalties are valid which conflict with domestic loyalties, that no activities are admirable which do not immediately conduce to domestic welfare, that private and familiar interests are, rightly and inevitably, the prime interests of man.
>
> — Van Wyck Brooks, *The Ordeal of Mark Twain*

Clemens recorded the following observation in his notebook while in Australia during his 1895–96 world lecture tour: "It is the strangest thing that the world is not full of books that scoff at the pitiful world, and the useless universe and violent, contemptible human race. . . . Why don't I write such a book? Because I have a family. There is no other reason" (*Mark Twain's Notebook* 256).

While biographers have recognized that family held an esteemed place in Clemens's life (Van Wyck Brooks calls it "the hub of Mark Twain's universe"), no attempt has ever been made to connect it with his fiction-writing capability (*The Ordeal of Mark Twain* 135). For Clemens, home and family constituted the core of his life, and with the stability and security they provided he was free to create. It was during the period in which his female family unit was intact, between 1876 and 1895, that Clemens produced much of what are considered to be his best writings: *The Adventures of Tom Sawyer* (1876), *The Prince and the Pauper* (1882), *Life on the Mississippi* (1883), *Adventures of Huckleberry Finn* (1885), *A Connecticut Yankee in King Arthur's Court* (1889), *Pudd'nhead Wilson* (1894), and *Personal Recollections of Joan of Arc* (1896).

Clemens wrote his novels under carefully controlled conditions. He required two outwardly paradoxical elements: quiet isolation for concentration, and the comforting, boisterous presence of his family. He had both elements at Quarry Farm in Elmira, New York, home of Olivia's adopted sister, Susan Crane. At this isolated retreat, Clemens could bathe in the atmosphere he required in order to write. In her manuscript, "What I Know About Mark Twain," Hattie Lewis Paff recalled that Clemens used

Quarry Farm for writing as early as the summer of 1869. Jervis Langdon purchased Quarry Farm earlier that same year, and he later gave it as a present to his daughter Susan when she married Theodore Crane. Hattie Paff, his niece, reminisced about her uncle's summer residence.

> [Jervis Langdon] had a summer residence about two miles from the city, and there Mr. C. would go in the morning and in a summer house covered with vines and a view which every way you looked was beautiful enough for an artists [sic] canvas, he wrote all day on this book. . . . In the evening he would come back, and read to us what he had written. (5 MTP*)

Settled in the octagonal study Susan had built for him in the summer of 1874, and removed from the main house, Clemens could write undisturbed. Every morning after breakfast he would ascend the hill to his windowed study, complete with fireplace, cigars, cats, desk, and divan, and work straight through until dinner. The family left him alone while he was working; at the end of the day, a bell would summon him, and Clemens would descend the hill to find Olivia, Susan Crane, Mary Ann Cord (a formerly enslaved African-American who worked as a cook for Susan Crane), and his three daughters waiting for him.[1]

A crucial part of Clemens's composing process would come later in the day, with the interaction of his female family members. After returning to the main house, he would read his day's work out loud and receive the varied opinions that, for Clemens, constituted his literary wellspring. Alan Gribben stresses the importance of such audiences to Clemens's writing:

> Nothing else known about Clemens's reading habits seems as significant as his preference for oral readings before other people, a practice that surely helped develop the flexible narrative voice he strove to reproduce in his fiction. He read his daily output of prose to his family and friends. . . . When he discovered material that elicited favorable audience responses under varied conditions, he stuck with it gratefully. ("Unsatisfactory," 55–56)

Yet this reading before a female audience resulted in more than a honing of Clemens's narrative voice; the women became, in a sense, co-constructors of his text. Clemens received the insights and opinions of individuals who were in their own way as rebellious toward restrictive Victorian society as the Southerner Clemens was toward literary, Brahmin New England or as Huckleberry Finn was toward the slaveholding society of St. Petersburg, Missouri.

In a draft of a memorial piece Clemens wrote about Susy several years after her death (the piece never progressed beyond draft form), he plainly stated how integral Olivia and his daughters were to his composing process:

> My first book, *The Innocents Abroad,* was edited & revised in proof by my prospective wife. Several later books were criticised [sic] & edited in manuscript before going to the press, by my wife & Mr. Howells. About 1880 Susy joined the staff and helped to edit *The Prince and the Pauper.* She was eight years old, then. In 1884 Clara, aged ten, joined the staff, & helped the others edit *Huckleberry Finn.* The children were a valuable reinforcement for my side. . . . They remained on the staff continuously thence forward, & helped as well as they could to edit all the subsequent books chapter by chapter nightly, as each day's work was completed. ("Memorial" 29–30)

Clemens's young daughters granted him instant feedback regarding his prose's effectiveness in sustaining interest, and they provided Clemens with a conduit to his childhood memories. When *Adventures of Huckleberry Finn* was published Susy was twelve, Clara ten, and Jean four.

Clemens obviously enjoyed having his daughters and Olivia take an active part in his writing, and he often engaged them in verbal games. He would insert deliberately inflammatory passages in his manuscripts which would be sure to attract their attention; Olivia and the children would then pounce upon and censor them. In an autobiographical dictation, Clemens fondly remembered his game:

> The children always helped their mother to edit my books in manuscript. She would sit on the porch at the farm and read aloud, with her pencil in her hand, and the children would keep an alert and suspicious eye upon her right along, for the belief was well grounded in them that whenever she came across a particularly satisfactory passage she would strike it out. Their suspicions were well founded. . . . For my own entertainment and to enjoy the protests of the children, I often abused my editor's innocent confidence. I . . . interlarded remarks of a studied and felicitously atrocious character purposely to achieve the children's brief delight and then see the remorseless pencil do its fatal work. I often joined my supplications to the children's for mercy and strung the argument out and pretended to be in earnest. They were deceived and so was their mother. . . . Now and then we gained the victory and there was much rejoicing. Then I privately struck the passage out myself. It had served its purpose. (Feb. 9, 1906, No. 64, MTP*)

Here Clemens turned the composition process into his own brand of child's play, well in keeping with the childlike side of his personality. (This method of composition would be difficult to imagine being employed by, say, Bret Harte, a contemporary of Clemens.) Clemens's "prank" highlights an important feature of Clemens's fiction-writing process, for it was essential that Clemens have direct, vocal feedback for his work. In order to check to see whether his writing instincts were valid, he had only to observe his wife and daughters' reactions. He recognized his family's contribution as his ideal audience by dedicating *The Prince and the Pauper* to Susy and Clara.

Another way in which Clemens would sharpen his creative faculties was in succumbing to his daughters' demands that he construct a narrative (with the theme dictated by the children) around the bibelots that lined the Hartford home's library shelves and fireplace mantelpiece:

> The children required me to construct a romance — always impromptu — not a moment's preparation permitted — and into that romance I had to get all that bric-a-brac. . . . It was not permissible to introduce a bric-a-brac ornament into the story out of its place in the procession. These bric-a-bracs were never allowed a peaceful day . . . a restful Sabbath. . . . If they brought me a picture in a magazine and required me to build a story to it, they would cover the rest of the page with their pudgy hands to keep me from stealing an idea from it. . . . If they heard of a new trade or an unfamiliar animal or anything like that, I was pretty sure to have to deal with those things in the next romance. Once Clara required me to build a sudden tale out of a plumber and a "bawgun strictor," and I had to do it. (Neider 204)[2]

Olivia's part in co-creating Clemens's texts was not so much in functioning as an editor, although that is the role to which she has been traditionally relegated, as in providing an educated audience familiar with transforming and reforming social standards. Olivia was concerned with the scope and treatment of the fictive subject, not with censoring the end product. In effect, she acted as Clemens's "didactic" audience. With Olivia as guide, Clemens could not overindulge in the burlesque; to elicit her approval he had to provide finesse behind the fireworks. Clemens described Olivia's crucial role in a letter to Archibald Henderson:

> She would say to me. . . . "You have a true lesson, a serious meaning to impart here. . . . Be yourself! Speak out your real thoughts as humorously as you please, but — without farcical commentary. Don't destroy your purpose with an ill-timed joke." I learned from her that the only right thing was to get in my serious meaning always, to treat my audience fairly, to let them really feel the underlying moral that gave body and essence to my jest. (Henderson 183)

The connection between the expectations of Clemens's familial audience and *Adventures of Huckleberry Finn,* for example, is readily apparent. The burlesque is left intact for the amusement of the children, as in Jim's soothsaying prowess with the ox hairball; Olivia's "serious meaning" takes precedence with this one sentence by Huck: "All right, then, I'll go to hell." Leland Krauth observes in his article "Mark Twain: The Victorian of Southwestern Fiction" that, in keeping with Olivia's advice to Clemens, the climax of the book represents "both [Huck's] greatest moment of pathos and one of the most humorous moments" (382). This moment is so effective because "of course we know that no one of such fine and tender feeling can be damned" (383).

Olivia's support and the sense of security she provided also allowed Clemens to remember his childhood days and commit them to writing. In a letter to his childhood friend Will Bowen two years before his marriage, Clemens remarks that he has "been thinking of schooldays at Dawson's, & trying to recall the old faces of that ancient time — but I cannot place them very well — they have faded out from my treacherous memory" (*Mark Twain's Letters to Will Bowen* 17). However, four days after his marriage, Clemens wrote again to Bowen, this time a remarkable letter recounting in meticulous detail the people and events of his youth. Six years after the letter celebrating the return of his memories, Clemens again writes to Bowen, this time to chastise him for remaining in the world of his youth. Clemens labels Bowen's habit "mental and moral masturbation" and claims he wants none of it (*Mark Twain's Letters to Will Bowen* 24). Particularly provocative is the timing of this third letter: Clemens wrote Bowen during the summer he began writing *Adventures of Huckleberry Finn*. Clemens simply may have been expressing some writerly frustration or he may have been warning Bowen off the subject. But, as James M. Cox observes, it was Olivia's influence that allowed Clemens the mental freedom to remember and revise his childhood experiences for use in his most successful works, including *Adventures of Huckleberry Finn*. "Under the protection of the reverent spirit of Olivia, the old vices and shameful habits of the intervening years are falling away, leaving the past free from evil and available to the memory. . . . She represents the presence of a grace which blesses the memory, opening a window upon the territory of boyhood" (79). Cox is the only critic to cite Olivia's positive influence, claiming that Olivia, "far from restricting [Clemens's] imagination, actually freed it to move toward the 'approved' world of childhood" (80–81).[3]

On the Farm: Audience and Sentiment

Another female-influenced facilitator of Clemens's creativity was Quarry Farm, where the Clemens family summered for more than twenty years.

The farm's owner, Susan Langdon Crane, referred to Quarry Farm as "go as you please hall," a place where new ideas were encouraged and frequently debated. The farm's enlightened atmosphere reflected the values of the liberal Langdon family. Susan, born in 1836 in Spencer, New York, was adopted in infancy by the Langdons after the deaths of her parents, Elijah and Mary Dean. Susan and Olivia were extremely close, attending school and church together, and remaining confidantes until Olivia's death. On Dec. 7, 1858, Susan married Theodore Crane, a business associate of Jervis Langdon's. Crane was well known for her church and reform activities and is remembered as a Park Church leader. In 1902, at the age of sixty-six, and having been a widow for three years, she became a businesswoman: She established the Quarry Farm Dairy, an experimental dairy that became the first in the region to receive certification for producing germ-free milk. Susan Crane died in 1924, at the age of eighty-eight.

As Clemens's contemporary, the religious but quite intrepid Crane enjoyed a *sympatisch* relationship with the writer — this despite (or perhaps because of) their opposing views on philosophy and religion. Clara later recalled the walks her aunt (who was only three months younger than Clemens) and father would take together while playfully debating religion. Clemens referred to the farm as the home of Tom Sawyer and Huckleberry Finn, revealing that the farm's atmosphere help spark their creation.[4]

In Susan Crane, Clemens found a woman who shared his sense of humor and who was supportive of his activities. Crane was an important source of information for Clemens; she kept him apprised of the various kinds of reform activities with which she and other women were directly involved. Crane also provided a sounding board for Clemens's writing in much the same way that Jane Clemens and Mary Fairbanks did. Clemens had known Crane since he was betrothed, and when Langdon, the Clemens's first child and only son, was born in Buffalo, Crane was in attendance. (Langdon would die at nineteen months.) All of Clemenses' daughters were born at Quarry Farm, and Crane was the only family member present at Susy Clemens's death. Indeed, Clemens and Crane enjoyed a close rapport, and this is reflected in their correspondence. One particularly revealing letter was sent to Clemens by Crane after the death of his daughter, Jean. The letter reveals Crane's awareness of Clemens's tendency to castigate himself: "Katy tells me you blame yourself for Jean's long absence from home. Do not. . . . I cannot bear to have you condemn yourself. . . . I do long to have you free from these burdensome thoughts of upbraiding" (Jan. 1910, MTP*). Crane was one of the few people Clemens always trusted.

Mary Ann Cord also played a crucial role in the shaping of Clemens's fiction. Born enslaved in Virginia, Cord had been sold twice and had all her children taken from her before she escaped to the North (Jerome and Wisbey 8). Charles Langdon's daughter, Ida Langdon, in an address delivered to the Elmira College Convocation in 1960, remembered Cord as a "dogmatic Methodist" (Jerome and Wisbey 62). Cord was very likely a member of the African Methodist Episcopal Zion Church, the first African-American church founded in Elmira in 1841 (Sorin 15). And indeed Cord's denomination is shared by Roxana in *Pudd'nhead Wilson*; it is Roxana's recent conversion to Methodism that saves her from being sold down the river by her master.

While summering at Quarry Farm, Clemens composed a short story written partly in black dialect, which was probably influenced by Cord. As Sherwood Cummings notes, this story later gave rise to the main plot and theme of the first section of *Adventures of Huckleberry Finn*. This short story, entitled "A True Story Repeated Word for Word as I Heard It," related the travails of "Rachel" Cord, and it provided Clemens with an entrée into the November 1874 issue of the *Atlantic*. William Dean Howells praised the story: "I think it extremely good and touching with the best and reallest kind of black talk in it" (*Mark Twain-Howells Letters* 24).

The crossover from "A True Story" and *Adventures of Huckleberry Finn* is readily apparent: in "A True Story," Rachel scolds a young man (who, unbeknownest to her, is her long-lost son) and says, "I wa'nt bawn in de mash to be fool' by trash!" (*The Unabridged Mark Twain* 408); in *Adventures of Huckleberry Finn*, Jim utters a similar line when he rebukes Huckleberry for playing a cruel trick on him: "Dat truck dah is *trash*; en trash is what people is dat puts dirt on de head er dey fren's en makes 'em ashamed" (72). "A True Story Repeated Word for Word as I Heard It" is of particular importance not only because it marked the beginning of Clemens's contributions to the *Atlantic*, but also because this oral history of an African-American woman's road to freedom may have served as a prototype for one of Clemens's greatest works.

Quarry Farm's inhabitants varied in terms of temperament, education, experience, culture, race, and age; this meant that in order for Clemens to maintain his disparate audience's attention, he had to produce fiction that was multigenerational, multicultural, and multiracial. Clemens also needed to provide characters and themes that would appeal particularly to this disparate female audience. Viewed within the context of Clemens's family, the absence of overtly masculine themes in *Adventures of Huckleberry Finn* should not come as a complete surprise. Leland Krauth isolates the various elements that traditionally comprise Southwestern humor and remarks that *Huckleberry Finn* is striking for what it is not:

> [*Adventures of Huckleberry Finn*] ignores, first of all, those subjects, like court-ings, frolics, dances, weddings, and honeymoons, that naturally involve adult sexuality. And secondly, it omits entirely or else skims over those activities, like hunting, fighting, gambling, gaming, horse racing, heavy drinking, and mili-tary maneuvering, that are the traditional pastimes of manly backwoods living. (Whenever such activities do appear briefly they are targets of ridicule.) In short, Twain purges from the Southwestern tradition its exuberant celebration of rough-and-tumble masculinity. (374)

While *Adventures of Huckleberry Finn* may lack traditional Southwest-ern masculine themes, what it is striking *for* is its similarity to the themes and plot structures that comprised female-authored fiction of the mid-nineteenth century. Nina Baym comments in *Woman's Fiction: A Guide to Novels by and about Women in America, 1820–1870* that many of the novels written by prominent women writers (such as Louisa May Alcott, Susan Warner, E.D.E.N. Southworth, Fanny Fern, Mary Jane Holmes) told with some modification a single story: "It is the story of a young girl who is deprived of the supports she had rightly or wrongly depended on to sustain her throughout life and is faced with the necessity of winning her own way in the world" (11). Baym claims that although men could have also au-thored such stories, "only women did so" (13). That men did not, Baym views as no mere coincidence: "[Male authors] assumed an audience of men as a matter of course, and reacted with distress and dismay as they discovered that to make a living by writing they would have to please female readers" (13).

Baym may be a bit too sweeping in her indictment against male authors. Baym argues that once male writers realized that in order to be published they would have to start writing for a female audience, one of the strategies they used to attract readers was "insulting or shocking them. Mark Twain is the most obvious example" (13–14). But, arguably, Clem-ens had always written to please a female audience, beginning with his mother and continuing with Mary Fairbanks in the late 1860s and most successfully with Olivia and his three daughters during the 1870s and 1880s.

Glenn Hendler's article, "The Limits of Sympathy: Louisa May Alcott and the Sentimental Novel," asserts that sentimental narratives played an essential role in perpetuating the Victorian belief in the sexes' "separate spheres," and that the "exigencies of sentimental fiction and the ideological imperatives of domesticity exist in tension with one another" (685). That Clemens utilized what was an exclusively female format to write his realistic novel may well suggest that Clemens was challenging the doctrine of the spheres and encouraging an epistemological shift. The plot of *Adventures of Huckleberry Finn* appears to fit neatly within Hendler's paradigm of the relationship between sentimental fiction and the "ideological imperatives of domesticity":

> The sentimental narrative has a surprising tendency to disarticulate domestic spaces. Rather than insistently fixing heroines in their families, many senti-mental plots begin with young girls leaving their homes, either by being orphaned or by their own choice. And instead of concluding . . . by restoring their heroines to normatively defined families — in which case the initial depar-ture from the family could be read as ultimately supportive of domestic values — the novels often place their heroines in situations that are notable for their deviations from that norm. While the new stasis that resolves the novels' narrative tensions is still described, at least metaphorically, as a "family," it always represents a transformation — sometimes a radical one — of the group initially designated by the term. Sentimental plots repeatedly transgress both the internal and the external limits of the family structure which domestic ideology held up as its overt ideal. (685–86)

Louisa May Alcott's *Work: A Story of Experience* (1873) begins with the orphaned heroine leaving her home in search of greater autonomy.[5] The orphan was a staple of Clemens's novels, and a parallel can be drawn between Alcott's heroine and Huckleberry Finn. Huck, too, leaves home in search of an autonomous self, although at the time of his departure he is not yet aware of this. After Pap kidnaps Huck, Huck thinks he cannot return because in doing so he, and possibly the Widow Douglas and Miss Watson, would suffer Pap's wrath. Pap falls within the group of characters Baym identifies as "abusers of power" in sentimental women's novels: "Abusers . . . run a gamut from fathers and mothers to step-parents, aunts, uncles, grandparents, guardians, and matrons of orphanages. They are the administrators or owners of the space within which the child is legally constrained" (*Woman's Fiction* 37).

What Pap has is legal control over Huck, and despite Judge Thatcher's and the Widow Douglas's protests to the contrary, he will retain that right. Baym comments that men in sentimental fiction "are less important to the heroine's emotional life than women. Chiefly, they are the controllers and dispensers of money" (39). Interestingly, Clemens has Pap attempt to claim

Huck's money, yet Huck manages to outsmart his father. Pap's chief role in the novel is to remove Huck from his "home" (a home that deviates from the Victorian norm, as both heads of the family are female), and he is able to do so because, however unfit, he is recognized as Huck's legal guardian. Once Huck has been removed from the Widow's house and Huck has removed himself from Pap's sorry dwelling, Pap's usefulness as a character has come to an end and he is killed off.

In Susan Warner's *The Wide, Wide World* (1850) (one of the best-selling books of the nineteenth century, with sales surpassing one-hundred thousand copies), the orphan Ellen Montgomery rejects blood relatives and instead elects to form her family ties with her neighbors, the Humphreys. Glenn Hendler notes that throughout the genre of the sentimental novel, "the voluntary affinities of sympathy prove stronger than the ties of kinship" (687). On the raft, Huck forges his family with Jim. When Jim exclaims: "'good lan'! is dat you, honey? Doan' make no noise,'" Huck comments, "It was Jim's voice—nothing ever sounded so good before" (*Adventures* 95). Huck and Jim form a bond that proves stronger than any other relationship in the novel, including Huck's friendship with Tom.

By the end of *Adventures of Huckleberry Finn,* Huckleberry has no viable option of returning to society in the manner of the sentimental heroines. He cannot return to the Widow Douglas because he has already learned how powerless she is within the constraints of patriarchal society. He cannot remain at Aunt Sally's farm because, "Aunt Sally she's going to adopt me and sivilize me" (229). After concluding such a long journey, Huck cannot allow this to happen because, however benign, Aunt Sally is representative of the slaveholding South he has rejected. As for allying himself with any of the male characters in the novel, Huck has witnessed Judge Thatcher's impotence in protecting him; the majority of the males in the Shepherdson and Grangerford families are murderous idiots; the Duke and the Dauphin are revealed to be frauds; and by the end of the novel, Huck painfully recognizes Tom's continued alliance to the South when Tom helps to free Jim only because Jim already has been freed. The only possibility that Huck has to rejoin a family structure, which Clemens does not offer the reader in the text, is if he and Jim were to remain together and find and rejoin Jim's biological family—in the antebellum South, an impossibility.

Huck's plight resembles that of the sentimental heroines, but his choices are even more limited than theirs. Clemens's solution to the problem (of the self in opposition to society) may well have been having Huck choose as the subject for his story what he cannot rejoin in the usual sense — society. In his telling, therefore, Huck does effect a kind of return.

Leland Krauth's discussion is particularly cogent in view of Clemens's immediate female audience. According to Krauth, what Clemens does with the character of Huck is unprecedented within the genre of Southwestern humor: Clemens departs from the archetype of the "Man of Feeling" to make Huck "a *comic* Man of Feeling. Huck never feels good about his goodness; his altruistic emotions — with the possible exception of his aid to Mary Jane — never give him egoistic satisfaction" (381). Krauth asserts that this altruism is one of the reasons *Adventures of Huckleberry Finn* is still so intriguing today, because the portrayal of the "Man of Feeling" still challenges conventional stereotypes of manhood. Krauth also points out, quite rightly, that while Huck is a lost boy afraid in a man's world, he is never frightened by the world of women. Clearly both Huck's and Clemens's angst was reduced when they were in the company of females. During Huck's trip down the river, he evolves into the student he was never allowed to become in St. Petersburg, and he learns about natural humanity from Jim and about the falsity of gender roles from Judith Loftus. These lessons result in a radically changed conception of the traditional Southwestern character.

Krauth ends his article with this intriguing statement: "[Huck's] kind of manliness seems to elude our language for it, even today" (384). This elusiveness may be attributed to Clemens's female collaborators who helped create Huck's "sense of manliness" combined with "delicate sensitivity," and to the influence of contemporary women's sentimental novels. Clemens was pragmatic enough to incorporate his audience's experience as females and the themes of female-authored sentimental fiction into his writing. This female audience, indeed, also helped him gain financial success. Clemens met with spectacular failure in most of his earlier business dealings; however, with the help of his "charmed circle," he realized that if he incorporated themes and characters that a female audience would find appealing, his market might increase. It is important to note, however, that while Clemens's reliance on women was unquestionably productive for Clemens, it was also a positive experience for his wife and daughters who, during the Hartford and Quarry Farm years, were able to take part in his composing process and reap the benefits of his success. At this time, Clemens was at his creative apex, and his family was integral in bringing about this achievement. Clemens realized the impact his family had upon his writing and they became a willing part of his composing process.[6]

In the Marketplace

The literary product created by Clemens and his family was clearly subject to what Elaine Showalter terms the "operations of the marketplace" (12). For instance, Clemens wrote to William Dean Howells to declare that he had written *The Adventures of Tom Sawyer* for adults: "It is not a boy's book, at all. It will only be read by adults" (*Mark Twain-Howells Letters* 91). Howells replied: "I think you ought to treat it explicitly as a boy's story" (110). Clemens wrote back to Howells, in agreement: "Mrs. Clemens decides with you that the book should issue as a book for boys, pure and simple — and so do I" (112). (In view of his listening audience, Clemens's uncertainty as to whether *The Adventures of Tom Sawyer* and *Adventures of Huckleberry Finn* should be considered children's books or adult books is understandable; after all, he had written them most immediately to please an aesthetically diverse group of female listeners of disparate ages.)

But Clemens changed his mind yet again, after Howells informed him that "the book consumer[s] par excellence in Victorian America" were young women (Wecter 172). Howells was correct. By the 1850s the works of female authors represented approximately half of all popular fiction published, and by the 1870s women had outdistanced male writers and authored almost three-quarters of all published novels (Coultrap-McQuin 2). Clemens ultimately took Howells's advice to heart, for he finally wrote him that "the book is now professedly & confessedly a boy's & girl's book" (*Mark Twain-Howells Letters* 122), and in the preface to *The Adventures of Tom Sawyer,* Clemens was careful to include this note: "Although my book is intended mainly for the entertainment of boys and girls, I hope it will not be shunned by men and women on that account" (*The Unabridged Mark Twain* 437).[7]

Clemens need not have feared the loss of an adult market, as *The Adventures of Tom Sawyer* was read by an audience of children and adults, females and males. It is noteworthy that the book agents enlisted to sell the novel reflected this gender diversity. Many of the booksellers were female — females who, according to the mores of the time, were considered by many to be of questionable character. One female book agent describes her experiences selling subscription books:

> "Who was it Cora?" "Only a woman with a book," responded the waiting girl to her mistress's interrogation regarding a summons to the front door. "Well, I declare! I cannot, for the life of me, see how any woman that has the least sort

of respect for herself can engage in such an occupation. Why the very idea is enough to repel a pure-minded person, let alone actually working in the capacity." (*Facts* 7)[8]

This bookseller recounts reading an announcement in the local paper for agents "to canvas 'Tom Sawyer,' Mark Twain's new book" (35). Prior to this the agent had been selling, unsuccessfully, an automatic plaiting machine: "I seized my writing material immediately and wrote to the firm, asking for the prospectus book, and the town of Oroville as territory to work upon" (35). She was hired for the position, traveled extensively throughout Northern California, and, despite some public censure regarding the propriety of her employment, sold *The Adventures of Tom Sawyer* to both men and women with great success.

Clemens targeted the female book-buying public within his own publishing firm, as the Charles L. Webster & Company offered a selection of texts written by women that would appeal to a distinctly female audience. Among the twelve women writers Webster published were Martha Jane Crim ("Matt Crim") whose novels featured strong, intelligent women characters and predictable romantic story lines (all her narratives ended happily); Elizabeth Cavazza ("Elizabeth J. C. Pullen"), a short story writer who offered Italian settings and female protagonists; Madeleine Vinton Dahlgren, who wrote a novel about a young woman named Alma and her supposedly psychic dog Chim; Annie E. Holdsworth, a novelist whose single female protagonist, Johanna, possessed philanthropic instincts and reformist politics; and Mary Russell Mitford, who authored a regional novel about the pleasures of small-town life.[9]

In addition to female-authored fiction, Webster published Civil War widows' memoirs, including Elizabeth Bacon Custer's *Tenting on the Plains, or, General Custer in Kansas and Texas* (1889) and Madeleine Vinton Dahlgren's *Memoirs of John A. Dahlgren* (1891), as well as a beauty book by Annie Jenness Miller, *Physical Beauty and How to Obtain and How to Preserve It* (1892), where Miller asserts that "above all other charms, [a woman] must possess that of mentality" (217).

There was also apparently some crossover by women who bought titles intended for a male audience. A prospectus copy of *Personal Memoirs of U.S. Grant* lists the names of individuals who signed up as possible subscribers. Of the twenty-nine names listed, four belonged to women subscribers (Sanderson).

One cannot underestimate Clemens's awareness of what was successful within the literary marketplace. In a sense, too, Clemens's family comprised his personal "test group" on which he could practice a form of what today we would call market research. This in part accounts for the level of decorum in Clemens's texts — he would not want to offend the sensibilities of his daughters, and he would obviously balk at offending the majority of his potential customers. Ann Douglas, in her discussion of the position writers occupied in Victorian society, comments regarding the burgeoning commercialism of the time, "In very real ways, authors and clergymen were on the market; they could hardly afford to ignore their feminine customers and competitors" (8). A man with Clemens's ambitions for wealth certainly could not ignore his female readership.

A Sense of Place

While it is clear that Quarry Farm's female community influenced Clemens's work, the farm has not received critical attention as the locus of creativity it became. Apart from *Mark Twain in Elmira* (a locally produced compilation of accounts featuring Elmira and its environs [Jerome and Wisbey, eds.]), there are no other texts that feature Quarry Farm. Everett Emerson is among the few scholars who have, even in passing, recognized its importance. In *The Authentic Mark Twain,* Emerson cites Quarry Farm as a place where Clemens composed "much of his best work" (64), yet he mentions only the site and not the other people besides Clemens who inhabited it. Both *The Adventures of Tom Sawyer* and *Adventures of Huckleberry Finn* were composed at Quarry Farm during the period 1874 to 1885, and it was there that Clemens spent his happiest and most secure moments. Clemens refers to his contentment in a letter sent from Quarry Farm to Dr. John Brown in 1874: "If there is one individual creature on all this footstool who is more thoroughly and uniformly and unceasingly *happy* than I am I defy the world to produce him and *prove* him. In my opinion he doesn't exist" (Paine 505).

Quarry Farm was Clemens's favorite place for composing, and he grew ever more aware of the vital link between Quarry Farm and his fiction. In a letter to Mary Fairbanks dated April 23, 1875, he mentions his capacity for work:

> We have determined to try to sweat it out, here in Hartford, this summer, and not go away at all. That is Livy's idea, not mine; for I can write ten chapters in

Elmira where I can write one here. I work at work here, but I don't accomplish anything worth speaking of. . . . I can't succeed except by getting clear out of the world on top of the mountain at Elmira. (*Mark Twain to Mrs. Fairbanks* 191)

As Resa Willis records, Hartford was where the Clemens family socialized and where Clemens primarily conducted his business affairs; Hartford was not a place Clemens found conducive to writing.

During the Quarry Farm years Clemens was so sure of his fiction-writing abilities that, in an often quoted metaphor, he bragged: "When the tank runs dry you've only to leave it alone and it will fill up again in time — while you are asleep — also while you are at work at other things and are quite unaware that this unconscious and profitable cerebration is going on" (*Mark Twain in Eruption* 197).

There would come a time, however, when Clemens's tank of inspiration would cease to replenish itself. The prolific days at Quarry Farm would come to an abrupt halt with the onset of Clemens's financial difficulties.

Notes

1. Justin Kaplan sees Clemens's favorite workplace as reinforcing the image of the solitary artist: "Everything lay below the study and beyond. . . . He was isolated — from Livy, children, servants, the entire domestic context" (178). Kaplan quotes part of a letter Clemens wrote to Dr. John Brown: "it [the study] is remote from all noises" (Sep. 4, 1879, MTP*). According to Kaplan's interpretation, Clemens was relieved to be isolated from familial interruptions.

At first glance, Kaplan's view appears valid. Removed from petty interferences, Clemens is free to create; the dichotomy is left intact. But Kaplan does not take into consideration that composition for Clemens was not restricted to the eight walls of his study. Nowhere in the letter does Clemens state that the isolation of the study is a welcome relief from the closeness of his family. The single sentence Kaplan quotes comes in between two paragraphs in which a gleeful Clemens describes at length the location and details of his retreat.

2. In Notebook 30, dated from August 1885 to March 1886, Clemens wrote: "Jean requests me to tell a story to be based upon a kind of business copartnership between a 'bawgunstrickter, & a burglar'" (No. 30, MTP*).

3. Apparently Olivia was not the only person who enabled Clemens to unlock his memories of the past. On March 4, 1869, Clemens wrote Olivia that his childhood minister had paid him a surprise visit, and that their conversation had "filled my brain with trooping phantoms of the past — of dead faces & forgotten forms — of scenes that are faded — of old familiar voices that are silent forever, & old songs that are only a memory now" (*Mark Twain's Letters, 1869,* vol. 3: 135).

In addition, Alan Gribben argues in his essay, "'I Did Wish Tom Sawyer Was There': Boy-Book Elements in *Tom Sawyer* and *Huckleberry Finn*," that within Thomas Bailey Aldrich's book, *The Story of a Bad Boy* (1869), there lay "the incidents that apparently prompted Mark Twain to value at last the wealth of literary materials lying unclaimed in his recollections of prewar Hannibal" (155). In a letter Clemens wrote to Olivia on December 31, 1868, he thanked her for sending him a "sketch" from the New York *Independent* (*Mark Twain's Letters, 1869,* vol. 3: 370). The clipping probably came from the December 24 issue. In the advertisement section of that December 24 issue is a prospectus for a new magazine entitled *Our Young Folks.* Prominently advertised as the "leading Serial Story . . . for the year 1869" was Aldrich's *Story of a Bad Boy.*

4. Biographical information on Susan Crane supplied in an interview with Gretchen Sharlow, Director of the Center for Mark Twain Studies, November 15, 1991.

5. In Gribben's *Mark Twain's Library: A Reconstruction,* two works by Alcott are listed as belonging to Clemens: *Little Women* (1869) and *Little Men* (1871) (14). Olivia quoted Fanny Fern in her commonplace book (MTP).

6. After the onset of financial difficulties in 1891 and the subsequent deaths of Susy and Olivia, Clemens adversely affected the lives of the remaining women in his life. He also became very aware that he could write extended narratives only under certain circumstances: "one can't write a book unless he can banish perplexities and put his whole mind on it" (Gerber 45). Clemens's awareness, though, did not lessen his bitterness when he realized that his days of sustained writing were finished.

7. The four letters in question are dated July 3, 1875; November 21, 1875; November 23, 1875; and January 18, 1876.

8. Another female agent, Elizabeth Lindley, described her experiences selling the novel on the East coast in *Diary of a Book Agent* (New York: Broadway Publishing Co., 1911).

9. Webster published *Adventures of a Fair Rebel* (1891), *Elizabeth: Christian Scientist* (1893), and *In Beaver Cove and Elsewhere* (1892) by Crim; *Don Finimondone: Calabrian Sketches* (1892) by Cavazza; *Chim: His Washington Winter* (1892) by Dahlgren; *Johanna Traill, Spinster* (1894) by Holdsworth; and *Our Village* (1893) by Mitford.

3. "Youth" and "Gravity"

> Praise is his meat and bread — it is his life. And there never was such an unappeasable appetite. So long as you feed him praise, he gorges, gorges, gorges, and is obscenely happy; the moment you stop he is famished — famished and wretched; utterly miserable, despondent, despairing. You ought to know all about it. You have tried to keep him fed-up, all of his life, and you know what a job it is.
>
> — Mark Twain, "Hellfire Hotchkiss"

Critics have had considerable difficulty reconciling the amount of influence Olivia may (or may not) have had on Clemens. One group argues that Olivia "tamed" Clemens to such an extent that his fictive voice was extinguished, while the other side contends that Clemens created a role of ideal womanhood and then forced Olivia to fulfill it, unquestionably to her detriment. Yet Clemens himself had practically foretold the sequel in a love letter of 1869. Shortly before their marriage Clemens wrote his fiancée: "Livy, you are so interwoven with the very fibers of my being that if I were to lose you it seems to me that to lose memory & reason at the same time would be a blessing to me" (*Mark Twain's Letters, 1869,* vol. 3: 206). After 1904, this virtually came to pass.

Controversy and Contradiction

Guy Cardwell includes an excellent summary of the current state of critical affairs in his article, "The Bowdlerizing of Mark Twain":

> The influence for good or bad that Clemens's wife exerted on his mind and writings has become a celebrated topic among the critics. For half a century it has resembled for them a compulsory figure in skating or diving: each contestant must go through his version. Most renditions divide along the Brooks-DeVoto fault line. . . . Alternatively and sometimes concurrently they may hold that Livy exerted little or no influence. (186)

One critic who charges that Olivia did have an effect on Clemens is Everett Emerson, who concludes that her influence was a decidedly negative one. Emerson states that "there were major losses for 'Mark Twain' when Clemens married Olivia" (115), although in a later passage he notes, paradoxically, that Olivia's death "did not make a great difference in the literary career of Mark Twain" (250). One year after Emerson's biography saw print, E. Hudson Long and J. R. LeMaster's *The New Mark Twain Handbook* (1985) was published. In their opinion, "The major charge against Livy . . . of emasculating Twain's style, [is] an indictment no longer taken very seriously by Twain scholars" (92). Long and LeMaster point to Edward Wagenknecht's concurrence and cite (incorrectly, as we will see) Wagenknecht's contention that Clemens was never in any danger from Olivia's influences since he simply possessed too much "vitality" to be "pushed very far from his native bent" (173).[1] Yet Long and LeMaster unintentionally go one step further than Wagenknecht in a revealing "Freudian slip." Whereas Long and LeMaster state, "It is Wagenknecht's conviction that Twain had too much *virility* to be 'pushed very far from his native bent'" (92), Wagenknecht's text actually reads "There was too much *vitality* in him" (173) (emphasis added).

The other side of the controversy surfaces in James Cox's contention that Clemens invented a role Olivia was to act out. Although Cox allows that Clemens gave Olivia "a more important role in his creative life than any subsequent critic has been willing to grant her," Cox nevertheless asserts: "She lacks personality because her identity has been relocated in her husband's image of her" (64–65). Perhaps a more accurate statement would be that, considered apart from her husband, she "lacks personality" in past appraisals because *critics* have located her identity solely in *their* image of her husband. Joyce Warren, who largely praises Cox's work in her chapter devoted to Clemens's relationships with women ("Old Ladies and Little Girls"), objects to his defense of Olivia because it is based on her usefulness to Clemens: if his marriage freed him to write of the past, he was, in a sense, exploiting her for his creative ends.

Determination

The plethora of critical opinions and disagreements suggests that, in order to gain an understanding of the Clemenses' relationship, we must first explore the patterns of Clemens's life before he met Olivia, then proceed to an analysis of Clemens and Olivia's early encounters. Since his days as a riverboat pilot, Clemens was determined to become both financially and socially successful. When his course toward realizing this goal was threatened or altered, the full extent of his wrath would descend upon the person Clemens held responsible. Often, Clemens would consider neither the consequences of his actions nor whether they were justified; instead, he would concern himself with removing, with all expediency, the barrier that inhibited his progress. (An example of Clemens's vindictiveness is evident in the sad fate of Charles Webster, Clemens's partner in the Webster Publishing Company. After the publishing house failed, Clemens, in a move that brings to mind Jane Clemens's "dislike list," blackballed him.) A cursory examination of Clemens's business dealings attests to his fondness for litigation when his demands were not summarily met.

Clemens's own family was not exempt from his fury when he suspected they might be impeding him. Clemens sent this icy warning to his brother Orion in 1862:

> I shall never look upon Ma's face again, or Pamela's, or get married, or revisit the "Banner State," until I am a rich man — so you can easily see that when you stand between me and my fortune (the one which I shall make, as surely as Fate itself,) you stand between me and home, friends, and all that I care for — and by the Lord God! you must clear the track, you know! (*Mark Twain's Letters, 1853–1866*, vol. 1: 195)

Clemens was not the one to cross while he was on the road to social prosperity and prominence. From San Francisco to Redding, Clemens was always on the watch for individuals attempting to take what he considered to be rightfully his. Like his mother, once Clemens considered himself wronged the individual in question was banished to his personal hate list, with little hope of reinstatement to his good graces. One person who was surely among the top five on the list was Lilian Aldrich, wife of Clemens's close friend, the writer Thomas Bailey Aldrich.

Upon first meeting Clemens, Aldrich was so repulsed by his appearance and mannerisms that she refused to invite him for dinner.[2] For a man as sensitive as Clemens, Aldrich's repudiation must have been embarrassingly painful. Indeed, this was obvious enough when the Aldriches paid the Clemenses a visit at their Hartford home, and Clemens exacted his revenge. On the morning of the first day of their visit, Clemens appeared at the Aldriches' bedroom door and sternly requested that they cease their nocturnal merrymaking and be more considerate in the future, as the Clemenses' bedroom was directly below theirs and Olivia was suffering from a terrible headache, which had been made all the worse by the Aldriches' midnight ruckus. Humiliated, Mr. and Mrs. Aldrich came to breakfast and begged Olivia's forgiveness. An astonished Olivia replied that she was perfectly well and that, since her room was in another wing of the house, she had not heard a sound. Mrs. Aldrich reports that during this exchange Clemens sat "at the other end of the table . . . looking as guileless as a combination of cherubim and seraphim — never a word, excepting with lengthened drawl, more slow than usual, 'Oh, do come to your breakfast, Aldrich, and don't talk all day'" (*Crowding Memories* 147–48). On the last night of their stay, Clemens put on a pair of cowskin slippers and imitated the African-American folk dances he had witnessed in his youth.

Clemens never forgot a slight, and here, on his home ground, he exacted the full measure of his anger toward Mrs. Aldrich. Indeed, Clemens nurtured a lifelong antipathy toward her; Clemens termed it an "aversion," and its culmination came in autobiographical dictations in which he devoted five days in 1908 (July 3–4, 7–9) to describing her in highly pejorative terms, giving a scathing account of her organization of and behavior during her husband's memorial service.

As to Clemens's amorous pursuits, we find that the romanticism that has surrounded Clemens and Olivia's courtship has all the trappings of the kind of short story Clemens would savor, but the reality was radically different. Despite his later protestations to the contrary, Clemens had been looking for a suitable marriage partner for some time. By age twenty-six Clemens was living in Carson City, Nevada, with his brother Orion, and he had already envisioned the place his future, as-yet-unfound wife would hold within their marriage. In a letter written to his sister-in-law Mary "Mollie" Clemens in January 1862, Clemens stated that he would not marry until he could maintain his wife "in the position for which I designed her, viz: — as a companion. I don't want to sleep with a three-fold Being who is cook, chambermaid and washerwoman all in one" (*Mark Twain's Letters, 1853–1866,* vol. 1: 145). Clemens was aware of the social rung this statement implied, one that would allow both him and his spouse to escape the rigors of a working-class life. More importantly, Clemens's expressed desire also implies an adjustment in attitude: he would not as a matter of course follow in the tracks of prescribed middle-class Victorian marital relations: rather, he would view his mate as a partner who had an equal role in the relationship. He continued: "I don't mind sleeping with female servants as long as I am a bachelor — by no means — but after I marry, that sort of thing will be 'played out,' you know" (*Mark Twain's Letters, 1853–1866,* vol. 1: 145). In other words, Clemens's sexual license external to marriage would be revoked with his engagement.

Past portrayals of Clemens have depicted him as a shy virgin upon his marriage to Olivia, but it is not unreasonable to assume that Clemens was sexually active before his marriage ("I don't mind sleeping with female servants as long as I am a bachelor," he had laconically remarked.) But at the same time that Clemens could have been sleeping with servants, he courted women belonging to what he deemed an appropriate social rank. One of his finest early letters, written at the age of twenty, was to a young woman, Ann E. Taylor, of whom Clemens was fond. In the letter Clemens anthropomorphizes a collection of insects that had been flying around his light and interfering with his writing by conducting a revival service presided over by a "Venerable beetle, who occupied the most prominent lock of my hair as his chair of state" (*Mark Twain's Letters, 1853–1866,* vol. 1: 60–61).[3] The anecdote was a tour de force creation that allowed Clemens to "show off" his written skills for Taylor. Clemens, of course, would continue to use his skills to attract attention to himself, and also to impress women.

When he was twenty-eight Clemens wrote to his one-time roommate, *Territorial Enterprise* editor William Wright, to relate an anecdote their former landlady had told Wright's father: "They always had women run[n]ing to their room — sometimes in broad daylight — bless you, they didn't care" (*Mark Twain's Letters, 1853–1866,* vol. 1: 304). And indeed Clemens took these proclivities with him when he traveled to Hawaii. At age thirty Clemens wrote to his mother and sister about going to call on a young woman while he was visiting Maui. Despite a hurt leg, Clemens made the trip on horseback:

> If I hadn't had a considerable weakness for her she might have gone to the devil under the circumstances, but as it was, I went after her. . . . If I were worth even $5,000 I would try to marry that plantation — but as it is, I resign myself to a long & useful bachelordom as cheerfully as I may. I had a pleasant time of it at Ulupalakua Plantation. It is 3,000 feet above the level of the sea . . . two pretty & accomplished girl's [sic] in the family & the plantation yields an income of $60,000 a year — chance for some enterprising scrub. (*Mark Twain's Letters, 1853–1866,* vol. 1: 337)

Clemens had always played to the ladies, and eventually this came back to haunt him. By the time he was wooing Olivia, his reputation was such that Olivia's mother was clearly worried. In a letter she wrote to Mary Fairbanks on December 1, 1868—a carefully worded exercise in nineteenth-century decorum—Olivia Lewis Langdon wonders about the man Clemens was, questions the kind of conversion Clemens had supposedly undergone, and asks whether this transformation is religious in nature:

> What I am about to write, must be plainly & frankly spoken. . . . what I desire is your opinion of him as a *man*; what the kind of man he *has been,* and what the man he now is, or is to become. I have learned from Charlie . . . that a great change had taken place in Mr. Clemens, that he seemed to have entered upon a new manner of life, with higher & better purposes actuating his conduct. — The question, the answer to which, would settle a most wearing anxiety, is, — from what standard of conduct, — from what habitual life, did this change, or improvement, or reformation; commence? Does this change, so desirably commenced make of an immoral man a moral one, as the *world* looks at men? — or — does this change make of one, who has been entirely a man of the world, different in this regard, that he resolutely aims to enter upon a new . . . Christian life? I think my dear friend that to you my meaning will not be obscure. (*Mark Twain's Letters, 1867–1868,* vol. 2: 286–87)

This line of questioning by Mrs. Langdon finds its echo in a sermon entitled "In Christ, or Not!" by the Reverend Theodore L. Cuyler. The tract was published on December 31, 1868 (one month after the above letter was written), in the New York *Independent.* The issue of conversion was a crucial one for Congregationalists, and it was a topic the Langdon's minister, Thomas Beecher, had often addressed in his sermons. In the first line of his sermon, Reverend Cuyler defines what the term "new" means to a Congregationalist: "If any man be in Christ, he is a new creature." Cuyler argues that one can only become a "new creature," if religious conversion has taken place (1).

Elements of Mrs. Langdon's letter also surface in a letter Clemens wrote to Olivia on December 27, 1868. In the second paragraph of the letter, Clemens assures Olivia that he has been reading Henry Ward Beecher's sermons, and he cites this quotation: "A Christian is a fruit-bearer — a moral man is a vine that does not bear fruit" (*Mark Twain's Letters, 1867–1868,* vol. 2: 353). Here Clemens refers to a particular sermon, "The Duty of Using One's Life for Others," wherein Beecher is careful to differentiate between a "moral" man and a "Christian" man. According to Beecher, moral men represent negativity, as their lives are filled with unthinking abnegation; in contrast, the Christian man lives a life of positivity as he "acts out of himself and upon others" (*Mark Twain's Letters, 1867–1868,* vol. 1: 356).[4] The last third of Mrs. Langdon's letter directly addresses this fine distinction: does Clemens's "great change" mean that he will "make of an immoral man a moral one," or does this mean he will "enter upon a new . . . Christian life?" For the Langdons this question was of extreme importance.

Earlier in his life Clemens treated the issue of reform as an elaborate form of game-playing; later, after meeting the Langdons, Clemens realized that if he was to marry the woman he loved, he would have to embrace a culture that held reform as its highest aspiration. Reform was at the core of the Langdon's belief system, in keeping with their religious, educational, and hydropathic background, and Clemens knew it. But whereas Clemens recognized that there was room for improvement in his character, he insisted that any improvements or alterations would be done on his terms—not other peoples'. In a courtship letter dated December 27, 1868, Clemens thanks Olivia for just "*suggesting* reforms when you could be such an absolute little tyrant if you choose" (*Mark Twain's Letters, 1867–1868,* vol. 2: 354).

While Clemens was willing to accept "tuition" from the women he trusted, he refused to be forced into anyone's conception of what he should be, and the women close to him understood this. Evidently the Langdons were eventually persuaded that Clemens was intent upon entering a new Christian life, since they finally consented to the marriage, but later events suggest that they might have been deceived. The culmination of Clemens's desire for wealth and status came on his wedding day in 1870, when he arranged to have a royalty check for four thousand dollars from the sales of *The Innocents Abroad* delivered to him that morning. Does this mean that Ambrose Bierce's cynical observation regarding Clemens's motivations was correct? Bierce observes that Clemens's marriage was "not committed while laboring under temporary insanity . . . it was the cool, methodical, cumulative culmination of human nature, working in the breast of an orphan hankering for some one with a fortune to love—some one with a bank account to caress. For years he has felt this matrimony coming on" (Rather 26). Was Olivia Langdon to be principally Clemens's "coal mine"?

A Literary Life

When Clemens was introduced to Olivia on December 31, 1867, he met a woman who was far better educated than he was. Judging from the contents of her personal letters to friends and from her commonplace book, she was a learned woman, relatively well-versed in classic and modern American and British literature.[5] Olivia and her mother were avid readers who "read continuously, alone as well as together, one reading to the other," and following the example set by her mother, Olivia organized reading and study groups throughout her life (B. Taylor, "Education" 47). In a letter to her best friend, Alice Hooker, Olivia lists the members who attended the second meeting of her reading circle in 1868: "Last night Emma Sayles, Henry, John and Mr. Yates spent the evening here. . . . We are now reading the *Vicar of Wakefield*. The boys have never read it" (Sept. 29, 1868, SDF).[6]

Olivia raised her daughters to be readers as well. Susy Clemens's biography of her father describes the family's reading habits at Quarry Farm:

> Mamma . . . reads or studdies [sic] or visits with aunt Susie for a while, and then she reads to Clara and I until lunch times things connected with English History for we hope to go to England next summer, while we sew. . . . She studdies [sic] for about a half an hour or visits with aunt Susie, then reads to us an hour or more, then studies write reads and rests till supper time. (Neider 146)

In addition to having read William Shakespeare, John Milton, Jane Austen, Margaret Fuller, Alphonse Lamartine, Maria Gowen Brooks, and Daniel Webster, Olivia recorded in her commonplace book abstracts from contemporary American, British, Scottish, and French writers: feminist Gail Hamilton; abolitionist Theodore Parker; journalist Horace Greeley; historian Thomas Carlyle; essayist John Ruskin; clergymen Charles Kingsley and Henry Ward Beecher; poets Jenny Marsh Parker, Jean Ingelow, Henry Wadsworth Longfellow, Elizabeth Barrett Browning (whom she particularly admired), James Russell Lowell, Robert Browning, and John Greenleaf Whittier; philosophers Henry David Thoreau and Ralph Waldo Emerson; and novelists William Makepeace Thackeray, Nathaniel Hawthorne, Victor Hugo, Fanny Fern, Charles Dickens, Harriet Beecher Stowe, Oliver Wendell Holmes, Anna Brownell Jameson, and William Dean Howells.

The range of authors and subjects in Olivia's commonplace book, which she kept from November 12, 1863, until March 9, 1871, is impressive. Particularly striking is the fact that, in contrast to most journals, the majority of writers Olivia quotes are contemporary, not classical, and many of the authors represented were associated with progressive interests. Olivia was drawing upon the writers and thinkers of her day, not of times past, to form her sense of self.

The commonplace book opens with poems by Jenny Marsh Parker and
Mary Abigail Dodge (known to her readers as Gail Hamilton). The first
poem, by Parker, is entitled "Archie Dean" and is an anguished, emotional
tribute to unrequited love.

> Would you laugh, or would you cry?
> Would you break your heart and die,
>   If you had a dashing lover
> Like my handsome Archie Dean —
> And he should forget his vowings
>   By the moon, and stars, and sun,
>   To love you forever more —
> And should go to Kitty Carrol —
>   . . . .
> Prithee, tell me, would you cry,
> And grow very sad, and die?
>   . . . .
>   Archie Dean! Archie Dean!
>   I remember that once you said
> Your name should be mine, and that I should be
>   The happiest bride ever wed.
> I little thought then of a day like this,
>   When I could wish I were dead.

The second poem is a rebuttal by Dodge entitled "What You'd Better Do,
Jenny Marsh," and it has a decidedly satiric cast. Dodge's response mocks
the pathos of Parker's poem.

> Break your heart for Archie Dean,
>   Jenny Marsh, Jenny Marsh
> Break your heart for Archie Dean,
>   Not a bit!
>   . . . .
>   Now, If I were a man,
>   Jenny Marsh, Jenny Marsh,
>   If I only were a man
>   For a day
>   (I'm a woman so I can't
>   Always do just what I want),

But if I were a man I would say,
   "Archie Dean, go to thunder!
   What's the use of sighs, I wonder?
Your oaths and vows and mutterings
   Are awfully profane!
Hie away to Kitty Carrol,
   Your loss is but a gain."

   . . . .

Take this advice and get him back,
   My darling, if you can,
And if you can't, why — right about,
   And take another man!

The two poems were apparently published in the women's magazine *Home Journal* during the 1850s (Endicott). At the time Olivia wrote this entry, Dodge was publishing "opinion pieces" on such topics as politics, religion, and women's rights in *The Independent* as well as in other popular periodicals of the time (Coultrap-McQuin 108, 110). *The Independent* was a weekly Congregationalist magazine that advocated abolition, temperance, and equal rights for women; it published stories and essays by such leading women writers and suffragists as Dodge, Harriet Beecher Stowe, Helen Hunt Jackson, and Elizabeth Stuart Phelps (another of Olivia's favorites). Dodge was well known during the mid-nineteenth century and, upon her death in 1896, she was eulogized in *The Independent* as "the most brilliant American woman of her generation" (Coultrap-McQuin 106). Decidedly iconoclastic, Dodge maintained that women needed to develop themselves without interferences from men and free from social dictates. In a chapter devoted to Dodge in *Doing Literary Business,* Susan Coultrap-McQuin maintains that Dodge "thought that in either career or marriage a woman needed to improve herself" (115). With Dodge so prominently located in her commonplace book, it appears that Olivia found her views to be of particular relevance.

A possible connection also might be made between Dodge and Olivia's future spouse. Alan Gribben lists two works by Dodge in the Clemens library: *Stumbling Blocks* (1864) and *Skirmishes and Sketches* (1865). When Clemens was courting Olivia, he wrote her a letter containing the following lines: "what we want is a *home* — we are done with the shows . . . of life. . . . At least *I* am — & 'I' means both of us, & 'both of us' means I of course — for are not we Twain one flesh?" (*Mark Twain's Letters, 1869,* vol. 3: 103). This latter line is strikingly similar to one found in Dodge's book, *A New*

Atmosphere (1865): "Neither is the man superior to the woman, nor the woman to the man, but they twain are one flesh" (Coultrap-McQuin 114). In this line Dodge is rewriting Matthew 19:5: "For this cause shall a man leave father and mother, and shall cleave to his wife: and they twain shall be one flesh." Dodge reworks Matthew to include the embracing and incorporating of each individual's gender. It is possible that Clemens, aware of Olivia's reformist beliefs and of her previous reading and recording of Dodge, employed this outspoken writer to assist him in his wooing.

If one assumes the Dodge link to be a viable one, light may be shed on the kind of woman Clemens was pursuing and the type of relationship they were creating. Susan Harris, in *Mark Twain's Escape from Time,* pronounces Olivia "provincial" and "avowedly conventional," and argues that Clemens "transform[ed] a real woman into an ideal one by shaping contemporary stereotypes of the good woman to fit his particular needs" (115–16). But popular Victorian stereotypes of the "good" woman very likely would have been at variance with the Langdons' definition. A "good" woman in the Langdon family would leave her church if it did not agree to sign an abolitionist pledge — as Olivia's mother did in 1846. This rebellious act obviously would not have fit within "contemporary stereotypes" of proper Victorian womanhood. According to Harris, the line "are not we Twain one flesh" was written to "accomplish several purposes":

> [Clemens wishes] to tell Livy what he expects her to want, to strengthen his association of her with home, and to absorb her into the manifold splits in his personality. The playful tone and clichéd language do not disguise the real message of this letter, which is that the Clemenses' home will constitute the core of Mark Twain's life, the innermost circle of the sphere around which his multiple personalities will revolve. (117)

Harris's interpretation of the "twain" line thus fits within the parameters of traditional scholarship, as she views Clemens as the sole initiator of action and Olivia as his passive receptor. Yet instead of interpreting the line as a forewarning of Clemens's attempt to "transform" Olivia, one can offer an alternate translation: that Twain was proposing a relationship whose structure would be symmetrical, not hierarchical in nature.

Courtship and Exchange

Olivia's sources for fiction by contemporary women writers were found in such periodicals as the *Phrenological Journal, Home Journal,* and *The In-*

dependent. The Independent, which was stridently supportive of women's rights, published an article entitled "Authoresses to the Rescue" on December 24, 1869. The piece identified women authors who supported the suffragist movement (Julia Ward Howe, Louisa May Alcott, Stowe, and Elizabeth Peabody), and scolded those writers (both female and male) who did not. The article concluded by stating: "On the whole, it may safely be declared that the literary women of America have now taken their rightful place at the head of the suffrage movement" (1).

Olivia may well have introduced Clemens to the pages of the *Independent.* During their courtship she mailed him a story from the December 1868 edition. Clemens commented on the piece in a letter to Olivia: "You are a malicious little piece of furniture, Livy, to send me that sketch from the *Independent,* when you knew perfectly well it would make me cry" (Dec. 31, 1868, *Mark Twain's Letters, 1867–1868,* vol. 2: 370). Olivia probably had sent him Augusta Larned's "Parson Fielder's Christmas Visit," a tale about a country parson too poor to give his large family gifts and who fears dismissal by church deacons.

Clemens wrote to the *Independent* in January 1874 requesting that they send him back issues beginning in November 1873 and continuing until the first of January. On January 28, Clemens received a bill charging him for five extra copies. Evidently, Clemens continued his subscription until the end of January (Gribben, *Mark Twain's Library* 343). Represented within the twelve issues Clemens received is a virtual pantheon of nineteenth-century female writers: along with Phelps writing on "The Female Education of Women" and "A Word for the Silent," there are poems and short stories by Rose Terry Cooke ("Thanksgiving Then: Remembered for Polly," "Thanksgiving," "Willow," and "Now"), a chapter from Louisa May Alcott's "Unwritten Romance," and a deft short story by Sarah Orne Jewett entitled "The Turtle Club."[7]

In "The Turtle Club" Jewett tells the tale of five little boys who, led by Joe Hunt, form "The United Turtle Club" and spend the summer collecting specimens with great success. In her conclusion, Jewett includes a school theme written by one of the members of the gang, Ned Crawford, who relates in first-person detail the epistemology of turtles. Ned describes his two remaining captives (the rest of the turtles had escaped their pen in an August rainstorm), and ends his composition with a self-reflexive comment: "I have two Turtles to sell—shiny, high-storied backs, first rate pocket-size and warranted lively snappers. This is the longest composition I ever wrote" (*Independent,* Nov. 27, 1873). Obviously, Huckleberry Finn's story was a great improvement on Ned's one-paragraph effort, yet there is a similarity between the two texts in that Huck, too, concludes his narrative by describing the act of writing: "and so there ain't nothing more to write about, and I am rotten glad of it, because if I'd a knowed what a trouble it was to make a book I wouldn't a tackled it" (*Adventures* 229).

Also contained within the issues Clemens ordered was a piece by Jenny Marsh Parker decrying "The Culture of Pauperism" (Nov. 6, 1873), and two essays by Gail Hamilton, "A Soul Saved" (Jan. 1, 1874) and "The Gentleman of Genesis" (Nov. 13, 1873) wherein Dodge/Hamilton again ironically comments on religion: "Adam had dominion over the earth; but he attempted to shield himself from the Divine displeasure by laying the blame on his wife, which no gentleman would ever do. Noah was a just man and perfect in his generations, if you do not mind an occasional fit of drunkenness."

It is quite likely that Clemens read the pieces authored by these women, and if he continued reading he would have been dismayed to find, in the first issue of the new year, a book review of *The Gilded Age*. Clemens's work was not kindly received by the anonymous critic: "The impression made — and this is our main objection to the book — is one of unrelieved venality and corruption. There is enough of this in Washington, no doubt; but to represent it as a general and pervading feature is terribly exaggerated" (*Independent,* Jan. 1, 1874).

But Clemens garnered praise in the last issue for the month of January in a review by Moncure D. Conway, who was in the audience during a London performance of the "bucking horse": "The talk of literary London just now is Mark Twain's account, in his new lecture, of the 'bucking' horse which he purchased in Nevada. . . . As I have said, the way in which this story is told is inimitable, and, indeed, the whole lecture is . . . one of the most unique pieces . . . ever known in these parts" (*Independent,* Jan. 29, 1874).

Olivia was obviously widely read in contemporary American women's fiction, and she must have been cognizant of the themes and images which Sandra Gilbert and Susan Gubar claim constitute the nineteenth-century female literary tradition. Gilbert and Gubar contend that "images of enclosure and escape" are representational of Victorian women's novels (xi). The elements of entrapment, enclosure, and escape that Gilbert and Gubar identify also comprise the primary themes and images of *Adventures of Huckleberry Finn*. This should not be viewed as mere coincidence; Olivia, with her extensive (and shared) reading of contemporary women's fiction, contributed to Clemens's awareness of these themes of estrangement, which he in turn incorporated in his fiction.

A writer whose works both Clemens and Olivia knew well was Charles Dickens (Clemens and Olivia's initial meeting took place at a Dickens reading in New York), and Clemens may have found Olivia's familiarity with Dickens's works a valuable asset for his own writing. There are certain similarities between Clemens's and Dickens's narrative structures: Dickens was a master at sustaining the public's interest in the monthly magazine installments of his novels, and Clemens's primary material for *The Innocents Abroad,* his first full-length book, consisted of the letters he sent back to be published in the *Alta California.*[8] When Clemens assembled the letters into his book, he still had to contend with attracting and sustaining the public's interest as his book was to be sold by subscription. During their courtship, Clemens asked Olivia to read proofs of *The Innocents Abroad.* Olivia's knowledge of Dickens's format might have aided her in her first editorial work for Clemens, a job she performed so well that he subsequently appointed her editor for all of his books. In a letter written to Elizabeth Jordan on March 10, 1905, Clemens emphasized the power of Olivia's influence: "She edited all my manuscripts, beginning this labor of love a year before we were married, continuing it 36 years" (New York Public Library, MTP*).

After their first meeting, and despite Clemens's fame as the author of "The Jumping Frog of Calaveras County," Olivia remained unintimidated. Hattie Lewis, Olivia's first cousin on her mother's side, recalled that during Clemens's first visit to Elmira, while the two were nervous about entertaining an author and unmarried man, "at least we were not overawed by his presence, or greeting" (Paff 2, MTP*). Olivia must have possessed a strong sense of self-confidence, for almost immediately she was assigned the job of reading proof for *The Innocents Abroad.* Clemens wrote Mary Fairbanks about an upcoming visit to Elmira and said Olivia and he would "read 500 or 600 pages of proof together—two or three weeks. Think of it! Splendid girl" (*Mark Twain's Letters, 1869,* vol. 3: 168). Concerning the interaction between Olivia and Clemens, Hattie ruefully commented: "I soon discovered that my quickness at seeing the point of a joke and the witty sayings that I had considered almost irresistible were simply nothing in comparison with my cousin's gifts. Mr. C. evidently greatly preferred her sense to my nonsense" (Paff 2, MTP*).

Hattie also noted in her memoir that Olivia "was rich, beautiful and intellectual, but she could not see through a joke or see anything to laugh at in the wittiest sayings unless explained in detail" (2 MTP*). Olivia effectively functioned as Clemens's "straight man," and the nickname Clemens gave her attests to her subtle delivery: "Gravity." An excellent example of

Olivia in the role of Clemens's comic foil occurs in a letter written by both of them to Mary Fairbanks shortly after their marriage. Olivia's "commentaries" are in parentheses:

> We are settled down & comfortable, & the days swing by with a whir & flash & are gone, we *know* not where and scarcely care. . . . But there is no romance in this existence for Livy. (False) When things don't go right she breaks the furniture & knocks everything endways. . . . We got off to church at last, the ladies (no ladies but the wife of the writer) within & I outside with Patrick. . . . And we two will get along well together—I feel it, I know it. We have been married eleven days, & not thirty-five (not one) cross words have passed between us. (*Mark Twain to Mrs. Fairbanks* 123–125)

In a postscript to the same letter, the raillery between the two is given free rein:

> P.S. The parenthesis refers to the
> manner of erasing words—not to Allie. S.
> [referring to a section Olivia crossed out in
> a portion of the letter not quoted]
> How thankful I am that you have some one
> to interpret my letter for you L.
> It is a sort of grammar that renders
> interpretation very necessary. S.
> I don' think so—*because*—L.
> And I *do* for the same reason. S.
> *No.*—L.
> Go to bed, Woman! S.
> I am not sleepy—L.
> This it *is* to be married. S.
> Yes indeed—woe is me! This it is to be
> married L.
> Go on-jaw-jaw-jaw. S.
> I don't *think* so—L.
> Well, take the last word. S.
> (*Mark Twain to Mrs. Fairbanks* 123–26)

Olivia did not lack a sense of humor; rather, she was subtle enough to know when and how best to display it.[9]

Correspondence

Critics have argued that Clemens inhibited Olivia's personal growth by the emphasis he placed on her "purity." This ideal of purity, according to some, determined the very structure of their courtship, as indicated in Clemens's correspondence. But this is a fundamental misreading of the nature and genesis of the couple's love letters and, by association, of the strategy *Olivia employed* in their wooing.

As early as their first meeting in Elmira, Olivia knew that Clemens intended to propose. (Hattie Lewis assures us that it was she who informed the "unsuspicious" Olivia of Clemens's intentions, but one can deduce that Olivia was far ahead of Hattie in realizing this.) From that point on, Olivia composed the movements of Clemens's suit: it was Olivia who rejected Clemens's first proposal but left the relationship intact; it was Olivia who insisted he write to her as a brother would a sister; it was Olivia who engaged in subterfuge by having Clemens address his letters to her brother; it was Olivia who installed Hattie Lewis as a romantic decoy so she could ponder Clemens's overtures without public pressure; and it was Olivia who had Clemens prove his sincerity about his intentions by writing scores of letters. It was a carefully thought-out wooing, and Olivia neatly concluded it in her methodical way when she wrote on the envelope of his final letter before they married: "184th — Last letter of a 17 months' correspondence" (*The Love Letters of Mark Twain* 139).

Indeed, Clemens viewed his intended as an independent, mature woman fully capable of making her own decisions. In a letter dated November 28, 1868, after Clemens chastises Olivia for overtaxing herself and becoming ill, he quickly apologizes for his tone:

> I am not talking to you as if you were a feeble little child, for on the contrary you are a brave, strong-willed *woman,* with no nonsense & no childishness about you — but what I am providing against is your liability to indulge in troubled thoughts & forebodings. Such thoughts *must* come, for they are *natural* to people who have brains & feelings . . . & so *you* must have them. (*Mark Twain's Letters, 1867–1868,* vol. 2: 289)

A reading of the courtship letters will bear out the fact that Clemens often engaged in flowery prose that sometimes seems overbearing. One sample of this can be found in a letter dated February 27, 1869, three weeks after the couple became engaged: "Don't be hurt at my solicitude, & my anxiety about your health, darling, for it is born of my strong, deep, deathless love for you, my worshipped idol" (*Mark Twain's Letters, 1869,* vol. 3: 118). Here, however, Clemens's prose is in keeping with the sentimental dictums of the day; Clemens's love letters are, indeed, good examples of nineteenth-century hyperbolic discourse of which Clemens, still active in the field of journalism during his courtship, was doubtless well aware, as was certainly Olivia.[10] In Clemens's love letters to Olivia, then, one should read his ecstatic proclamations on her virtue and perfection with the understanding that this rhetoric was typical of the pronouncements of the Victorian upper-middle class. This was the artificial language of courtship, not necessarily the beginning of Clemens's domination.

It seems likely that Clemens found working within these strictures to be stifling, as indeed one of the strategies Clemens employed in order to compensate for this stilted dialogue was his use of humor. There is an abundance of affectionate banter and amusing anecdotes in his letters. In a letter dated February 27, 1869, Clemens teases Olivia about her spelling, "(Livy, they spell Plymouth without the u—take courage, my darling)" (*Mark Twain's Letters, 1869,* vol. 3: 116), and he concludes by complimenting her on her wittiness: "The ring continuing to be 'the largest piece of furniture in the house' is a burst of humor worthy of your affianced husband, Livy, you dear little Gravity" (ibid.: 118). When Clemens joked with Olivia, his true voice, not the formal, sentimentalized version, emerged.

As the courtship progressed, the letters changed in tone, and Clemens's lover's prose gradually subsided. Although he never failed to express his affection, Clemens largely wrote of practical concerns after their marriage. In a sense, his sentimentalized rhetorical discourse had served its purpose; Clemens was no longer a suitor—he was a married man with responsibilities. A literary parallel can be drawn here to the Emmeline Grangerford episode in *Adventures of Huckleberry Finn.* Just as Clemens ceased using artificial discourse in favor of a more direct, simply articulated language to communicate with Olivia, he also reflected the decline of the lugubrious doggerel that Emmeline employs, which is to be replaced by more realistic prose.

Clemens's intention to love a flesh-and-blood Olivia, not an ethereal, purified deity, is made plain in a letter to Mary Fairbanks where he writes about how frustrated he became after receiving Olivia's first letter (most likely the one in which she stated that the only possible relationship between them could be as siblings), and how happy he is with his current engaged status.

Makes me feel awful to think of that first letter she wrote me—remember it? And that poem in the *Atlantic*—representing her out of reach—"And all my life shall lift its hands / In earnest longing toward thy face"—I wasn't going to regard her at *that* distance. (*Mark Twain's Letters, 1869,* vol. 3: 169)

Notwithstanding her love for Clemens, Olivia remained candid even when she realized that the truth might distress him. To an aggrieved

Clemens she wrote that during his first two-week visit in Elmira he had come close to overstaying his welcome. Clemens first responded to this news in a letter dated January 21–22, 1869, in which he stated that he nearly decided to travel from Chicago (where he had been lecturing) to Elmira on impulse to spend one day with Olivia, but that he was stopped by the knowledge that the "visit would have been unexpected & therefore a surprise, & you know surprises . . . are not always enthusiastically received" (*Mark Twain's Letters, 1869*, vol. 3: 59). Clemens made a second reference to Olivia's criticism on March 6, 1869:

> (It is funny that I am so willing to be in the way at *your* house — isn't it Livy? But then I have always felt perfectly comfortable there, & never once suspected that you so regretted my concluding to stay a fortnight that first time I visited Elmira — why it even touches my pride yet to think of it! — what did you want to go & tell me that, for, you dear little persecutor?) (*Mark Twain's Letters, 1869*, vol. 3: 139)

On March 12, 1869, Clemens recalled a dream in which Olivia refused to meet him, marking yet a third reference to Olivia's criticism:

> I remember that in a dream, last night, even *you* snubbed me in the most cruel way. . . . I thought I arrived at the side gate in a carriage, & walked around to the front of the house . . . as I neared the front door I saw you run . . . toward the drawing-room window, making gestures with your hands which I took to be gestures of gladness & welcome. . . . But alas! they were to warn me not to enter yet, because the philosophy lesson was going on. . . . Why do you treat people that way in dreams, I want to know?
> So don't you bother about that first visit, Livy dear. But for that remark of yours, I would have fancied I was quite a pleasant addition to the family circle at that time! (*Mark Twain's Letters, 1869*, vol. 3: 162)

Before their marriage, Olivia and Clemens discussed one couple whom they considered to be a loveless match — Thomas and Julia Jones Beecher. Clemens elaborated at length on his opinion of Thomas Beecher's insensitivity in a letter to Olivia:

> Mr. Beecher robs himself of the best happiness of his life when he enjoys his pleasures in solitude. . . . And then the glaring *wrong* of the thing: for Mrs. Beecher shares his sorrows, & this earns the *right* to share his pleasures. But it seems that when the two are done carrying all the *burdens* of the day, he has no more use for her — she may sit down in sadness & weariness, while he loses the memory of the drudgery in the happy relief of pleasure. It is selfish — though, superbly gifted as he is, let us charitably try to fancy that he don't [sic] know it. Only, my dear, I will suggest that his heart & his brain would not have been so

dull in these matters with his first wife. . . . It is the native *instinct* of *our* love to have no secrets, no concealments . . . we never will have to *reason* ourselves into doing a thing that necessarily comes natural to us. . . . Mr. Beecher . . . will have the *corpse* of the marital love. (*Mark Twain's Letters, 1869,* vol. 3: 241)

Here the flowery prose characteristic of Clemens's early love letters is absent. Judging from the contents of this letter, Clemens and Olivia had openly discussed, and thus decided *together,* the type of relationship they desired. They appear to have been well aware of the difficulties inherent in marriage. In a letter dated December 4, 1868, Clemens eloquently compliments Olivia on the type of relationship the two are constructing:

You are building up this love as I would have it built — upon a basis of *reason,* not *passion.* You are raising this edifice gradually, course by course, & proving each as it is laid. . . . *Passion* springs *full-grown* from the heart . . . & when lagging Reason follows & strips off its finery & exposes the skeleton beneath, Passion dies. The love that lasts, & is genuine, is that love which is born of both *heart & brain.* . . . Livy, was *ever* the love of an ill-matched couple born of both heart & brain? . . . Hardly, I think. (*Mark Twain's Letters, 1867–1868,* vol. 2: 300–301)

It is significant here that Clemens views Olivia as the individual in control of their future; this is in contrast to the view of biographers who have traditionally considered the distribution of power within their relationship as an unequal one. Unquestionably, Olivia entered her marriage with a clear sense of the union she wanted to have with her husband. Katy Leary, Olivia's maid, recalled that Olivia had "made up her mind when they first married, that her husband was going to be *free* to *say* anything and everything that he wanted to — no matter what it was; that he wasn't ever going to dread her criticizing him. . . . that his home was going to be a place where he could say and do what he wanted" (Lawton 240). What Olivia and Clemens desired (and here Clemens was a willing pupil for Olivia's tutorials) was a relationship based on a meeting of intellects; in other words, a love that would outlast mere passion.

Collaborator and Organizer

Olivia's control did not end at the altar. When the Clemenses decided to build a home in Hartford, Olivia took charge of planning its construction. She also drew the initial sketch of the house and, like her mother and adopted sister before her, held sole title of the land. All the negotiations regarding the house and land were carried out in Olivia's name, not Clemens's.[11] Olivia wrote to her husband concerning her handling of the house and its construction while he was away on James Redpath's lecture tour during the winter of 1871: "I think I have about decided what we shall do about building. I have *decided* so you will not have to decide. . . . We will put if it is necessary the 29000. into house, grounds and what new furniture we may need" (*The Love Letters of Mark Twain* 168).

Olivia was not a genteel, helpless victim of Clemens's misogyny; instead, she was instrumental in organizing and determining the direction of their lives. It was Olivia who decided the family's movements — whether they were to summer in Hartford or Elmira, and whether they would return to Hartford after their sojourn abroad. It was also Olivia who was in charge of educating and disciplining the children, and Olivia (with Henry H. Rogers) who insisted after Clemens's bankruptcy that he repay his creditors in full.[12]

At times, all of this responsibility and activity overwhelmed Olivia. Although her upper-class status protected her from much everyday drudgery, the Clemenses' lifestyle produced its own kinds of strain. In 1879, three days after her thirty-fourth birthday, Olivia wrote to her mother expressing her frustration over the social expectations for women.

> I told Mr. Clemens the other day, that in this day women must be everything: they must keep up with all the current literature, they must know all about art, they must help in one or two benevolent societies — they must be perfect mothers — they must be perfect housekeepers + graceful gracious hostesses, they must know how to give perfect dinners[,] they must go and visit all the people in the town where they live, they must always be ready to receive their acquaintances — they must dress themselves + their children becomingly and above all they must make their houses "charming" + so on without end — then if they are not studying something their case is a hopeless one — (Nov. 30, 1879, MTM)

According to Ann Douglas, the nineteenth-century woman was forced by Victorian social norms to become a "saint and consumer." These two roles were "interlocked and mutually dependent; the lady's function in a capitalist society was to appropriate and preserve both the values and the commodities which her competitive husband . . . had little time to honor or enjoy; she was to provide an antidote and a purpose for [his] labor" (60). Although on the surface Olivia may appear to fit Douglas's definition, by virtue of her background she was well aware of the restrictiveness of

Victorian society, and she attempted to operate both within and outside of accepted standards of behavior for women of her class. Her rejection of the more rigid aspects of Victorian society can be seen in her constant quest for education (as exemplified by her extensive reading), her friendships with suffragists, and her involvement with Clemens's writing. Olivia could of course play both "saint and consumer"—there are enough testimonials to that effect (among them those of Howells and Clemens's close friend Joseph Twichell). But Olivia did not merely function as an "antidote" for Clemens's work; she labored with him to create his works.

A common notion among the handful of studies conducted by female critics regarding Clemens and women is that Olivia has not been granted her true "personhood." Because Clemens's relationship with his spouse has been found lacking by the few female scholars working in the field, Olivia by association has been negated. Mary Ellen Goad, in her thesis, "The Image and the Woman in the Life and Writings of Mark Twain," falls within the "Brooks-DeVoto fault line" with her rendition of an Olivia pushed, pulled, and ultimately molded into Clemens's ideal woman. Clemens's machinations began, claims Goad, before he had even met Olivia: "Having seen her picture, Twain proceeded to create her personality" (25).

Goad's work as well as other studies by women are undermined by their excessive dependence on other biographies for primary source material. Like Goad, Resa Willis adopts the position that Olivia "was another of Clemens's [fictional] creations" (*Mark and Livy* xii). Willis views Olivia as a conventional, idolized, hypochondriac who believed her husband needed and wanted to be "tamed" (xiii). This stance by and large is not original; Goad had raised this point more than twenty years earlier. Most problematic about both critics' reliance on previous biographers for information is that this earlier research is often flawed. Goad and Willis, in attempting to portray Olivia as an individual in her own right, use as the foundation for their arguments the very same scholarship that contributed to the current dichotomous debate in Twain studies. As a result, their work becomes inherently biased: a balanced study of Olivia's personality and her interaction with Clemens becomes impossible.

Susan Harris and Joyce Warren, two literary critics who have published work on Clemens's relationship with Olivia, rely heavily on Goad for their formulations. Harris, writing eleven years after Goad, echoes her when she claims that "Twain projected the woman he wanted Livy to be . . . he could create the woman and the relationship he wanted just as he could create any other fictional situation" (115). This view invests Clemens with a great deal of power, and at the same time renders Olivia helpless. In *The American Narcissus* Warren refers to Goad as "the only critic I have found who discusses Livy as a person separate from Mark Twain" (166). But this discussion is nowhere to be found, for Goad constantly assures the reader that there *is* no Olivia — only a fabrication of Clemens's imagination — and Warren and Harris both seize upon this. Harris in particular argues that Clemens fictionalized Olivia by emphasizing her "purity." (For Twain scholars, this manifests a progression of sorts with reference to Olivia: she moves from Paine's unawakened child, to Van Wyck Brooks's castrator, to Kaplan's whining, parsimonious figure, to Harris's "conventional girl.") Warren's final pronouncement on the foundation of Clemens and Olivia's relationship effectively summarizes the critical positions taken by Goad, Willis, and Harris: "With this preconceived idea of what his wife should be, Twain proceeded to mold Olivia Langdon according to the image he desired for a wife; in a sense, he created her" (160). We are left with an image of Olivia Langdon Clemens as a helpless automaton, and of Clemens as a Machiavelli. One cannot help wondering where Olivia and Clemens went.

Finally, one point must be clarified regarding the issue of Olivia's editing. Although she has been generally viewed as acting principally as editor, in fact Olivia had a much greater role. Olivia's interaction was crucial in all phases of Clemens's writing process. Cox summed up Olivia's influence on Clemens's writing by saying "she was both [Clemens's] muse and censor, or, to put it more precisely, his muse *as* censor" (64–65), thereby implying that somehow Olivia curtailed Clemens's imagination. But a more appropriate candidate for the role of "censor" — that is, one who works only to suppress, not create — would be Isabel Lyon, for when Lyon was unable to provide constructive critical feedback, Clemens's creativity suffered. Olivia's value to Clemens's work was not so much as "editor" as it was "facilitator," for it was through Olivia's sensibilities that Clemens was able to create characters that transcended the traditional fictional female and male stereotypes. While Clemens was free to let his imagination roam, Olivia gave focus to his tremendous sense of play and provided him with an informed, intelligent, female perspective.

Guy Cardwell challenges Hamlin Hill's assertion that the loss of Olivia's editorial supervision proved a great blow to Clemens, but Hill is quite right. On September 15, 1902, Clemens wrote to Frederick Duneka at *Harper's Magazine,* "My wife being ill, I have been — in literary matters — helpless all these weeks. I have no editor — no censor" (MTP*). Cardwell labels this well-known quotation "a curiously self-pitying, provocative passage, rife with possible suggestions concerning the wellsprings of Clemens's creativity, but how seriously a critic should expand upon it is, I think moot" ("Bowdlerizing" 187). The critic who regards this statement by Clemens as inconsequential is the critic who fails to understand the genuine basis of Clemens and Olivia's relationship, as well as the powerful effect it had on his writing.

Notes

1. This odd reassurance is reminiscent of Joseph Hergesheimer's 1921 *Yale Review* article, "The Feminine Nuisance in American Literature," in which the essayist laid out his definition of the desired masculine author/hero: "I must return to the word vitality, for that alone explains my meaning: such men have perceptibly about them the air, almost the shock, of their force" (719–720).

2. Mrs. Aldrich was particularly appalled by Clemens's ensemble. In her memoir, *Crowding Memories* (1920), she recalls with a genteel shudder that Clemens was wearing

> a coat of seal skin, the fur worn outward; a seal skin cap well down over his ears; the cap half revealing and half concealing the mass of reddish hair underneath; the heavy mustache having the same red tint. The trousers came well below the coat, and were of a yellowish-brown color; stockings of the same tawny hue, which the low black shoe emphasized. Was it dress for winter, or was it the dress for summer? . . . Winter disappeared with the removal of the guest's fur coat and cap, and summer, or at least early springtime, emerged in the violet tint of the carelessly tied neck-knot, and the light grey of under coat and waistcoat. (129–30)

Clearly, Clemens's later affectation of the white suit was not the first of his experiments with dress; indeed, perhaps the white suit should not be seen as so shocking in view of this earlier raiment. Clemens had apparently been breaking fashion rules for most of his adult life. According to one account, when Clemens first came to Elmira to call on Olivia, Charles Langdon, who met him at the train station, was so alarmed by his shoddy dress that he insisted he change before seeing his sister.

3. An excerpt from Clemens's autobiography, written September 26–29, 1892, in Florence, Italy, harkens back to this early letter. Here Clemens describes his battles with insects after he had his head shaved.

> Got my head shaved. This was a mistake. . . . But the main difficulty is the flies. They like it up there better than anywhere else. . . . These appear to have talons. Wherever they put their foot down they grab. They walk over my head all the time and cause me infinite torture. It is their park, their club, their summer

resort. They have garden parties there and conventions and all sorts of dissipation. (Neider, *Papa* 33)

4. Information about Henry Ward Beecher's sermon and an excerpt from the
sermon are from *Mark Twain's Letters, 1867–1868,* vol. 2: 356. Another example of
Clemens's awareness of Mrs. Langdon's concern that he become a "new man" can be
found in a letter he wrote to Olivia on December 10, 1868. Clemens tells Olivia he
has added a new closing to his lecture, "& one gentleman said that that gave the
lecture a sort of Sabbath-school cast. I said if he meant that it gave it a religious cast,
it was precisely what I intended" (*Mark Twain's Letters, 1867–1868,* vol. 2: 356).

5. In *The Man Who Was Mark Twain,* Guy Cardwell charges that Olivia had
practically no "formal education" and that "she had read little; her taste was insipid."
Nevertheless in the face of all these glaring inadequacies, Cardwell wonderingly
notes that Clemens "implored this incompetent young woman to reform his western habits and attitudes and to purify his works" (99). Cardwell *is* accurate regarding one aspect of Olivia's education: Olivia was deficient in ancient Greek literature,
since she had studied only Latin in college (whereas both Latin and Greek were
emphasized at men's colleges).

6. Barbara Taylor supplies an appendix to her master's thesis, "Education in
the Life of Olivia Langdon Clemens to 1870," where she records the dates and titles
of books Olivia mentions in her correspondence. Several genres are represented,
including biography (Washington Irving's *Life of Washington*); history (John
Lothrop Motley's *A History of the United Netherlands* and W. Carlos Martyn's *A
History of the Huguenots*); drama (William Shakespeare's "Tempest," "Much Ado
About Nothing," and "King Henry V"); as well as poetry and novels (Robert
Southey's "Poem," Edward Young's "Night Thoughts," Elizabeth Barrett Brown-
ing's "Aurora Leigh" [apparently a favorite poem of Olivia's], Laurence Sterne's *The
Life and Opinions of Tristram Shandy,* and Nathaniel Hawthorne's *The Scarlet Letter*)
(82).

7. Publication dates for these various writings are as follows: "The Female
Education of Women" (Nov. 13, 1873); "A Word for the Silent" (Jan. 1, 1874);
"Thanksgiving Then: Remembered for Polly" (Nov. 27, 1873); "Thanksgiving,"
"Willow" (Dec. 4, 1873); "Now" (Jan. 8, 1874); "Unwritten Romance" (Dec. 18,
1873); "The Turtle Club" (Nov. 27, 1873).

8. For further information on Clemens's roots in Dickens see: Howard
Baetzhold, "Mark Twain and Dickens: Why the Denial?" *Dickens Studies Annual* 16
(New York: AMS Press, 1987); Joseph H. Gardner, "Mark Twain and Dickens"
PMLA 84 (Jan. 1969): 90–101; "Dickens and Twain Presented by The University of
California Dickens Project" (ts. Mark Twain Project, University of California,
Berkeley).

9. Jeffrey Steinbrink's recent study regarding Clemens's brief residence in
Buffalo, *Getting to be Mark Twain* (Berkeley: University of California Press, 1991),
quotes extensively from Olivia and Clemens's correspondence and does an admi-
rable job of documenting the Clemenses' fledgling marriage.

10. A typical example of Victorian prose is this excerpt from a fashionable
women's periodical (circa 1830) called *Ladies' Magazine.*

See, she sits, she walks, she speaks, she looks — unutterable things! Inspiration springs up in her very paths — it follows her foot-steps. A halo of glory encircles her, and illumines her whole orbit. With her, man not only feels safe but is actually renovated. For he approaches her *with* an awe, a reverence, and an affection which before he knew not he possessed. (Douglas 46)

11. There are two excellent sources regarding the building and restoration of the Hartford home: an unpublished typescript by Walter K. Schwinn entitled "The House That Mark Built" (Hartford, Connecticut: Mark Twain Memorial) and Wilson H. Faude's *Mark Twain's House: A Handbook for Restoration* (Larchmont, N.Y.: Queens House, 1978).

12. Justin Kaplan uses this fact as an indictment against Olivia, for having Clemens assume the risks of business but refusing him "the recourse of the business-man" (330). Louis Budd, on the other hand, in *Our Mark Twain: The Making of His Public Personality* (Philadelphia: University of Pennsylvania Press, 1983), views Clemens's repayment of his debts as "the best investment he ever made" because it made him a paragon of personal integrity in the eyes of the public (201).

4. Elmira, Queen of the Southern Tier: Era of Reform, Part 1

> I reached Elmira after seventy-five miles of traveling and was relieved to find myself in a comfortable hotel in a large and thriving village. Elmira is the most business town of its size I ever saw. . . . When the iron horse startles the echoes of these hills with its shrill scream, come out and you will feel proud of the people, their intelligence, enterprise and love of free institutions and liberty.
> — *New York Courier and Enquirer,* July 14, 1849

Little has been written about Olivia Langdon's life prior to her meeting Clemens, or about the place where she grew up. Without such background information, Olivia has been something of a blank figure, an outline too temptingly easy to fill in or leave as a void. Without knowledge of her youth, it has been difficult to interpret with any certainty the events of Olivia's adulthood, or to gauge the amount and kind of influence Olivia eventually wielded with Clemens. The following will attempt to piece together, for the first time, the cultural surroundings, upbringing, and character of Clemens's future spouse.

Olivia Louise Langdon, the adored second daughter of Jervis and Olivia Lewis Langdon, was born on November 27, 1845, in Elmira, New York. Elmira was a hotbed of social reform during Olivia's childhood. Between the years 1852 and 1855, there occurred three events that would determine Elmira's *Zeitgeist* for the rest of the nineteenth century and well into the first decades of the twentieth. During the decade of the 1850s Elmira was captured, set afire, and ultimately transformed by the winds of reform: the city underwent major changes in health care, religious and social activism, and women's education. At issue, then, is how and to what extent the Langdon women were involved in this period of social upheaval.

The Langdon family's involvement with Elmira's social reform played a crucial role in shaping Olivia's perspective as well as her future life with Clemens. The Langdon family was deeply involved in all of the aforementioned reforms, and in two cases served as their instigators and primary supporters. One can state with some certainty that without the influence and commitment of the Langdons, this period of marked social upheaval and change in Elmira would not have taken place.

Of particular interest to me in researching Olivia Langdon Clemens's relationship to the social history of Elmira was an exploration of the Langdon women's role within the public sphere. How did these women, for example, negotiate the nineteenth-century dichotomy between the "public" or "masculine" and the "private" or "feminine"? The doctrine of the separate spheres as a central paradigm for examining gender division is particularly applicable for studying women who, like the Langdons, belonged to "the newly privatized households of an emergent middle class" (Peiss 818). In "Going Public: Women in Nineteenth-Centry Cultural History," Kathy Peiss argues that the public sphere for these women of the middle and upper classes represented "virtually any form of activity" outside of the home (818). Whereas past scholars have mistakenly positioned the Langdon women and their friends solely within the domestic arena, my analysis will attempt to place these women in the public milieu of reformist Elmira. I begin, first, with a discussion of the rapid changes that took place in Elmira during the nineteenth century.

A New Town, Reborn

Early biographers portrayed Elmira as a stifling backwater of nouveau riche conservatism. Van Wyck Brooks, in *The Ordeal of Mark Twain,* originated the characterization that future treatments of Elmira would perpetuate: "A provincial fresh-water aristocracy, resting on a basis of angular sectarianism, imposed its own type upon all the rest of society, forcing all to submit to it or to imitate it. . . . We can imagine how Mark Twain must have been struck dumb in such a presence" (102). Brooks quotes Albert Bigelow Paine's description of Elmira in *Mark Twain: A Biography* as supporting evidence for his own condemnation; but while most of what Paine wrote was similarly imprecise, he at least managed to avoid Brooks's shrill tone:

> Elmira was a conservative place — a place of pedigree and family tradition; that a stranger, a former printer, pilot, miner, wandering journalist and lecturer, was to carry off the daughter of one of the oldest and wealthiest families, was a thing not to be lightly permitted. The fact that he had achieved a national fame did not count against other considerations. The social protest amounted almost to insurrection. (Vol. 1: 378)

Clearly, Samuel Clemens was not "struck dumb," as Brooks would like to persuade us; in Paine's passage, one can almost hear Clemens, éminence grise, dictating his version of his infiltration and ultimate conquest of Elmira.[1] To gain an understanding of the place where Olivia Langdon came of age and where Clemens happily took up summer residence for three decades, we must turn to the historical record of the town itself, and away from the corpus of Twain biography.

In 1828 the south-central New York village of Newtown was re-christened "Elmira." At the time it boasted a population of 1,246 and its economy was agriculturally based (Sorin 8). By the end of the nineteenth century, Elmira had matured into a city of over 35,000 inhabitants, and its former agricultural origins were buried beneath the weight of industry. In a sense, the story of Elmira's growth is the perfect parallel to Samuel Clemens's own rise from rural obscurity to worldwide renown. What changed Elmira from a sleepy farming community to a prosperous industrial city was the opening of the Erie Canal in 1833 (the Erie connected with the Chemung Canal). This made Elmira a regional center for the transportation of lumber and coal. (Indeed these two commodities by 1860 formed the bulk of Jervis Langdon's business.) In 1851 the next economic boom hit Elmira with the arrival of the railroad. During the next thirty years the main lines of the Erie, Lackawanna, Lehigh Valley, Delaware, and Western Railroads all stopped at Elmira's depot. Business and industry exploded. An indication of Elmira's wealth can be found in a notice in the town's newspaper, dated January 14, 1860, which lists the deposits in the local bank, "published in report to-day," as totaling $158,110,66.00. The increase since the last report, published just four months earlier in September 1859, was an enormous $44,488,82.00 ("Elmira Bank" 5). All of this growth and wealth led logically to Elmira's designation as the Chemung county seat. As an outgrowth of the canal and railroads, by the mid-1890s Elmira boasted four main industrial sectors, housing such businesses as the Rolling Mills, B.W. Payne & Sons Engine and Boiler Works, Elmira Bridge Company, American LaFrance Fire Engine Company, tanneries, glue factories, breweries, woolen mills, freight houses, coal and lumber yards, and the Hope-Jones Organ Company (which eventually listed Clemens as one of its investors).[2]

With the rapid growth of business, laborers came to Elmira in droves, and the town's population soared. Between the years 1870 and 1890, Elmira's population more than doubled.[3] The new labor force contributed to Elmira's remarkably heterogeneous population. The African-American population had been the earliest minority to settle there, with free blacks living in the area as early as 1800. Most African-Americans arrived after 1840, and they fell into three main categories: formerly enslaved African-Americans who had escaped by way of the Underground Railroad; free African-Americans who had moved from Pennsylvania or New York City; and freedmen who had come North during the Reconstruction period in order to find work.[4] (Both Mary Ann Cord, Susan Crane's cook at Quarry Farm, and John T. Lewis, who worked as a handyman at the farm, fall into the first category.[5]) The African-American community in Elmira was deeply involved in the operation of the Underground Railroad: Elmira was a regular "stop" due to its strategic position between Philadelphia and St. Catherines, Canada.[6] In 1848 Frederick Douglass visited and lectured on African-American rights at Elmira's Temperance Hall. The vast majority of working African-American men worked in local factories, on farms, for the railroad or canal, and in road and building maintenance in and around Elmira. Black working women were employed primarily as domestic servants who, if single, often lived with their white employers (as did Mary Ann Cord).[7]

Irish immigrants first arrived in sizable numbers in Elmira between 1820 and 1860. The men worked primarily as laborers, digging the Chemung Canal and laying tracks for the railroad; the women worked largely as domestics. The Langdons employed several Irish women as servants.[8] Olivia Langdon Clemens drew from the same labor pool as her mother had and in the mid-1870s hired Katy Leary as the family housekeeper and caretaker. Leary, a second-generation Elmira native of Irish descent, worked for the family for more than thirty years.

By the close of the nineteenth century, Elmira boasted a thriving cultural scene. In 1885 the town had more than forty-five hotels, nine local papers (including two temperance papers, the *Elmira Sentinel* and the *Temperance Gem*), an Opera House (known later as the Lyceum Theater, where on November 23, 1868, Clemens delivered "The American Vandal Abroad"), an Academy of Music, and several assorted music halls and theaters. The Victorian era's best actors and lecturers trod Elmira theater boards: Edwin Booth, in "Julius Caesar," Laura Keene, appearing in the 1867 production of "Our American Cousin," and Frank Mayo, playing the lead role he created for "Davy Crockett." Elmira was also a regular stop on the lyceum circuit, with such lecturers as John B. Gough, Louis Agassiz, and Anna Dickinson appearing there.[9]

In stark contrast to the prosperity and cultural attractions of the town, Elmira was also the site of one of the most infamous prison camps of the

Civil War. Labeled the "Andersonville of the North" (after the notorious Southern camp), the Elmira prison camp at its peak held 9,499 men in an area designed to contain a maximum of five thousand prisoners. The groundwork for the Elmira prison camp was begun in May 1864, and it opened on July 6, 1864. The conditions there were horrendous; the Confederate prisoners lacked adequate food, housing, and medical treatment (Towner 265). During the one year and four days of its existence, the camp's death rate averaged eight men per day.[10] When the camp closed on July 10, 1865, a total of 3,022 men had died (Horigan 3,449–57).[11]

During its existence, the camp became something of a lurid attraction for the local townspeople and for sightseers from throughout the county. A viewing platform was built at the camp's northwest corner, and for a small fee the curious could ascend a ladder and gawk at the imprisoned men. Along the camp's perimeter, concession booths were built, and cakes, lemonade, beer, and peanuts were sold to spectators. Reportedly, local citizens would walk or drive by the camp as part of their "regular exercise" (Towner 270–71). One can only speculate what kind of effect this specter of misery had upon the Langdon family; at this time, Olivia Langdon was eighteen years old, a young woman. The family must have known about the camp, for it was located less than a mile away from their home, and their minister, Thomas Beecher, took aid to the camp's inmates (Holmes 36).

Elmira had been designated a "military depot" on July 30, 1861, because of its strategic railroad connections. It thus became a staging area for Union troops. A total of 20,796 men departed for battle from Elmira. On May 17, 1865, Mrs. Langdon wrote in her diary that the entire family, minus Olivia, "rode up to see the grand Review of the troops stationed here" (MTM). Without a doubt, the war and the camp must have had a tremendous impact on Elmira; at the time, the town's permanent population was just 13,130.

A Family's Progress

Jervis and Olivia Lewis Langdon were recent arrivals in Elmira, having moved there from Ithaca, New York, in 1845 (Beecher, *Jervis Langdon Eulogy Memorial Pamphlet* 8). Jervis was originally from Vernon, New York, and was born on January 9, 1809; Olivia Lewis was born on August 19, 1810, in Lenox, New York. They married on July 23, 1832.[12] The Langdons lived in Millport, New York, from 1838 to 1843 (Beecher, *Jervis Langdon*

Eulogy Memorial Pamphlet 8). They adopted Susan Dean sometime around 1838, when she was two years old; Olivia Louise was born in 1845; and their son Charles was born four years later in 1849. The Langdon family was part of a large circle of Elmira friends, and their home was a popular gathering place for social functions. The entire family enjoyed a robust sense of humor, and the Langdon children apparently adored their parents.

Jervis and his daughter Olivia shared a particularly close relationship. Alice Hooker, during one of her extended stays with the Langdon family, wrote home to her mother Isabella with this observation: "His [Jervis's] love and Livy's is remarkable — they seem more, almost, like lovers than father and daughter — he is bound up with her and she loves him with a great love" (Apr. 14, 1867, SDF). Their close relationship was well known to family members. Olivia's daughter Susy, in a biography of her father she wrote when she was thirteen, commented, "Mamma loved Grandpa more than any one else in the world. He was her idol and she his; I think mamma's love for grandpa must have very much resembled my love for mamma" (144, Feb. 13, 1906, Autobiographical Dictation, No. 64, MTP*).

Olivia's father was a self-made success who became wealthy late in life. Jervis Langdon's business instincts have been underplayed in the past in favor of his philanthropic activities,[13] but Jervis's business acumen emerges in a letter written by Isabella Beecher Hooker to her husband John on January 28, 1863. Isabella repeats Jervis's advice to her concerning future investments:

> he said this coming year was the time to sell real estate & invest in govt. [government] securities — there would not be such another time for selling for *ten* years he *thought*.
>
> I am sick of hobbling along with him [John Hooker's business partner] — when I think of how such a man as Mr. Langdon would put things through, it makes me ready to fly with vexation. (SDF)

Olivia's mother, Olivia Lewis Langdon, came from a family of eleven children: Olivia Lewis was the sixth oldest child and had a twin sister.[14] Clemens, when still courting Olivia, commended Mrs. Langdon's "native dignity" in a letter to his friend Joseph Twichell, observing that she was "born for a countess" (*Mark Twain's Letters, 1867–1868,* vol. 2: 332). The type and extent of her education is an area yet to be researched; however, it is known that Mrs. Langdon was an avid reader who possessed great intellectual curiosity. (A faithful member of the Tuesday Morning Club as well as the Shakespearian Circle, she also donated books to her church library.) In

Mrs. Langdon's personal diaries, she lists and comments on such varied texts as "Enoch Arden," "Much Ado About Nothing," and Irving's *Life of Washington.*

Whereas nineteenth-century women's literary clubs, such as the ones to which Mrs. Langdon belonged, have been frequently criticized as intellectually superficial, historian Karen Blair argues that the clubs had a polemical purpose that has heretofore gone unrecognized:

> The study of culture represents the culmination of the Domestic Feminism which grew in women's clubs and the story of its development is the story of women's successful attempt to exert their influence on the world at large. . . . By the end of the century . . . culture became absorbed into [women's] sphere and they ruled the domain as they ruled the home. (133)

Mrs. Langdon clearly "ruled" the Langdon home, but a larger issue is the nature of her relationship with her husband and the kind of model this provided for their daughter Olivia. There are two documents that shed some light on this question. One is a brief notation Mrs. Langdon made in her diary on December 9, [1865], stating that Mr. Langdon had given her as a present "the deed of this House" (MTM). This unconventional act would be repeated when Susan Crane gained the deed to Quarry Farm and when Olivia took possession of the deed to the Clemenses' Hartford home. (Susan, in turn, transferred her property to Susy, Clara, and Jean when she deeded to them the grounds of their playhouse "Ellerslie" in 1886, thus creating an instant matriarchal lineage [Lanmon 20].)

A second significant clue is found in the sermon the Reverend Thomas Beecher gave at Mrs. Langdon's memorial service in November 1890. The first line of the eulogy pamphlet reads: "'The woman question' for the last forty years has challenged attention, and more and more engaged the pens of brilliant writers." Beecher emphasized that he considered Mrs. Langdon an equal partner in her marriage to her husband, and he concluded his sermon by stating that he viewed "with grief and alarm the growing schism between man and woman. . . . I stand saying Mr. Langdon was a very strong man, and Mrs. Langdon a notable woman" (Beecher, *Olivia Langdon Eulogy Memorial Pamphlet* 5, 11–12). While Mrs. Langdon was representative of her generation in her adoption of the tenets of "domestic feminism" (in which she must have been well-versed, as she maintained a close relationship with Catharine Beecher), her active support of abolition and temperance, her membership in reading groups, and her friendships with women from the suffragist factions of the women's movement, including

Isabella Hooker and Anna Dickinson, signaled her openness to what lay beyond the private sphere.[15]

Additional insight into Mrs. Langdon's upbringing and her strength of character can be gleaned from the letters that her sister, Mary Anne Lewis, wrote to her. Lewis was an itinerant teacher who worked between the years 1836 and 1841 in and around Cleveland, Ohio. That she worked as a teacher reveals much about the Lewis family and what they considered acceptable in terms of women's roles. Keith Melder, in *Beginnings of Sisterhood,* comments that in the early nineteenth century the prevailing opinion was that "the vocation of a teacher demanded . . . special qualifications of strength sufficient to apply corporal punishment and learned preparation, possessed only by men. . . . Men teachers dominated most American education before 1840" (24). Early female teachers, such as Mary Anne Lewis, had to confront society's view that the teaching profession was analogous to medicine or the ministry, and therefore closed to women. By the early 1830s women had begun to gain acceptance as teachers, first in the New England states, and by the 1840s in states such as Ohio. Thus Mary Anne Lewis was a pioneer, and her family was unusually tolerant.

In a letter to Olivia dated August 23, 1841, Mary Anne writes to her sister Olivia that she must seek a position at another school due to the lack of students, and she describes in detail her ten-day visit to Oberlin College. Here Mary Anne is traveling by herself at a considerable distance from her family, and, judging by her tone, she is devoted to her vocation and proud of her independence. The letter reveals a woman who is clearly well educated, confident, and outspoken. She is unabashedly critical of Oberlin's student body when she comments on the men and women she has seen. Lewis bluntly describes the male students at Oberlin as "outright dolts" and labels the women as "buxom, uncorsetted, unpolished, unintellectual, and exceedingly unethical company." While she concedes that these observations are based upon "*appearances,*" her final pronouncement is that she will gladly amend what she has said about Oberlin students "if I find under a rough exterior real refinement and intellectuality" (CCHS).

The year 1841 was important in the context both of the history of Oberlin College and of women's education. This marked the first time a coeducational college would award bachelor of arts degrees to women, degrees which were to be considered equal to those granted to male students. Mary Anne Lewis commented in her letter: "Three young ladies are to graduate who have taken the regular college course" (CCHS). Mary Anne Lewis stayed with the Langdons during visits to Elmira, and young Olivia had in her aunt a decidedly atypical Victorian role model.

The Roots of Reform: Abolition and the Underground Railroad

Jervis Langdon and his wife were staunch abolitionists well before they moved to Elmira. Langdon was a "conductor" on the Underground Railroad, and Frederick Douglass was an honored guest in the Langdon home. Upon Langdon's death in 1870, Douglass sent a condolence note to Olivia Lewis Langdon (quoted in part here): "If I had never seen nor heard of Mr. Langdon since the days that you and himself made me welcome under your roof in Millport, I should never have forgotten either of you. Those were times of irreffaacable [sic] memories with me, and I have carried the name of Jervis Langdon with me ever since" (Nov. 9, MTM). At Olivia Lewis Langdon's memorial service, the Reverend Thomas Beecher reminded those gathered that the Langdons had always been "at the service of fugitives from slavery," and that the Langdon home had always been open to abolitionists such as "Garrison, Phillips, Quincy, Johnson, Gerritt Smith, Foster, Frederick Douglass" (Beecher, *Olivia Langdon Eulogy Memorial Pamphlet* 7).

An intriguing notice in the *Elmira Advertiser,* titled "Noble Donation" and dated November 30, 1864, gives testimony to the Langdon family's support for abolition. The announcement calls attention to the "noble donation" Jervis Langdon made to assist "white refugees who are fleeing from the ravages of Southern rebels." Langdon, along with other Elmira personages such as the Reverend Thomas Beecher, Dr. Silas Gleason, and Judge Ariel S. Thurston, donated $650 to this cause. What makes the item noteworthy is that the collected funds were given to a certain Reverend E. Folsom, a hospital chaplain in Cairo, Illinois. This money very likely funded Underground Railroad activities in the area, and the "white refugees" were possibly abolitionists who had been discovered and were forced to escape. At the time, Cairo was solidly pro-Confederacy, and activities such as those being carried out by Reverend Folsom would have been cloaked with great secrecy ("Noble Donation").

Hydropathy and the Elmira Water Cure

June 1, 1852, marked the official opening of the Elmira Water Cure, and heralded the first wave of social reform that would soon crest over the city of Elmira. The proprietors, Dr. Silas Gleason and Dr. Rachael Brooks Gleason, introduced a new era of health reform to the entire region. The

Gleasons believed in the power of hydropathy: that pure, cold water could be used to prevent and to cure most bodily illnesses. Hydropathy, let it be noted, was a gentler alternative to the established school of allopathic medicine. Allopathic practitioners took what could be termed an aggressive, often brutal, stance toward fighting disease, and their treatments included bloodletting, purging, blistering, cupping, leechings, cauterization, and the application and prescription of such "medicines" as laudanum, mustard baths, rhubarb, mercury, and morphine. The goal of allopathic curatives was to rid the body of disease and to restore health by removing from the body any "ill humours."

The result of these kinds of "heroic" medical practices — medication, bleeding, and surgery (performed without benefit of anesthesia, antiseptics, or hemostasis) — was that many people, not surprisingly, came to fear doctors and began to look for alternatives. By the mid-1850s these alternatives could be found in "irregular" schools of medicine, of which hydropathy was a leading representative.[16] Hydropathic medicine claimed that allopathy undermined the body's natural ability to fight disease and that the treatment often (especially in cases involving gynecological disorders) was more debilitating to the patient than the initial illness. Hydropathic therapeutic treatments included the sitting bath, the pouring bath, the sitz bath, the plunge bath, and frequent washings. The most widely used remedy was the wet-sheet pack: A patient would be wrapped in a wet sheet, covered by blankets, and left until the body was thoroughly warmed.[17] (The vestiges of hydropathy are apparent today in bottled water, jacuzzis, and home spas.)

The basic tenets of hydropathic medicine involved self-help and prevention. Kathryn Kish Sklar comments on the practice and philosophy of hydropathic medicine:

> Hydropathy was based on the belief that water was the natural sustainer of life. From the time of its founding . . . the *Water Cure Journal* . . . popularized the cure . . . and promoted many corollary doctrines such as temperance, women's rights, dress reform, and medical reform. It strongly endorsed the need for women medical practitioners. (246)[18]

Hydropathic medicine offered women (including both female doctors and female patients) a far more active role in determining the diagnosis and treatment of disease than did allopathic medicine. A result of hydropathic medicine's openness to women was that some of the earliest women doctors became water cure physicians.[19]

Rachael Brooks Gleason (1820–1909) was one of these medical pioneers. Rachael Brooks was born in Winhall, Vermont, on November 27, 1820. At age eighteen, despite some initial protest from those opposed to hiring a woman, Brooks took on a schoolteaching position, and she continued to teach for six years. Brooks married Dr. Silas Orsemus Gleason on July 3, 1844, and for a time studied medicine privately with her husband. On November 20, 1849 (according to the date printed on her matriculation card), she entered the Central Medical College of Syracuse, New York. She stayed at Syracuse until the fall of 1850, when she transferred and completed her medical studies in 1851 (according to the date and place on her hand-written diploma) at the Central Medical College in Rochester (Gleason File, CCHS).[20]

While the Gleasons lived in Syracuse, where Silas Gleason held the position of professor of hygiene at the Medical College, the New York State Eclectic Society called a meeting in Rochester to plan the opening of a similar institution there. Gleason attended the meeting and offered a resolution that the college also accept female students. The resolution passed, and in the first term of 1850, seventy-five men and five women were admitted; Rachael Gleason was one of those five. Of her minority status, Rachael commented: "Our seats were in front near the rostrum, and the quiet courtesy with which we were treated by professor and students saved us unnecessary embarrassment." She added, "They [the female students] were too earnest and too grateful to be troubled by any unavoidable annoyance" (Gleason File, CCHS). Rachael Brooks Gleason is listed in *Medical Women of America* as the fourth woman to receive her medical degree in America; just two years earlier, in 1849, Elizabeth Blackwell was granted the first such degree (Hard-Mead).

When one ascends Watercure Hill Road today nothing remains of the Cure except two stone posts, partially covered by vines, which mark the former entrance to the main drive, and some rusted pipes. The site where the Cure used to stand is vacant and overgrown; power lines hum overhead. Yet one hundred and thirty years ago the Cure was a thriving place: Carriages arrived full of patients who had traveled to the Elmira railroad depot located at the base of East Hill. The rural location was a deliberate choice; hydropaths were convinced that nature's restorative powers would enhance the cure, and hydropathic doctors encouraged patients to visit rural establishments. In addition to the natural surroundings and proximity to major transportation, there was another reason for the selection of East Hill as the site for the Elmira Water Cure — the excellent quality of the spring water.

ELMIRA WATER CURE.

This Cure has been open nearly eight years. Its Physicians have had a large experience in the treatment of Chronic Disease. For more than Fifteen years they have given their best energies to the Study and Practice of the Medical Profession. During this time more than 10,000 cases have been prescribed for.

This Season *entirely new* Bath-Rooms have been made in the Ladies' Department, equal to one room 60 feet long by 16 wide and fitted up in good style. The increase of our business demanded better facilities, and we have spared no pains to meet the necessities and comfort of our guests.

Our location has ever elicited the admiration of all our visitors and guests. It combines the bold and romantic with the more quiet and gentle phases of Nature. The city and country are at one view represented. The walks in the ravines and groves back of the Cure have been greatly improved this season. There is a new foot bridge spanning a deep ravine—paths, with nice seats for resting places, embowered in deep shade for retreats from the scorching Summer's sun.

We do not pursue the extremes of Hydropathy or of Vegetarianism. We intend the condition of the patient shall indicate the diet and regimen necessary to promote health in each case. We seek, *first of all, to cure our patients*. WATER IS OUR CHIEF REMEDY. But we not hesitate to use Homœopathic remedies, Electricity, or any other means within our knowledge, to facilitate the recovery of the Sick. We are Electic in our practice—using all means that in our judgment shall do good to any patient. Those who come to us shall have the benefit of our best skill and care.

Mrs. R. B. GLEASON, M. D., gives her attention to the specific treatment of the *Special Diseases of Females*. Her large experience in this department of practice—her eminent success in the cure of many who have been confined to the bed for years, entitle her to public confidence and to the *large practice* she has already made ; having under her care all the time from thirty to sixty ladies from various States in the Union.

We invite the Sick to our HILL-SIDE HOME, and pledge ourselves to do them all the good that lies within our power.

TERMS—$7, $7,50, $8, $9, $10, per week, according to size and location of room required. Each patient is expected to furnish, for bath purposes, 2 Comforters, 1 Blanket, 2 Sheets—linen preferred—and 6 bath Towels. But these may be rented at the Cure.

Address   S. O. GLEASON, M. D.,
Mrs. R. B. GLEASON, M. D.
Elmira, N. Y.

2. Gleason Water Cure advertisement. (Courtesy of the Chemung County Historical Society)

When the Cure was first established, conditions were primitive: guests were expected to "'rent at the Cure or to furnish' two comforters, one blanket, two sheets, linen preferred—and six bath towels" (Gleason File, CCHS). Water for the treatments and baths was hand-carried in pails and heated on wood stoves. The price for a week-long stay, depending on whether one was in a private or common room, was a steep seven to ten dollars.[21] The Gleasons constituted the entire medical staff and were assisted in carrying out their services by a corps of servants.[22]

In 1862 Julia Beecher, Reverend Thomas Beecher's wife, reported to her sister-in-law Isabella Hooker (the half-sister of Harriet Beecher Stowe) on the Elmira Water Cure's progress: "Cure has prospered in its slow sure way all through the hard times—30 patients I guess at present" (June 6, SDF). The Cure continued to grow and expanded its therapeutic offerings. Eight years after the Cure's opening, the Gleasons announced the addition of "entirely new bathrooms fitted in good style" (Gleason File, CCHS). Tallow and wax candles were replaced first by oil lamps, then gas, and finally electric lights. The original wooden structure was enlarged with the addition of north and south wings and an annex. Land surrounding the Cure was purchased, and much planting was done to cover the area that had been laid bare by construction. By 1875 the Cure boasted grounds adorned with "evergreens, shade and fruit trees and flowers, while the forests and glen behind afford delightful recreation in the open air" (Gleason File, CCHS). A turn-of-the-century advertisement lists the Cure's latest comforts: electric bells in every room, an elevator, a billiard room, and a gymnasium (Gleason File, CCHS). The Gleasons eventually abandoned strict adherence to hydropathy alone and began to include an eclectic mixture of various therapeutic models. By the 1890s, advertisements for the Cure mentioned such treatments as electricity, Swedish movements, a Swedish rest cure, and homeopathic medicines (Cayleff 103–4).

The Elmira Water Cure attracted patients from all over the country. By 1900, more than twenty thousand patients had been treated there (Gleason File, CCHS). Many of the Cure's patients were authors, physicians, activists, Quakers, and clergy who shared the Gleasons' devotion to reform. The Gleasons treated a clientele that included Jervis Langdon, Susan Langdon Crane, Olivia Lewis Langdon, Elizabeth Cady Stanton, Susan B. Anthony, Vice-President Schuyler Colfax, Congressman Samuel Cox, Catharine Beecher (who retired at the Cure), Emily Dickinson's mother, the family of the son of Brigham Young, Mary Riley Smith (a popular poet), Virginia Townsend (a popular author), the Reverend James Beecher, Isabella

Beecher Hooker, Mary Hooker, Alice Hooker Day, Mollie Clemens (Samuel Clemens's sister-in-law), Annie Beecher, and Samuel L. Clemens (Gleason File, CCHS).[23]

Much of the Elmira Water Cure's success was due to Rachael Gleason's indefatigable energy and spirit. Dr. Gleason specialized in the diagnosis and treatment of women's diseases, and her record of success attracted many female patrons. Throughout the 1850s and 1860s, Rachael traveled widely in the upper New York state region to proselytize on women's health. She became a popular platform lecturer, and her essays were regular features in health journals. In 1871, she published a compendium of her parlor addresses on women's health entitled *Talks to My Patients*. The book was immediately successful and quickly passed through eight editions garnering substantial profits for its New York and London publishers.

Gleason did not restrict her reform sympathies solely to the practice of hydropathy. She also advocated enlarged opportunities for women, and to that end eighteen women served their internships with her. One, Dr. Anna Stuart, later founded Elmira's Arnot-Ogden Hospital. Gleason was also a committed abolitionist and, after emancipation, an active supporter of freedmen's schools. One grateful recipient of Gleason's medical care was a young missionary, Maria Waterbury, who had harmed her health while working long hours in freedmen's schools in the South. In an 1872 journal entry, Waterbury provides an invaluable glimpse into life at the Cure, the lives of people treated there, and the professional character of Rachael Gleason. Waterbury recorded that during her stay she shared a "lovely room" with "three room-maties" from West Virginia. After her initial panic upon realizing that they were Southerners, her anxiety was somewhat lessened when she found that her companions were also Quakers. In one remarkable passage, Waterbury writes about her conflicting emotions at confessing her profession to the Quaker women:

> Query: Wonder if I am to be haunted with southerners the rest of my life? Now if I wasn't a "*nigger teacher*", and had worlds of money, I could have a room alone.
>
> The duty of one of us is plainer and plainer. These sweet Quaker women must know their associate is a "nigger teacher", and the teacher must tell them. Wonder if they'll bounce down the stairs, or pitch her out the window. "Ha! ha! Thee needn't vex thyself with our *displeasure, for thy calling is from heaven*," says the old mother Quaker lady. After years of boiled down scorn, we have swallowed at the South, this tonic of the God-fearing Quaker family, is almost too much. The tears are about to fall. (Waterbury 120–122)

Waterbury also includes a written record of Rachael Gleason's diagnosis of her condition and her prescribed treatment. This is the only first-person account of the "water cure" found to date.

> "Your throat is bad, madam. You ought to have been here six weeks ago; I don't know as I can prevent it from going to your lungs. What have you been doing?" "Teaching" "Where" "In Mobile, Alabama." "I thought so. We have the most trouble with teachers of any class of patients. They are worn out. They wear out faster than any other class of people. Orders: Hot baths; high diet—beefsteak, eggs, milk, fruit, oysters, everything the health cure has on the table; ride for exercise; sleep late in the morning; never mind the breakfast bell. You can have your breakfast sent up when you waken. We'll see if you can be toned up, for some more teaching. Lizzie, show the lady to her room," says the old doctor. (120)

Gleason was also outspoken on the issue of dress reform. In February 1851 she wrote to the *Water Cure Journal* urging it to print articles and give examples of healthful clothing for women. The *Journal* complied, and a "Dress Reform" column appeared in most issues. Susan Cayleff contends that hydropaths demonstrated their support for women's expanded roles in American society by their advocacy of dress reform, "which involved a fundamental critique of cultural concepts of femininity through the ignoring of fashion's dictates. . . . Tight-lacing corsets, stays, high heels, voluminous yardage, heavy materials that trapped moisture against the body, and certain hats and shawls all came under scrutiny and then attack" (126). Hydropaths advocated dress reform for two primary reasons: for the improvement of health and for the advancement of women.[24]

Julia Beecher was one woman who Dr. Gleason made into a dress reform convert. Beecher wrote to Mrs. Langdon (obviously regarding Mrs. Langdon as a sympathetic ally) to complain about her mother's attempts to have her dress fashionably and her own determination to dress healthfully: "She [Julia's mother] has various plans—I see them at work in her brain, & get hints of them in her speech. But there is one stand I make and that is, against corsets, and a waterfall. Outside of those she may have her way—but this thing—if I can help it, I will never become" (May 5, 1870, SDF).

Kathy Peiss maintains that women's assault on the public sphere was not restricted to public demands for political representation and economic independence, but that their entrance to these can be traced "through a number of symbolic acts, such as . . . wearing bloomers or comfortable dress" (818). Julia Beecher, Olivia Langdon, and Isabella Beecher Hooker would all share in the benefits of comfortable clothing, and daughters

a waterfall — Outside of those she
may have her way — but this
thing — if I can
help it, I will
never become!

I had much rather be
in my own good time a motherly
personage like this.

3. Illustration from a May 5, 1870, letter from Julia Beecher to Olivia Lewis Langdon.
(Courtesy of the Stowe-Day Foundation, Hartford, Conn.)

Olivia and Mary Hooker would don what was called "gymnastic dress," or bloomers. A letter by author Gail Hamilton describes "gymnastic dress": "Mrs. Hooker gave me a dress which she had made several years ago, in order to practise in at a gymnasium. It is a kind of bloomer, full Turkish trousers, etc." (Feb. 7, 1855, Dodge 84).

Along with urging women to become better informed and more self-determined about their raiment, Gleason also believed women needed practical training in home management. In an article that appeared in the July 1867 issue of *The Herald of Health and Journal of Physical Culture,* Gleason advises young women about how they can more effectively use their time and labor in organizing their domestic responsibilities. Here Gleason expands on the principles of domesticity Catharine Beecher outlined in her text, *A Treatise on Domestic Economy,* published in 1841. Gleason recommends that young women serve what she terms "apprenticeships" in the kitchen before being pressed into service on their own. If young women did not learn the principles of domestic management, Gleason warned, they risked becoming broken in health and in spirit. Should this occur, the "husband and wife [would] grow unconsciously less and less to each other, instead of more and more indispensable" (Gleason, "Letters" 11–12). That readers took Gleason's advice seriously is clear from a letter Julia Beecher wrote to her sister-in-law Isabella Hooker, offering her home as a place where Isabella's daughter, Alice, and Olivia Langdon could do their apprenticeships. On December 2, 1866, Hooker wrote to Alice to tell her of Beecher's offer:

> I enclose a letter from Aunt Julie, which came tonight & which I have read . . . I find it, very like her. I would answer it, immediately — assuring her of your entire willingness to come & help her economise & assuring her, that you really want to learn how to work & this would be just the chance. I have no idea that Mr. Langdon will let her [Olivia] do it, but if he does, it will be just the thing for you to take hold & learn many things, that you can get so much better from & with her than anywhere else. (SDF)

Both young women spent the week of April 1, 1867, with Julia to become educated in the ways of successful home management (Olivia Lewis Langdon to Isabella Beecher Hooker Apr. 4, 1867, SDF).

Health, Hydropathy, and the Langdons

The Langdons were apparently familiar with hydropathic principles long before the opening of the Elmira Water Cure. Mary Anne Lewis discussed

her sister Olivia's new health care regimen in a letter dated August 23, 1841:
"Olivia I am exceedingly glad to hear that your health is so comfortable and
that your habits are so good. As it regards frequent ablutions in cold water
or sponge baths as this may be termed I am sure of their good effects upon
myself—intend to follow the practice and hope you will do the same"
(CCHS). Lewis wrote the letter from Oberlin, where alternative medicine
was endorsed and practiced. Silas Gleason, who was attending Oberlin
College at the time, may have received his first lessons in the benefits of
hydropathy during the same period.

Mrs. Langdon suffered from poor health throughout her adult life. (In
his eulogy, Thomas Beecher remembered her as "always weak in the flesh,"
and in her letters and diaries there is a constant refrain of illness [Beecher,
Olivia Langdon Eulogy Memorial Pamphlet 7].) Hydropathy appears to have
been the treatment she found most effective, and when her daughter Olivia
fell ill in the summer of 1860, Mrs. Langdon duly dispatched her to the
Gleasons. Beginning in approximately 1841, and for the remainder of their
lives, the Langdons were hydropathic devotees, and all the members of the
family spent time at the Elmira Water Cure.[25]

Throughout the course of Twain biography the issue of Olivia Clemens's health has been raised periodically. Biographers have always known
that *something* was wrong with Olivia, but the diagnoses given were usually
uncomfortably and quickly made. During the last sixty years of scholarship,
biographers have performed a curious kind of approach-and-avoidance
dance, with most commentators gingerly touching upon and then quickly
fleeing from the subject of Olivia's suspected "female problems." Since Van
Wyck Brooks's time, an unresolved question has been the issue of whether
Olivia's manifested symptoms were organic or hysterical in nature. Brooks
labeled Olivia "neurotic"; Bernard DeVoto termed her "neurasthenic," but
refused to elaborate. With the publication of Hamlin Hill's biography,
Olivia's health took a decided turn for the worse with his pronouncement
that "the truth is that Olivia's body was less frail than her mind" (xxiv). Hill
regarded Olivia's ailments as neurotic and viewed her illnesses as a strategic
device she used to gain control over her husband and daughters. Resa
Willis, in an article about Olivia's commonplace book, echoed Hill's as-
sumptions, repeating Hill's quotation from Erna Eskuche that Olivia "enjoy[ed] poor health all her life" ("'Quietly and Steadily,'" 18). With the
publication of Hill's book, Olivia went from being considered a harmless
hysteric to an unstable, manipulative schemer.

The foundation of these biographers' evaluations concerning Olivia's
health and state of mind is an entry Clemens made in his 1906 autobiogra-

phy. In this dictation Clemens told the story of Olivia's fall and her subsequent cure at the hands of a faith healer. The fall purportedly occurred as a result of a mysterious accident while sixteen-year-old Olivia was ice skating. Olivia injured her spine, was left incapacitated, and spent the next two years flat on her back in a darkened bedroom. There she was left until the day Dr. J. R. Newton, a traveling faith healer and newcomer to New York state's Southern tier, visited her and gave her the command to walk — whereupon she miraculously walked. What fine melodrama!

In light of the recent scholarly efforts toward deconstructing Clemens's reconstructions of other factual events, it is interesting to note that no critic has sought to determine whether Clemens's story of Olivia's two-year stint in bed is true. Hill never questions Clemens's tale. Kaplan speculates that this story owed as much to Clemens's boyhood in 1845 as it did to events in Chemung County in 1861. The tale of the fall and the miraculous cure appear to have originated in Clemens's imagination, however, for no factual trace can be found that would link this account to events of either Clemens's youth or Olivia's girlhood. When Clemens recounted Olivia's ice skating travail he used considerable exaggeration to heighten the dramatic effect: "All the great physicians were brought to Elmira, one after another . . . but there was no helpful result" (Feb. 13, 1906, Autobiographical Dictation, No. 64, MTP*). When one reads Clemens's dictation, it becomes clear — as it does for many of Clemens's supposedly true accounts — that hyperbole has been employed to the detriment of veracity: In other words, Clemens lied. A return to primary source materials reveals that Olivia did not spend two long years reclining in her Elmira bedroom; in fact, Olivia was not even in Elmira for much of this two-year period.

Olivia's physical difficulties began some time before her sixteenth birthday. In 1860, Isabella Hooker wrote to her husband John, commenting on fourteen-year-old Olivia's poor state of health and praising the quality of health care she was receiving at the Cure. For a total of five months during the spring and summer of 1860, Hooker was treated by Rachael Gleason for gynecological problems. Regarding Dr. Gleason's prowess, Hooker commented to her husband that "she is another demonstration of my theory that . . . women can do *anything* that men can do" (May 29, 1860, SDF). Hooker also told her husband about the tea she had attended at the Langdon home the previous day, and she describes her newest roommate at the Cure.

The only daughter, is my roommate for the present — Livy Langdon — she is a sweet young girl of Mary's age — but in very delicate health and I have helped persuade [Mr. and Mrs. Langdon] to place her under Mrs. Gleason's care—she has been living on her nerves instead of her muscles all her life so far—and will not have *any thing* left to live upon pretty soon, unless she is made over. Oh dear—how blind mothers are—.... (July 15–16, 1860, SDF)

This letter is quite significant, given that it was written two and a half years *before* Olivia's famous collapse at age sixteen. With a nervous disorder so readily discernible as early as age fourteen, Olivia's difficulties in her late teens and her subsequent periods of seclusion from Clemens hardly seem like sexual "power plays," but rather were almost certainly symptomatic of an illness that was organic in nature. Julia Beecher wrote to Hooker a week before Olivia's sixteenth birthday in 1861 and reported that Olivia was again staying at the Cure. She concluded: "Livy Langdon, I trust[,] will gradually *wear* out her complicated difficulties as she matures, in growth etc.—poor thing, she has a hard time of it, and is very patient" (Nov. 19, SDF). At this juncture, Olivia was likely being treated for what Dr. Gleason suspected was dysmenorrhea (difficult or painful menstruation).

Olivia's health worsened that winter, and by March 1862 she was taken from Elmira to a sanatorium in Washington, D.C. In June, Olivia's family moved her from Washington and brought her to the Institute of Swedish Movement Cure in New York City in hopes of obtaining more effective treatment. The illness—possibly worsened by the move—nearly killed Olivia. Beecher wrote to Hooker that Olivia's symptoms became so serious immediately after her trip that the family feared for her life:

Mr. Langdon with wife, Mary Lewis & Susy Crane are in N. York attending upon Livy who was brought to Staten Island & then to the city—for a change—direct from Washington—Her symptoms became at once acute. She retained nothing upon her stomach for days & vomited blood at last. At last acct [account] she was continually delirious and they are *almost certain* now that they cannot keep her many more days—Susy went day before yesterday Mr. Langdon had watched—& all had till very weary. This is all I can tell you about the Langdons. (June 6, 1862, SDF)

Olivia underwent treatment at the Institute for more than two years, not returning home to Elmira until June 15, 1864.

Movement and Cure

Olivia's New York City doctors, George and Charles Taylor, were brothers who specialized in kinesipathy and orthopedics. The brothers' expertise was in therapeutic exercises, mechanical orthopedics, and women's health. Dr. George Herbert Taylor had graduated from New York Medical College in 1852; after obtaining his medical degree he joined the faculty at Dr. R. T. Trall's New York Hydropathic School (Kelley 1,124; Weiss 36), where he taught chemistry, surgery, and obstetrics. A Water Cure Institute was located on the premises, and Taylor served as a consulting physician until 1863. From the fall of 1854 until the winter of 1855, Dr. Taylor practiced with another hydropathic pioneer, Dr. Shew (Weiss 70). Together they focused on treating gynecological disorders using hydropathic principles.

Dr. Charles Fayette Taylor was granted his medical degree in 1856 by the University of Vermont. That same summer he traveled to London, where he studied with a practitioner of the Ling method of movement (Kelley 1,123). Dr. Peter Henry Ling of Stockholm was the inventor of what was known as the "Swedish Movement Cure." The Ling method involved manual application of exercises to eliminate disease. (In a sense the Ling method can be viewed as a precursor of modern aerobics, although aerobics is considered preventive activity, whereas Ling movement exercises were considered curative.) The patient was prescribed eight to twelve movements all involving or relating to the afflicted area. Great emphasis was placed on stretching and bending the body. Charles Taylor later wrote that cases of "neuralgia, paralysis, spinal disease and curvatures," as well as "inveterate constipation" could all be cured using this system of movements (C. Taylor, "Kinesipathy," 54–55).

Charles Taylor returned to New York in November 1856, and the brothers opened a water cure located at 650 Sixth Avenue (Shands 811; Weiss 152). Together they practiced kinesipathy and were highly regarded within eclectic medical circles. At the time, the Taylors' water cure facility was the only place in the United States that offered the full course of Ling's system of movements. In the winter of 1858–59, George Taylor traveled to Dr. Satherberg's Institute of kinesipathy in Stockholm to continue his studies (Kelley 1,124). While his brother was overseas, Charles Taylor changed locations and established a new practice on 38th Street (Shands 812). When George Taylor returned from Sweden, he founded the Institute of the Swedish Movement Cure at 67 West 38th Street (Weiss 60) where, it appears, the brothers resumed their joint practice. It was to their Institute that a desperately ill Olivia Langdon was brought in 1862.

Although George Taylor was the better known of the two brothers during the latter half of the nineteenth century, it is his younger brother Charles who is remembered today in American medical histories and biographies. Charles Taylor is credited with two major accomplishments: the intro-

4. Undated photograph (circa 1861–63) of Olivia Langdon. Olivia's emaciated appearance supports the hypothesis that she suffered from Pott's disease. (Courtesy of The Mark Twain Project, The Bancroft Library)

duction of the Swedish Movement Cure, or the practice of kinesipathy, in America in 1857 and the development of a method for relieving and curing Pott's disease (more commonly known as tuberculosis of the spine).[26] Alfred R. Shands, in "Charles Fayette Taylor and His Times," wrote that Charles Taylor was involved with three "great investigations": "kinesipathy, surgical mechanics and common sense psychotherapy" (811). The Langdon family would avail themselves of the full range of his specialties.

Charles Taylor is remembered today as the first physician to develop a viable treatment for Pott's disease.[27] The most common sign signaling the onset of Pott's disease is persistent back pain or a general stiffness of the back that eventually leads to partial paralysis. Dr. Taylor recommended in *The Mechanical Treatment of Angular Curvature, or, Pott's Disease of the Spine* that Pott's disease should be suspected if "a child who a month before has had a fall, should complain of pains in the sides or bowels" (11–12).[28]

What little is known of Olivia's medical history appears to mirror the symptoms of Pott's disease. Clemens recounted Olivia's accident in his autobiographical dictation: "She became an invalid at sixteen, through a partial paralysis caused by falling on the ice, and she was never strong again while her life lasted" (Feb. 13, 1906, No. 64, MTP*). This information corresponds to Dr. Taylor's etiology, and as weight loss is also a common symptom of Pott's disease, an undated photograph taken of Olivia during this period (1861–63) supports this diagnosis.[29] The photograph displays an emaciated Olivia; her thinness is striking when the picture is compared to the plump child pictured in earlier photographs and to the miniature she would give as a present to her brother Charles just five years later.

When Olivia Langdon arrived at the Institute in June, the family held out little hope for her survival. It is unknown whether the trip from Washington to New York was the cause of Olivia's violent decline or whether this deterioration might have been another manifestation of Pott's disease or another illness. It appears, however, that when Olivia had sufficiently recovered from this acute stage, she began a treatment for spinal tuberculosis. Modern treatment of Pott's disease involves chemotherapy, limited bed rest, drug therapy, and, possibly, surgery (*Merck Manual* 125; Roy 502). Dr. Taylor's treatment revolved around mechanical immobilization of the afflicted area, possibly limited homeopathic drug therapy, and extended bed rest. Spinal braces were already in use, although according to Taylor, none was particularly effective. Taylor designed his own brace ("the spinal assistant") that immobilized the shoulders and pelvis so that no forward movement was possible. Taylor crafted many braces, each geared for a particular stage of treatment. Most likely, it was one of Taylor's spinal braces Clemens referred to in his dictation regarding Olivia: "Over her was suspended a tackle from the ceiling" (Feb. 13, 1906, Autobiographical Dictation, No. 64, MTP*).

Charles Taylor's inventions proved so successful that he became known as "the first great American surgeon-mechanic, planning and accurately fitting back braces and later many other types of orthopedic appliances" (Malone 318). Dr. Taylor wrote that he was most successful with cases where the disease was still in the early stages: "a treatment founded on these obvious indications [before curvature occurs or deterioration of the vertebrae] will in many cases be followed by complete arrest of the diseased action, and the saving of the patient from years of suffering as well as a lifelong deformity" (C. Taylor, *Mechanical Treatment* 10).

Charles Taylor's braces were discarded by doctors in the mid-1920s in favor of a plaster-of-Paris bed that ensured complete immobilization; today, a plaster-of-Paris jacket is used to support the spine in ambulant patients. The prescribed length of bed rest has also been revised. Olivia was in bed for approximately two years. By 1926, the recommendation was for not "less than two years and at least one year of complete freedom from all signs or symptoms of active disease . . . [before] this reassumption of the erect attitude" (Trumble 243). In an article published in 1976 in the *Journal of Bone and Joint Surgery,* the recommended length of bed rest was six months (Sedden 396). The 1987 edition of *The Merck Manual of Diagnosis and Therapy* cautions against extended bed rest, warning that "morbidity following prolonged immobilization is substantial" (125). This "morbidity," or difficulty in regaining full use of the body, may account for an unusually bitter outburst by Olivia in a letter to Alice Hooker in the summer of 1867: "Father and Mother are very anxious to have me vegitate [sic], as if I am not enough of a vegitable [sic] already—" (July 29, SDF). Even when patients had finally recovered freedom of movement, they were cautioned to remember that they would never fully regain their previous good health. *The Medical Journal of Australia* warned in 1926:

> For years to come, indeed for the remainder of his term of life he must be made to realize that his spine is no longer in class A1, but rather C3. It must be pampered; to its demands his whole scheme of living must be subservient. He should live in the open air as far as possible and should avoid any occupation calling for excessive physical exertion. When resting he should lie rather than sit down. (Trumble 244)

The only surviving written account by Olivia during her illness is her commonplace book. Olivia began her commonplace book on November 12, 1863, a year and five months after her arrival in New York. Just two weeks shy of her eighteenth birthday, Olivia neatly inscribed the following on the first page:

Livie L. Langdon
Elmira
N.Y.

Movement Cure N.Y.
Nov. 12th 1863

The commonplace book provides the Taylors' address, "61 W. 38th St. N.Y.," in addition to giving the names of some of Olivia's visitors during her period of convalescence in Elmira and during her second stay at the Institute: Emma Nye, Susan Crane, Thomas Beecher, Miss Warner. The commonplace book is valuable, for it provides a record of abstracts Olivia found sustaining, and it also provides an indication of her attempts to remain intellectually active despite her dire illness. Pinned to the first recto page is a quotation from John Ruskin: "it is no man's business whether he has genius or not; work he must, whatever he is, but quietly and steadily; and the natural and unforced results of such work will be always the thing God meant him to do, and will be his best. No agonies or heartrendings will enable him to do better." This inspirational passage would serve Olivia during her long, difficult recovery.

In a letter to her husband John dated January 28, 1863, Isabella Hooker wrote that she had just returned from Dr. Taylor's, where she had spent the day visiting with Mr. and Mrs. Langdon and "two or three other Elmira friends." Evidently, the Langdons were trying to persuade Isabella to stay and keep Olivia company: "Mr Langdon says I *must* come." Hooker closes her letter with her assurance that "I will tell you all about . . . *Livy Langdon*" when they are once again together (SDF).

Two months later, on the recommendation of his sister, Catharine Beecher, James Beecher arrived at the Institute for treatment of a nervous breakdown. James Beecher came under doctor's care due to marital woes (he was married to Annie Morse, who suffered from alcoholism; she would die of delirium tremens in April 1863) and regimental troubles (he was a lieutenant colonel of the 141st New York Volunteers and was being threatened with court-martial). Hooker described her half-brother James as

"broken down—seems just like a person half under the influence of morphine—eyes lusterless . . . ; [he is] utterly broken down & out of his head"
suffering from "'tension of the brain'" (Isabella Hooker to John Hooker,
Mar. 7, 1863, SDF; Isabella Hooker to Hon. Edwin Stanton, Apr. 1863,
SDF). Hooker wrote to her husband that as soon as they could afford it she
wanted to be placed "under treatment" herself (Mar. 7, 1863, SDF). Most
likely her main complaint would be exhaustion after all her machinations
on her brother's behalf. James Beecher remained at the Institute for two
weeks; during that period, on March 16, Isabella Hooker brought her
daughter Mary to the Institute for her first "movement." The movement
cure Mary learned and practiced gained popularity by the mid-1860s and
was rapidly adopted as a therapeutic device by water cure establishments.
By 1870, in the first edition of her book, *Talks to My Patients,* Rachael
Gleason recommended physical exercise as "a way as to improve appetite,
digestion, and assimilation" (18). Many of the Taylors' innovations were
adopted by Gleason's water cure. Olivia would not be physically able to
take part in the movement cure for three years.

Olivia finally completed her treatment and returned home to Elmira
on June 15, 1864. The next mention of Olivia in the Hooker correspondence comes four months later in a letter from Isabella to John; Isabella
urges John, passing through Elmira on business, to "give my best love to
Mrs. Gleason & the Langdon's—call & see Livy Langdon for me . . . try to
make Mrs. Gleason come with you—" (Oct. 16, 1864, SDF). Evidently,
Olivia had not completely recovered.

On November 30, 1864, the faith healer Dr. James Rogers Newton
entered the Langdon home and effected a cure. Here is Clemens's breathless telling of the well-known tale:

> In those days both worlds were well acquainted with the name of Dr. Newton,
> a man who was regarded in both worlds as a quack. . . . Notice of his coming
> was spread upon the dead walls in vast colored posters, along with his formida-
> ble portrait, several weeks beforehand. One day Andrew Langdon, a relative of
> the Langdon family [,] came to the house and said: "You have tried everybody
> else, now try Dr. Newton, the quack. He is down town at the Rathburn
> House, practicing upon the well-to-do at war prices and upon the poor for
> nothing. . . . Send for Newton."
>
> Newton came. He found the young girl upon her back. . . . Newton opened
> the windows—long [shut] & delivered a short, fervent prayer; then he put an
> arm behind her shoulders and said "Now we will sit up, my child."
>
> The family were alarmed, and tried to stop him, but he was not disturbed,
> and raised her up. She sat several minutes, without nausea or discomfort. Then

Newton said "Now we will walk a few steps, my child." He took her out of bed and supported her while she walked several steps; then he said: "I have reached the limit of my art. She is not cured. It is not likely that she will ever be cured. She will never be able to walk far, but after a little daily practice she will be able to walk one or two hundred yards, and she can depend on being able to do *that* for the rest of her life." (Autobiographical Dictation, Feb. 13, 1906, No. 64 MTP*)

Clemens was very much crafting a story here. In the original manu-script of his dictation there are several crossed-out passages that indicate revisions made to enhance the dramatic effect. In a brief article, "Mark Twain and Dr. Newton" (1972), Harold Aspiz was the first to verify Dr. Newton's identity. Aspiz provided Newton's biography and then pro-ceeded to link Newton with characters appearing in Clemens's fiction, most notably the Dauphin in *Adventures of Huckleberry Finn*. What Aspiz did not realize at the time of his writing was that just as Clemens created fiction out of fact, he also fictionalized Newton and the tale of Olivia's cure. In composing his autobiography, Clemens was in some sense attempting to see how convertible reality was to fiction (a device he experimented with in the Ashcroft-Lyon manuscript).

Dr. Newton was not the unique phenomenon Clemens made him out to be. At the same time that Dr. Newton was curing the townspeople of Elmira, there were two other healers in temporary residence there. One, Dr. J. W. Stewart, took up an entire column in the Elmira newspaper to advertise his healing prowess. Dr. Stewart claimed he could "describe and locate Diseases merely by the patient's coming into his presence" and only needed to touch a patient for five to thirty minutes for the cure to take place. Another visiting healer was the exotic Dr. Neebin, "the great Chippewa Indian Physician," who treated patients "decked out in the full costume of his native tribe." Dr. Neebin set up camp at the American Hotel in Elmira and planned on staying "For One Moon" ("Drs.," *Elmira Advertiser*, Dec. 1, 1864). By comparison, Dr. Newton's announcement was the epitome of understatement. Whereas Clemens claims that Dr. Newton's appearance in Elmira was heralded several weeks in advance by "vast colored posters," "spread upon . . . dead walls," "along with his formidable portrait," the only notice that appeared in the local Elmira newspaper consists of this modest line: "Doct. J. R. Newton will be at the Brainard House next Sunday to operate upon any of the afflicted that may call upon him" (Newton, *Elmira Advertiser*).

In *The Modern Bethesda, or The Gift of Healing Restored* (1879), Dr.

Newton's biographer, J. R. Newton, provides a brief mention of Olivia. Dr. Newton resided in Rochester and would travel to towns in the general area to heal the afflicted on weekends:

> One of these [cases] was at Elmira, N.Y., where Dr. N. went to treat Miss Libbie Langdon, whom he cured. . . . Dr. N. found her suffering with spinal disease; could not be raised to a sitting posture in her bed for over four years. She was almost like death itself. With one characteristic treatment he made her to cross the room with assistance, and in a few days the cure was complete. (294)

Yet no miraculous cure had occurred here. What Dr. Newton presumably did was to convince Olivia to shake off the malaise which still lingered from her prolonged bed rest and instill in her the confidence to again become active. Olivia's physical healing had taken place in New York at the Institute; what Dr. Newton completed was the psychological healing necessary to persuade Olivia that she was no longer an invalid and could again, after a period of four years, resume a normal life. Clemens's account of the healing would lead one to think that as quickly as he swept in, Dr. Newton mysteriously departed the scene, but this was not the case: Mrs. Langdon corresponded with Dr. Newton for two and a half years after his visit, and he returned to talk to Olivia again on June 3, 1865.

Over a period of one year and three months (January 30, 1865 to April 28, 1866) Olivia's mother poignantly records in her diary her daughter's valiant struggle to regain her health: "Livia bore her weight alone on her crutches." (January 30, 1865); "This morning Livia breakfasted with the family. The first time she has done so in *three years*." (February 11, 1865); "This *afternoon* we *moved Livia's bed into the sitting room,* + took possession of our old room again" (June 24, 1865); "Livia went to Mr. Spauldings to tea yesterday for the first time in about six years" (April 5, 1866); "Livia moved upstairs today" (April 10, 1866); "*Yesterday* Livia got out of her chair, walked to the bureau + back, + sat down again without help[.] It seems almost more than I can realise that my child can once more walk" (April 23, 1866); "*Livia went to church this morning for the first time in more than 5 years*" (April 29, 1866, MTM).

Despite her positive progress, Olivia returned to New York to seek treatment on October 10, 1866. By this time Charles Taylor had left his brother's Institute and founded the New York Orthopedic Dispensary with the help of such celebrated friends as Theodore Roosevelt, Sr. (Taylor successfully treated Roosevelt's daughter, Anna). Taylor served there as surgeon-in-chief for eight years. Olivia stayed again at Dr. George Taylor's Institute and was probably placed under his sole care. Years later, in response to a query from Elinor Howells, wife of William Dean Howells, Clemens recommended the Institute and Dr. George H. Taylor: "There are two Taylors in the business — Dr. George H. Taylor is the only right one — bear that in mind. — Livy had a high opinion of him & his methods & his establishment; he did her great good. But this was 12 or 15 years ago" (*Mark Twain-Howells Letters* 323). Apparently the Langdons and Clemens gave Dr. Newton and Dr. George Taylor the full measure of credit for Olivia's recovery — Dr. Charles Taylor was wrongly ignored.

This time Olivia's stay at the Institute was far shorter than her first visit. During her approximately three-month-long stint, Olivia took part in George Taylor's "movement cure." Isabella Hooker wrote her daughter Alice that Olivia had on a "gymnastic" dress the day she visited her there (Dec. 2, 1866, SDF). Clearly, Olivia's health had radically improved to the point that she was able to perform the various exercises demanded by the Swedish cure. Olivia finished her course of treatment by the end of January and made an unexpected return to her parents in Elmira: "This morning, we had a complete + joyous surprise," Olivia's mother declared in her diary. "When we were seated at the breakfast table . . . Livia walked into the Dining room. We could not have been more astonished + delighted. . . . How good God is to return my child to me in such mercy" (Jan. 27, 1867 MTM).

Mrs. Langdon continued recording Olivia's "firsts" in her diary. In February mother and daughter called on "Mrs. Robert + Fred. [Frederick] Hall. It is the first time in 7 years that she [Olivia] has been able to make a call. I could hardly believe my child to be by my side" (February 11, 1867, MTM). On Saturday, February 16, the Langdons held a party to celebrate Olivia's homecoming: "The party was very pleasant, + the eve. [evening] passed off delightfully[.] Livia was able to take part in all the amusements (except dancing)" (Olivia Lewis Langdon Diary, MTM).

By April 1867 Mrs. Langdon rejoiced in a letter to Isabella about Olivia's return to good health:

> Livy has improved rapidly since her return from Doct. Taylor's. . . . I hope there is much of enjoyment and happiness in store for her. So entirely has her life been one of confinement & privation. . . . In the long night of our trial & sorrow . . . as I look back into that darkness when my precious child lay *discoursingly* [sic] prostrate I only wonder how I sustained under it. (Apr. 4, 1867, SDF)

Olivia's recovery must not have been as complete as Mrs. Langdon wanted to believe, as Alice confided to her mother just ten days later that "Livy is not very well. . . . I am pained to see how frail she is and how sober and deeply thoughtful a thing life is to her" (Apr. 14, 1867, SDF). In her diary, on April 17, Mrs. Langdon took note that Olivia had "knelt at family worship for the 1st time in 6 years." (MTM). In July of that year, just five months before she met Clemens, Olivia confessed to Alice: "I . . . have not been very well" (July 29, 1867, SDF).

In retrospect it is hardly surprising that the Langdons brought their daughter to the Taylors for treatment. The Langdons and the Taylors held identical reformist positions regarding politics and medicine: both families were Republicans, both revered Lincoln, both were dress reform advocates, and the brothers were frequent contributors to the *Water Cure Journal* and the *North American Journal of Homeopathy,* to which the Langdons surely subscribed.

During her lifetime, Olivia Clemens suffered enormously from her lack of good health. Her documented illnesses ranged from frequent colds and tonsillitis to life-threatening influenza, typhoid, diphtheria, asthma, syncope, heart attacks, and hyperthyroid disease. The letters written by Olivia, Clemens, and Langdon family friends demand a reappraisal of current views on the sources for and significance of her ailments. Olivia's illnesses often have been removed from the realm of the physiological to the purely psychological without full documentation of their case histories. In *Backlash: The Undeclared War Against American Women,* Susan Faludi contends that "neurasthenia" was a term often invoked by nineteenth century male clinicians to "similarly link feminism . . . and hysteria": "the agitation of suffragists, charged a typical late Victorian counselor, had unleashed in the female population 'a nervous distress that has become universal'" (345). Perhaps Olivia's major ailment, which DeVoto uncomfortably labeled as "neurasthenia," might have indicated an acute case of suffragist fever.

It is telling that Hill should begin his discussion of Olivia's health with Clemens's story of the skating fall and the faith healer, then conclude with a young girl's remark that, in 1901, Olivia appeared to be "enjoying poor health" (35); in the first case Hill cites Clemens, who wanted to obscure the truth, and in the second case he quotes Erna Eskuche, a young girl at the time who could not have had much knowledge of the subject.[30] Moreover, the idiom "enjoying" health or the lack of health was well accepted at the turn-of-the-century, and had no negative connotations such as we might today infer.

In Sickness and in Health

It is very likely that Clemens was informed early on by Mr. and Mrs. Langdon about the supreme delicacy of Olivia's health. Beginning with his earliest courtship letters, Clemens constantly advises Olivia to conserve her strength, to sleep longer, to eat better. A possible explanation for Clemens's long delay before visiting Olivia in Elmira might be due to her health problems. Just three months after meeting Clemens, Olivia fell ill with diphtheria (Olivia Langdon to Alice Hooker, Apr. 22, 1868, SDF). The courtship letters also record Clemens's responses to Olivia's attempts at convincing him to embrace hydropathic principles. Clemens swears to Olivia that giving up liquor would entail "*no sacrifice,*" because he has "*never had,* any love for any kind of liquors, & not even a passable *liking* for any but champagne & ale, & only for these *at intervals.*" Clemens was not so quick to agree to give up smoking, but he assures Olivia that if she really wants him to stop "I shall be swindled into the notion that I [don't] *want* to smoke any more, anyhow!" (*Mark Twain's Letters, 1867–1868,* vol. 2: 354).

It would be an error to view these early attempts by Olivia to reform Clemens's smoking and drinking habits as mere Victorian niceties, or as portents of her future manipulations. One must consider the entire picture: It was Olivia's cultural milieu, rather than any self-serving motive, that provided the primary impetus for her efforts to persuade Clemens to accept personal and social reform. The two main causes for illness, according to hydropathic physicians, were alcohol consumption and smoking, and such popular periodicals as the *Water Cure Journal* were filled with admonitions against liquor and tobacco. Olivia grew up reading such didactic hydropathic poetry as this ditty, "How To Be Happy," published in the *Water Cure Journal* in 1857:

> Away with brandy, rum, and gin,
> With tea, with coffee, and hot sling.
> Break friends with sherry-wine and beer,
> You'll then live *happy through the year.*
> Then smash your old tobacco pipe,
> And be a worthy *Prototype*;
> Don't daub your friends, yourself besmear,
> And you'll be happy through the year. (55)

Clemens eventually came to embrace much of hydropathy, although he never quit enjoying good hard liquor and a smelly, cheap cigar. After the

Clemenses were married, Rachael Gleason and hydropathy would become a part of the family's health regime. Olivia's babies were delivered by Gleason, and the family often visited the Elmira Water Cure. In an auto-biographical dictation, Clemens recounted Gleason's tending to Olivia, after the birth of their first child, Langdon, and pronounced her "almost divine." The Clemenses spent July of 1872 in New Saybrook with infant daughter Susy (son Langdon had died in June), and Olivia included a note in a letter Clemens wrote to Mollie Clemens asking her to send some bathing necessities:

> Mr Clemens is determined that I shall bath so I shall *have* to ask you to get me a bathing suit they advertize them ready made caps & all — I would like quite a pretty one. . . . Mr Clemens is going to make me take sitz baths too so I shall have to trouble you for that black and white wrapper than hangs on the left in my closet. I use it for sitz baths — My back is troubling me so this is the reason that Mr C. is taking these vigorous measures — . (July 20–21, 1872, MTP*)

When living and traveling on the continent, the family received treatment at European spas and baths, which Clemens wrote about in "Aix, the Paradise of the Rheumatics" (1891) and "Marienbad — A Health Factory" (1891).

During the early 1900s Clemens also became interested in the growing health-food industry, and he invested in a food supplement called Plasmon. John Harvey Kellogg was a famous hydropath who invented such water cure health-foods as granola and peanut butter, and introduced soy milk to America. Clemens hoped that his Plasmon investment would catch on with the public's eating habits in much the same way. Health foods had become a big business by the end of the nineteenth century: Henry Perky's shredded whole wheat biscuits were a top seller. Unfortunately, following the precedent set by most of his earlier business investments, Clemens's high hopes for Plasmon were eventually dashed.

Even after Olivia's death, Clemens remained receptive to health reform. Clemens's secretary, Isabel Lyon, and his manager, Ralph Ashcroft, bought Clemens a vibrating chair for his birthday in 1908; the prototype for the chair had been invented by George Taylor in 1864 and was used to treat patients at Gleason's Water Cure (1908 Lyon Daily Reminder, Dec. 21, MTP). Clemens's decision to dress in white may also have received reinforcement from the health-reform movement. Kellogg advocated the wearing of white clothing, and as early as 1866 he began dressing entirely in white, explaining that "from the standpoint of health, white is superior to all other colors at all seasons" (quoted in Schwartz 141). Doubters questioned these supposed health benefits, arguing that Kellogg's chosen attire was based less on health concerns than on granting him an opportunity for some highly visual showmanship (Schwartz 141). Clemens, a fellow lover of the spotlight, probably found the idea of attracting attention as desirable as any perceived health gains, and to that end he directed Lyon in October 1906 to order five new white suits from his personal tailor: "The King is filled with the idea of defying conventionalities and wearing his suitable white clothing all winter" (1906 Daily Reminder, Oct. 8, MTP).

From the beginning of his novel-writing period, Clemens frequently alluded to health reform. In *Roughing It,* a bullet from a Smith and Wesson "seven-shooter" is likened to a "homeopathic pill." In a "Boy's Manuscript," written in about 1870, Clemens cites the various treatments included in the water cure, "douch, sitz, wet-sheet and shower-bath (awful)," (424); and in *The Adventures of Tom Sawyer,* there is a lengthy section where Clemens satirizes Aunt Polly's newfound hydropathic beliefs. Here Clemens refers to and benignly ridicules a catalog of health reform mainstays: the *Water Cure Journal,* the movement cure, dress reform, and homeopathic medicines. Mooning after Becky Thatcher, Tom becomes silent and morose; Aunt Polly fears the boy has taken ill and immediately begins treatment. Tom is subjected to hydropathic applications that come practically verbatim from Mary Gove Nichols's *Experience in Water Cure* (1850).

> The water treatment was new, now, and Tom's low condition was a windfall to her. She had him out at daylight every morning, stood him up in the woodshed and drowned him with a deluge of cold water; then she scrubbed him down with a towel like a file, and so brought him to; then she rolled him up in a wet sheet and put him away under blankets till she sweated his soul clean. . . . She added hot baths, sitz baths, shower baths and plunges. (*The Unabridged Mark Twain* 490–91)

Clemens did not restrict his hydropathic references to his fiction. In 1901 he spoke before the New York General Assembly in support of the Seymour bill which, if passed, would have granted licenses to osteopathic practitioners. During his speech Clemens claimed that his introduction to alternative forms of medicine had begun when his mother gave him his first cold water cure at the age of nine. Clemens humorously regaled his audience:

> I remember how my mother used to stand me up naked in the back yard every morning and throw buckets of cold water on me, just to see what effect it

would have. Personally, I had no curiosity upon the subject. And then, when the dousing was over, she would wrap me up in a sheet wet with ice water and then wrap blankets around that and put me into bed. I never realized that the treatment was doing me any particular good physically. But it purified me spiritually. For pretty soon after I was put into bed I would get up a perspiration that was something worth seeing. Mother generally put a life preserver in bed with me. (*Mark Twain Speaking* 386–87)[31]

The Gleasons and their hydropathic health spa were the first of a series of reforms that would transform Elmira. Two years after the Gleasons opened the Water Cure, Thomas Kennicut Beecher was hired as minister by the Independent Congregational church of Elmira. Beecher proved to be the catalyst for an era of tremendous religious and social reform.

Notes

1. The only other repudiation of Brooks's views that I have located is an article by Max Eastman entitled "Mark Twain's Elmira," published in *Harper's Magazine* (May 1938): 620–32. Eastman, the son of Thomas Beecher's personally appointed successor at Park Church, the Reverend Annis Ford Eastman, tactfully observed that Brooks, "being interested in ideas so largely because of their immediate flavor and the work of art that can be made of them, is often very cavalier about their relations to actual fact" (621).

2. Information concerning railroads and Elmira's businesses comes from the Chemung County Historical Society and from Thomas E. Byrne, ed., *Chemung County, New York, History, 1890–1975* (Elmira, N.Y.: CCHS, 1975).

3. The censuses taken during the years 1860 to 1900 illustrates the city's rapid expansion.

YEAR	POPULATION
1860	8,696
1865	13,130
1870	15,863
1880	20,541
1890	30,893
1900	35,672

(Federal Population Census, Elmira, Chemung County Census, Steel Memorial Library, Elmira, New York.)

The City of Elmira included 5 wards at its 1864 incorporation, and 6 from 1867 to 1872, it grew to 9 wards in 1895. In 1900 the 10th, 11th and 12th wards were added, testifying to the population growth, particularly around the Northern Central Railroad shops and the LaFrance Fire Engine Works. (Byrne 10)

4. Information about African-Americans in Elmira is taken from Gretchen Sullivan Sorin, "The Black Community in Elmira," in *A Heritage Uncovered: The Black Experience in Upstate New York, 1800–1925,* ed. Cara Sutherland (Elmira, N.Y.: CCHS, 1988): 8, 10.

5. In the 1870 Elmira census, John T. Lewis is listed as 35 years old (making Lewis and Clemens the same age), with his profession listed as farmer, the value of his owned real estate as $800.00, the value of his personal estate as $850.00, and his birthplace as Maryland.

6 For further information concerning Elmira's role in the Underground Railroad, see Clay Holmes, *The Elmira Prison Camp* (Putnam, 1912): 143–44.

7. A small proportion of African-Americans in Elmira held skilled positions. By 1875, the African-American population comprised 2.8 percent of Elmira's total population (Sorin 7). According to historian Charles Haley, the year 1875 also marked the first public appearance of the Ku Klux Klan in the Southern Tier. "The Klan in Their Midst: The Ku Klux Klan in Upstate New York Communities" *Afro-Americans in New York Life and History* 7 (Jan. 1983): 41–53.

8. Federal Population Census, 1860 and 1870, Elmira, Chemung County Census. Steel Memorial Library, Elmira, New York. In the census for 1860, Catharine Mahen is listed as living and working at the Langdon home. Mahen was twenty years old, a serving girl, and listed Ireland as her place of birth (Chemung County Census, 1860). In the 1870 census, there were three female servants listed as working for the Langdons; two were Irish: Laura McLean and Orna McLean, both age 20 (Orna McLean was listed as illiterate). The third servant was a Pennsylvania-born African-American woman, Laura McQuian, whose age is listed as 60.

Sizable groups of Germans arrived after the attempted revolution in 1848 and again after the Franco-Prussian war of 1870; Jews also emigrated from Germany due to the upheaval in 1848, and by 1862 the Jewish population numbered about 100. Other ethnic groups in Elmira included Polish settlers, who appeared in small numbers around 1871, and Ukrainians, who came during the 1890s. The last large group of immigrants were Italians, who began arriving in large numbers at the end of the nineteenth century. Information on Elmira's ethnic groups from the Chemung County Historical Society and from Byrne, ed., *Chemung County, New York, History, 1890–1975.*

9. Information on Elmira's social and cultural aspects and newspapers is derived from Byrne, ed., *Chemung County, New York, History 1890–1975,* and the *Elmira City Directory* from 1857 and 1885.

10. A formerly enslaved African-American from Virginia named John Jones was hired to bury the Confederate dead at $2.50 per body. By the time the camp closed, Jones had amassed a sizable fortune. Jones was a leader in the African-American community and served as a "station master" in the Underground Railroad, assisting many former slaves on their way to freedom (Sorin 11; Byrne 519).

11. "The [Elmira] camp's overall death rate was 24.4 percent. The overall death rate in Union-administered prisons was 11.7 percent. The overall death rate in Southern prisons was 15.3 percent" (Horigan 3,457). The figure of 3,022 total deaths is from Nat Daniel's article, "Confederate Graves Tabulated on Computer," *Chemung Historical Journal* (Dec. 1985): 3,532.

12. Beecher, *Jervis Langdon Eulogy Memorial Pamphlet* and *Olivia Lewis Langdon Eulogy Memorial Pamphlet*, CCHS. For information regarding Jervis Langdon's biography see Resa Willis, *Mark and Livy*, 13–15.

13. After reading "Mark Twain's Elmira" by Max Eastman, one is left with the impression that Jervis favored ethics sometimes to the detriment of his business.

14. Information about Olivia Lewis Langdon's genealogy comes from an interview with Gretchen Sharlow, Director of the Center for Mark Twain Studies, September 13, 1990. Olivia's twin sister's married name was Mrs. Sheppard Marsh (*Mark Twain's Letters, 1867–1868,* vol. 2: 292).

15. Domestic feminism is defined and discussed by Susan Coultrap-McQuin in her excellent text, *Doing Literary Business: American Women Writers in the Nineteenth Century* (Chapel Hill: University of North Carolina Press, 1990): 90–91.

16. Information concerning regular and alternative schools of medicine and the practices of regular physicians is based on Virgina G. Drachman's "Women Doctors and the Women's Medical Movement: Feminism and Medicine, 1850–1895" (Ph.D. diss., SUNY at Buffalo, 1976): 14–16.

17. For more detailed information concerning types of treatments offered at water cures, see Susan Cayleff's *Wash and Be Healed.*

18. Hydropathy became immediately popular in the Northeast upon its arrival from Europe in the 1840s, and between 1843 and 1900, 213 water cure centers were established, primarily in the New England area (Sklar 246). The Elmira Water Cure (later known as The Gleason Sanitarium and The Gleason Health Resort) was one of the longest-lived of the hydropathic institutions.

Silas Gleason practiced at three other water cures before coming to Elmira, including the Cuba Water Cure, Glen Haven Health Resort, and the Forest City Water Cure. In 1851, Gleason bought the Elmira site with his two partners, Fox Holden and N. Hale; the Gleasons personally operated the Cure for more than fifty years. The Elmira Water Cure was temporarily closed from December 1, 1860, to April 15, 1861, so that the Gleasons could rest from their ministrations. Silas retired to Florida in 1868 due to poor health. After Silas's death in April 1899, Rachael continued to work at the Cure and treated patients until 1905; she died in March of that year. The Gleasons were succeeded by their daughter, Adele Gleason, along with Rachael's sister, Dr. Zippie Brooks Wales, and Zippie's husband, Dr. Theron Wales. The Cure eventually passed out of family control and survived in various forms until 1959 (Susan Cayleff, *Wash and Be Healed,* 92–93; Harry B. Weiss, *The Great American Water-Cure Craze,* 158).

19. Virginia Drachman, in "Women Doctors and the Women's Medical Movement: Feminism and Medicine, 1850–1895," claims that women in medicine fit within the parameters of the nineteenth century's "woman movement": "The entrance of women into the professions of teaching and nursing, and their active fight for suffrage and marriage reform were all part of the Woman Movement. Similarly, women's entrance into medicine was part of this movement as well" (Ph.D. diss., SUNY at Buffalo, 1976, 27).

20. Silas Orsemus Gleason was born in Massachusetts on November 3, 1818, and grew up in Vermont. He was a student at Oberlin College for two years and received his medical degree in 1844 from Castleton (now Burlington) Medical College in Vermont.

Biographical material regarding the Gleasons was obtained from the following sources: a typescript of clippings about the Gleasons collected by Ada Gleason Bush (Rachael and Silas Gleason's granddaughter); document nos. 14, 15, and 22, Gleason file, Chemung County Historical Society; Susan Cayleff, *Wash and Be Healed*, 92; "Death in Buffalo of Mrs. Rachael Brooks Gleason," Gleason file, Chemung County Historical Society; and Adele A. Gleason, *In Memoriam, 1820–1905, Rachael Brooks Gleason* (n.p., n.d., obtained from the American Antiquarian Society).

21. Cayleff points out that in the mid-1850s workingmen's wages amounted to approximately six dollars per week (87). This effectively removed the Elmira Water Cure from the realm of the working class, although Rachael Gleason often permitted individuals unable to pay to be treated gratis.

22. Four of the Gleason's servants were native Irish (three women and one man), two were African-American women from Maryland, and eight were European-American women (six from New York and two from Pennsylvania). All of the water hauling was done by these women.

By 1870 the Cure had expanded, and the medical staff reflected this growth: there was a third doctor in residence (Lucy Brooks) and two female nurses. Also added to the staff were a female clerk, two female housekeepers, and one male attendant. Only one person, Patrick Burns, an Irish laborer, remained from the original staff of 1860. Most of the servants were white and from New York State, with three exceptions: one female Irish-American servant and two female African-American women from Pennsylvania and New York (Federal Population Census, 1860 and 1870, Elmira, Chemung County Census. Steel Memorial Library, Elmira, New York).

23. In a letter dated April 6, 1945, Rachael Gleason's granddaughter, Ada Gleason Bush, responded to an inquiry by the Cornell University Library asking for information about her grandmother. Mrs. Bush provided the following information about the connection between the Langdons, the Clemenses, and the Gleason Water Cure: "I know that grandmother stayed with them [Samuel and Olivia] in Buffalo for several weeks. Mrs. Clemens was a patient of grandmothers' before she was married, and her father [Jervis Langdon] was a patient of my grandfather also, so there was a long association in the families" (John M. Olin Library, Cornell University, Ithaca, New York).

24. Information regarding Rachael Gleason's commitment to dress reform is from Cayleff, 126.

25. In her diary Mrs. Langdon wrote that "Sue [Susan Crane] went with Zippie [Rachael Gleason's sister, also a physician] to spend the week at Spencer Springs" (May 14, 1866, SDF).

26. Both brothers wrote extensively about the Swedish Movement Cure and other various medical investigations. See Charles Fayette Taylor, "Kinesipathy, or the Movement Cure," *Water Cure Journal* (March 1857); "The Cure of Spinal Distortions by 'Movements,'" *Water Cure Journal* (May 1857); *The Pathology and Treatment of Some of the Diseases Incident to Women* (1859); *The Theory and Practice of the Movement Cure* (1861); *Mechanical Treatment of Angular Curvature, or Pott's Disease of the Spine* (1863); *Spinal Irritation or, the Causes of Back-Ache Among American Women* (1864); and *Mechanical Treatment of Diseases of the Hip* (1873).

See also George Herbert Taylor, *A Sketch of the Movement Cure, with Illustrated Cases* (1860); *An Exposition of the Swedish Movement-Cure* (1860); *An Illustrated Sketch of the Movement-Cure* (1866); *Diseases of Women: Their Causes, Prevention, and Radical Cure* (1871); *Paralysis, and other Affections of the Nerves: Their Cure by Vibratory and Special Movements* (1871); *Health for Women* (1879); *Health by Exercise* (1880); *Massage: Principle and Practice of Remedial Treatment by Imparted Motion — Description of Manual Processes* (1884).

27. Biographical information concerning Charles Fayette Taylor comes from the following sources: Dumas Malone, ed., *Dictionary of American Biography,* vol. 8 (New York: Scribner's, 1946); *Dictionary of American Medical Biography,* vol. 2 (Westport, Conn.: Greenwood Press, 1984); *Allibone Critical Dictionary of English Literature and British and American Authors,* vol. 3 (Philadelphia, 1871).

28. Taylor wrote extensively about Pott's disease and diseases of the spine: *Spinal Irritation or, the Causes of Backache Among American Women* (1864), *Infantile Paralysis* (1867), and *Mechanical Treatment of Diseases of the Hip* (1873). Injury as symptomatic of Pott's disease was corroborated in an article in *The Medical Journal of Australia*: "Many patients date their troubles from some particular fall or blow in the back. . . . A light injury serves to unmask a disease already present for some time, but previously causing no symptoms" (Trumble 240).

29 Information regarding the symptoms of Pott's disease is taken from Dr. Ronald J. Nelson, "Pott's Disease: A Resurgent Challenge to the Thoracic Surgeon," *Chest* 95 (Jan. 1989): 145–50; *Dorland's Illustrated Medical Dictionary* (Philadelphia: Harcourt Brace Jovanovich, 1988): 1,770; and *The Merck Manual of Diagnosis and Therapy* (Rahway: Merck Sharp and Dohme Laboratories, 1987): 125.

30. Mrs. Erna Eskuche, Documents File, 1901, MTP.

31. Here Clemens reused some of his earlier material from *Tom Sawyer.* The likelihood of such a childhood episode occurring is possible, but not as supportable as one might imagine. John C. Gerber, however, contends that Clemens's account of his mother administering the water cure to him in his youth is true. In "Explanatory Notes" to *The Adventures of Tom Sawyer,* Gerber explains that "Jane Clemens . . . had enormous faith in home remedies and patent medicines, and forced them on young Sam whenever he was ailing" (Berkeley: University of California Press, 1980): 484. Jane Clemens was indeed representative of her generation in her firm belief in the potency of family remedies and advertised "miracle pills." Paine writes in his *Biography* that when Clemens was young, "The doctor was summoned for him oftener than was good for the family purse — or for him, perhaps, if we may credit the story of heavy dosings of those stern allopathic days" (29). Doris and Samuel Webster (the son of Clemens's niece) recalled that Jane "was always eager to try new medicines, and [would] experiment on the children to a limited extent" ("Whitewashing Jane Clemens," *Bookman* 61 [July 1925]: 531–35). Clemens stated in his piece, "Jane Lampton Clemens," that in the early years of his childhood "I was sick the first seven years of it and lived altogether on expensive allopathic medicines" (91). Yet, nowhere in these three accounts is there any mention of hydropathic ministrations by Jane Clemens.

Hydropathy was an entirely different matter from allopathy or homeopathy. Hydropathy was an alternative medical movement that was not well-known outside of the Northeast until the mid-1850s and early 1860s. No water cures were ever established in Missouri. In his notes, Gerber lists several health periodical titles that provide a compendium of several health movements (homeopathy, phrenology, and hydropathy), yet Gerber does not distinguish among them. Gerber's note about the various nineteenth-century health journals is misleading in that he states that the journals listed were all published during the 1840s; they were not. *Water Cure World* ran from 1860 to 1861; *Phrenological Journal of Science of Health* was published in 1838, but dealt with a health movement separate from hydropathy. *Health Journal and Independent Magazine* (New York, 1843) fits Clemens's chronology, since he would have been eight at the time; however, the periodical lasted only for a single issue. A second periodical, *Water Cure World,* was first published in 1860 and would not fit the chronology. The best-known of the hydropathic periodicals which Gerber cites was the *Water Cure Journal* (New York), first published in November 1844, although the journal's circulation did not top ten thousand until 1849 (Weiss 26, 41).

While it is possible that Jane Lampton Clemens did hear of hydropathic treatments, this most likely did not occur until the 1850s — and by then Clemens was a spirited fifteen-year-old adolescent who probably would not have submitted to such a dunking. Available sources indicate that most of Clemens's knowledge concerning hydropathic practices came after his marriage.

5. Elmira's Cultural Influence: Era of Reform, Part 2

We have arrived at a point where East and West, gender, and taste come together. As we have seen, when Clemens married Olivia, she existed as a reflex of Elmira, that is, was a relatively ordinary, unindividualized young woman.

  — Guy Cardwell, *The Man Who Was Mark Twain*

An Abolitionist Church and Its People

In 1846, as Thomas Kennicut Beecher later recalled, a group of "thirty-one . . . men and only thirty-nine women," among them Jervis and Olivia Langdon, broke from the First Presbyterian Church of Elmira because of its refusal to issue a written condemnation of slavery and founded the Independent Congregational Church (Beecher, *Jervis Langdon Eulogy Memorial Pamphlet* 7).[1] After joining the Congregationalists, Jervis Langdon became deeply involved in church affairs. He was among the group of church elders who approved the hiring of Beecher (Harriet Beecher Stowe's half-brother) in 1854, and in 1862, he was elected to the "church committee," a position he held until his death. Silas Gleason was chosen as a church trustee.

  When an Elmira deacon first encountered Beecher in 1853, he had just been fired from his first position as minister at the New England Congregational Church in Williamsburg, New York. Beecher had discovered that certain church board members had been engaged in unethical business transactions, and he had refused to overlook their transgressions (Stowe 358). The deacon offered Beecher the Elmira Congregationalist ministerial position, and he responded by sending a unique five-item questionnaire addressed to Jervis Langdon and "Brethren." Among Beecher's demands were that church members understand that they would be free at the end of any month to ask him to leave without hurting his feelings; that they must remember Beecher came to them full of doubt as to whether any church could benefit from his services; and that they must keep in mind that his exclusive goal was to assist individuals in becoming Christians and that no church's prosperity could dazzle him (Taylor and Myers 12–13). Evidently the elders answered all the questions correctly, for Beecher came to Elmira and remained there for the next forty-six years (Jerome and Wisbey 114).[2]

In the original church charter, dancing and drinking were forbidden. However, when the Elmira Congregationalists hired Beecher, they gained a minister who played baseball, held his own at the billiard table (which must have endeared him to Clemens), played cards, and was known to drink a beer with his flock on occasion (his personal mug hung in a town saloon). Still, Beecher's views regarding alcohol did change over the years. At first he maintained that a liking for strong drink could be controlled, and he rejected temperance arguments. But after a stint "drying out" at the Glen Haven health resort in the mid-1850s, Beecher gradually allied himself with temperance forces. Beecher also approved of dancing, and when the Congregationalists new Park Church was being built, a "dancing hall" was included in the construction plans. The Langdons followed Beecher's lead, and in February 1867, Mrs. Langdon recorded in her diary the fun everyone had dancing at a party the Langdons held in their home.

Beecher possessed a driven personality and was prone to periods of depression. He always regarded himself as a working man; in Elmira he dressed in rough clothes and wore a railroad man's cap, which Susan Crane sewed for him. He was greatly interested in science and mechanics and for forty years was in charge of setting the town clock. Max Eastman, the son of Annis Ford Eastman, Beecher's successor, remembered that Beecher would set the town's clock by "keeping it in pace with the sun by means of observations made with his own instruments on the famous East Hill half way up to Quarry Farm" (Jerome and Wisbey 134). The sundial Beecher used to tell time still stands in front of the house he built on East Hill. In 1861, along with Dr. Farrar of Elmira College, Beecher established the Elmira Academy of Science, serving as its first president, and together they corresponded with such luminaries as Charles Darwin and Thomas Henry Huxley.

Every Tuesday Beecher would withdraw from his clerical responsibilities and engage in physical activities, such as painting or carpentry, to aid his parishioners. Prior to his marriage to Julia Jones in 1857, Beecher resided at the Gleason Water Cure. Three years after they wed, the Beechers moved across the street to the home Thomas designed and built. The Gleasons and Beechers became so close that they were buried in the same group of cemetery plots, which Thomas bought for ninety dollars on May 13, 1864. During the Civil War Beecher enlisted as chaplain in the 141st New York Volunteers; his tour of duty was brief—just four months—and he soon returned to Elmira.

Beecher quickly became well-liked by his parishioners, due in part to his common dress and his devotion to assisting those in need. Perhaps most important of all, Beecher made himself available to this congregation during the week. Beecher rented two rooms in town where parishioners could come to talk with him, women could hold their sewing circle, young men could play billiards, and interested parishioners could check out books from what was in effect the town's first public library.[3] Beecher's accessibility to and involvement with his congregation, however, was vehemently denounced by the other Elmira ministers (Jerome and Wisbey 115). Beecher's sermons attracted larger and larger crowds until his church ran out of space, a problem Beecher solved in his practical way by conducting services in the city's opera house. This act so enraged the Ministerial Association—an association of local ministers Beecher had resurrected when he first came to Elmira—that they expelled him from its membership. Beecher hardly took notice. Beecher further infuriated the Ministerial Association by conducting summer services in the city park while dressed in a white suit and hat (Stowe 370).[4]

One person who publicly voiced his disgust with the Ministerial Association's actions was Samuel Clemens, whose essay, "Mr. Beecher and the Clergy," appeared in the local Elmira newspaper on April 10, 1869 (*Mark Twain: Collected Tales, Sketches, Speeches, & Essays,* 1,008). Two months into his engagement with Olivia, Clemens wrote a scathingly funny piece defending the Langdon family's minister:

> Happy, happy world, that knows at last that a little Congress of congregationless clergymen of whom it had never heard before, have crushed a famous BEECHER and reduced his audiences from fifteen hundred down to fourteen hundred and seventy-five at one fell blow! . . . And miserable, O thrice miserable BEECHER!—for the Ministerial Union of Elmira will never, no never more be responsible to God for his shortcomings. (*Mark Twain: Collected Tales, Sketches, Speeches, & Essays,* 294–95)

Clemens's voice in support of Beecher was heard again on July 25, 1871, in an article describing the new church that was being planned. Clemens called the church "as variegated, eccentric and marked with as peculiar and striking an individuality as a Beecher himself." Clemens quickly pointed out two notable exclusions of the proposed church: "There is to be no steeple on the church — merely because no practical use can be made of it. There is to be no bell, because any ignoramus knows what time church service begins without that exasperating nuisance" (Jerome and Wisbey 124).

Included among the members on the planning committee for the new church were Charles Langdon and Susan Crane. By this time Theodore Crane, Susan's husband, had also joined the trustees as an appointed member. After the building of the new Park Church in 1875, toward which the Langdons matched funds raised and donated sixty-five thousand dollars, Beecher's ideal of his "Church Home" was realized. The town's first public library, to which the Langdons had donated books, now had a permanent home and a place where the librarian, Ella Wolcott, could teach literary classes and convene the Shakespeare Club. Beecher ran what resembled a social services office that provided for the town's aged and poor, and he operated an employment service for those in need of work. Among the most interesting features of the new church were six bathrooms (so that worshippers without their own facilities could avail themselves) and a church infirmary, for parishioners unable to afford private health care, which boasted what must have been a unique curiosity — water beds (an idea taken from the Gleasons' cure).

The Langdons and the Cranes formed the backbone of the church. The Langdons were known as the "First Family of Park Church," and the Langdon women enrolled as members of the sewing circle and literary clubs. Mrs. Langdon sang in the church quartette when the congregation was still meeting in Temperance Hall — a radical act considering that most Protestant churches at the time forbade women from performing music that formed part of the liturgy. Theodore Crane served as church treasurer, and Susan Crane decorated the pulpit and baked the Communion bread. Beecher officiated at both the Cranes' and the Clemenses' weddings (the Reverend Joseph Twichell assisted at the Clemenses' nuptials), and both Julia and Thomas Beecher became Langdon family intimates (Jervis Langdon eventually paid off the mortgage to the Beechers' home). Thomas Beecher and Clemens became close companions; in his autobiography, Clemens commented on Beecher's character: "He was deeply versed in the sciences, and his pulpit eloquence fell but little short of that of his great brother, Henry Ward. His was a keen intellect, and he was brilliant in conversation. . . . He was one of the best men I have ever known" (Mar. 1, 1907, Autobiographical Dictation, No. 68, MTP*).

Rallying for Reform

Abolition was a cause the Park Church congregation was involved in from the church's inception, and this initial participation led church members to sponsor a multitude of diverse social reform organizations. An announcement in the *Elmira Advertiser* on March 23, 1867, signaled the direction the female congregation of Park Church would follow toward the end of the nineteenth century. The announcement concerns the first annual meeting of the American Equal Rights Association (an organization that combined suffragist and African-American rights forces). The timing of this newspaper piece, signed by Lucretia Mott, Susan B. Anthony, and Henry Blackwell, was crucial — the New York State Constitution was slated to be revised in the spring of 1867, and reformers wanted to apply pressure in order to achieve suffrage for both African-Americans and women: "The black man, even the black soldier, is yet but half emancipated, nor will he be, until his full suffrage and citizenship are secured to him in the Federal Constitution. Still more deplorable is the condition of the black woman; and legally, that of the white woman is no better!" (Mott et al., "First Anniversary"). But women were not granted their voting rights in the revised state constitution, and were forced to step aside while African-American men were granted suffrage in a federal constitutional amendment.

Both Olivia Lewis Langdon and Jervis Langdon were deeply involved with the abolitionist movement. At Olivia Lewis Langdon's memorial service, Beecher stated that the primary reason for the church's formation was to enable individuals to meet, "talk and pray anti-slavery and 'reform'" (Beecher *Olivia Langdon Eulogy Memorial Pamphlet* 7). The men demonstrated their support for the abolitionist movement by becoming involved with the Underground Railroad; the women met weekly in a "sewing society," which was adapted to serve a variety of causes. The primary purpose of the Elmira Independent Congregational Church's female sewing society was to raise money for missionary or charitable activities, and its first cause was abolition. With the onset of the Civil War, the sewing circle demonstrated its support for the North by making clothing and uniforms for Union forces: in May 1863, "Mrs. Gilbert, Mrs. Crane, Mrs. Ballard and Mrs. Sayles cut 79 flannel shirts for the soldiers" (Taylor and Myers 33).

Remembered in Elmira histories primarily for her preparations for church functions, Susan Crane first emerged as a community activist during the Civil War. At age twenty-eight Crane was chair of the Soldier's Relief

Association Finance Committee in 1864, a position that required considerable organizational skills and involved managing large sums. A report of the finance committee in the local Elmira paper lists expenditures for November 1864 totaling $609.98, with remaining cash on hand at $3,693.53 — an enormous amount of money at the time ("Report," *Elmira Advertiser,* Dec. 7, 1864).

Park Church women also joined the Sanitary Commission, "which sent large kitchen, and linen and money supplies to hospitals in Virginia and Maryland, beside the great demand for home work" (Taylor and Myers 34). Karen Blair views the Civil War years as contributing to "the club spirit among women," and notes that the organizational skills honed in these church organizations would result in broader roles for women and resurface in future suffrage campaigns:

> Patriotism legitimated women's participation in the Sanitary Commission, a voluntary association of women which undertook the work of raising twenty-five to thirty million dollars, much of it for supplies for the Union soldiers — medical supplies, food, and uniforms. . . . Sanitary Commission women coordinated huge fairs in every big northern city, raising millions of dollars by selling donated gifts, and providing entertainment, refreshments, and exhibits. (26)[5]

The Park Church sewing circle continued its social activism in the post–Civil War years and broadened its range to encompass both foreign and home missionary work. Julia Beecher is credited with establishing the first foreign missionary society in Elmira in 1885. To raise funds for the missionary treasury, Julia created a doll made of old hose and yarn. Missionary society members sold the "Beecher dolls" at fairs for fifty cents. By 1895, the dolls had earned the society $1,111.89 (Taylor and Myers 34–35). The society actively supported freedman's schools, and in 1893 missionary members donated "twenty-five quilts and comfortables . . . a valuable box of bedding" to a freedman's school in Alabama (Taylor and Myers 34). With their missionary societies and Sunday schools, churches afforded women the opportunity to edge closer to the public sphere. The various church activities women organized, Kathy Peiss argues, "offered women an institutional base for public involvement and a model for their political association. The world of churches . . . a world dominated by women — must be understood as an alternative public arena" (820). Using their church as a power base, the Langdon women and their closest female friends in some sense were able to transgress established gender boundaries.

The Temperance Crusade: A Woman's Cause

With their women's network firmly in place by the latter half of the nineteenth century, Park Church women united during the mid-1870s for their
second great cause: temperance. In Elmira, the roots of temperance organizations ran deep. Before prohibition was first passed in 1854, local "friends
of Temperance" sponsored lectures in the Elmira area. In November 1850 a
group of these friends invited the public to come and hear W. H. Burleigh,
secretary of the New York State Temperance Society, speak on the evils of
alcohol consumption ("W. H. Burleigh," CCHS).

When prohibition was repealed in 1864, Elmira temperance organizers
once again became active. Temperance and abolition had always been
shared concerns of Park Church's congregation, and after the repeal Park
Church women became local temperance leaders. Temperance lecturers
often came to speak in Elmira, as did Susannah Evens in 1864 "at Rev. Mr.
Beecher's Church" ("Temperance Lecture," *Elmira Advertiser,* December 5,
1864, 3). The Langdons and the Cranes participated in and actively supported the temperance movement; in 1865 Olivia Lewis Langdon noted
in her diary that Susan and Theodore Crane and Lottie had gone to spend
the evening at a temperance meeting held at the local Methodist church
(Jan. 23, MTM).

The temperance movement slowly gathered momentum, and by the
winter of 1873–74, it exploded into what was called the "crusade." A
speaker well-known to temperance reformers, Diocletian Lewis, was lecturing that winter in Fredonia, New York, the home of Clemens's mother and
sister (Scott 93). On December 13, he delivered a speech that provided the
inspiration for the crusade (Crocker 55). In addition to his temperance
work, Lewis was also known as "an advocate of homeopathic medicine and
physical exercise for women" (Hardesty 145). Lewis was received with
tremendous enthusiasm when he lectured later that week in Jamestown,
New York, and again when he spoke on December 23, 1873, in Hillsboro,
Ohio, on "The Duty of Christian Women in the Cause of Temperance"
(Scott 94; Hardesty 145). The substance of Lewis's speech was not particularly new, but its effect was unprecedented. Upon hearing Lewis's
speech local Fredonia women, tired of ineffective laws and politicians who
gave lip service to regulating liquor traffic, took to the streets. Many of the
women viewed themselves and their children as the principal victims of
male drinking, which, they argued, was supported and encouraged by

liquor dealers. Fredonia women decided that the time had come for acts of civil disobedience. Their protest took two forms: The first was picketing bars. Women would stand outside the bars and sing hymns, pray, and request all individuals entering to cease their ruinous habits. The second was circulating petitions pledging abstinence for citizens to sign; these petitions were then published in the local papers. Jane Clemens and her daughter, Pamela Clemens Moffett, were among these Fredonia crusaders ("List of the W.C.T.U. Crusaders"). News of the Fredonia women's actions quickly spread, and groups of temperance women in surrounding states began similar crusades.[6]

The Fredonia crusade inspired Clemens to write an essay which, when first published, was entitled "The Temperance Insurrection."[7] (Paine mistakenly dated the Clemens piece 1873, but the Ohio crusade Clemens mentions in the first paragraph of his essay did not occur until late December 1873; the essay's actual date is March 12, and it first appeared in the London *Standard* on March 26, 1874 [*Mark Twain: Collected Tales, Sketches, Speeches, & Essays* 1,015].) When Clemens cites in his essay the "3,000 victories" the crusaders had accomplished, he may be alluding to those official abstainers who signed the temperance petition (25), and he is also careful to point out that the crusaders "are young girls and women . . . the very best in the village communities." Clemens was doubtlessly aware that these women included his mother and sister (Twain, *Europe and Elsewhere* 26). Considering how involved the Langdons, Jane Clemens, and Pamela Moffett were in the temperance movement, Clemens must have regarded them as important sources of information about the crusade.

The crusade came to Elmira in the spring of 1874. On March 4, Dio Lewis arrived and fired the opening salvo in the temperance war in a lecture he delivered to a packed Opera House ("An Appeal," *Elmira Advertiser,* Apr. 4, 1874).[8] One month later, John B. Gough, one of the era's most famous speakers on the evils of intemperance, related "the most thrilling events of his life" ("John B. Gough," *Elmira Advertiser,* Apr. 1, 1874). Gough was a recovering alcoholic who, as part of his performance, would act out for his shocked audience the fulsome horrors of delirium tremens. Following the example set by crusade organizers in other cities, an Elmira temperance executive committee was formed and local women began meeting in prayer groups; they signed "the women's appeal and pledge," and began to picket saloons ("John B. Gough," *Elmira Advertiser,* Apr. 1, 1874). While the local newspaper tried to console its tippling readers by pointing out that "the temperance crusaders have not run riot so madly here, as in most other places," this soon became an empty reassurance, as Elmira women took to the streets ("Temperance," *Elmira Advertiser,* Apr. 3, 1874).

Elmira temperance supporters authored an appeal demanding that "Dealers in Intoxicating Drinks" must "cease at once." More than three thousand women signed the petition, including Julia Beecher, Susan Crane, Rachael Gleason, and Olivia Lewis Langdon ("An Appeal," *Elmira Advertiser,* Apr. 4, 1874). Temperance meetings grew increasingly larger, and on April 13, more than four thousand men and women gathered for a public rally. The Elmira women's temperance crusade goes unmentioned in town histories.[9]

When the Clemenses arrived in Elmira for the summer in early May, just weeks after the Elmira women had published a petition and held a public rally, the Langdons, Cranes, and their many friends must have been full of news about the local crusade, and Clemens must have been fascinated to find that the crusade had surfaced at the local level. The Clemenses spent that entire temperance summer in Elmira and did not return to Hartford until September 10 ("Chronology," MTP).[10]

Temperance forces continued their work in a slow, steady way even after the pronounced activism that initially marked the crusade had ebbed. A "Temperance Headquarters" was established in Elmira by 1877, and the organization held regular meetings, sponsored temperance speakers, and conducted prayer groups ("Temperance Headquarters," *Elmira Advertiser,* May 11, 1877). A newspaper article dated February 23, 1880, mentions Theodore Crane as a member of the "friends of temperance and total abstinence" group, which urged the public to vote for Excise Commissioners sympathetic to temperance concerns ("Temperance Rally," *Elmira Advertiser*). Clemens was kept informed about the progress of the temperance movement by his sister and brother-in-law, and by the late 1870s and early 1880s, references to temperance began to appear in his fiction.

Clemens wrote jocularly but in detail about the movement in a fragment entitled "Autobiography of a Damned Fool," begun March 1877. Chapter 4 opens with a temperance lecturer coming to town; after some initial harassment, the speaker and his followers begin to convert the local populace. A major victory comes when a liquor dealer by the name of Lawson decides to smash his twenty barrels of whiskey and join forces with the reformers. The "do-good" temperance supporters, distressed at the thought that this loss of revenue might plunge Lawson's family into debt, decide to contribute money to make up for his losses. Everyone donates, and Lawson pockets an amount double the worth of his whiskey. Lawson's conversion turns out to be fake — the whiskey barrels the reformers smashed were filled with water — and after the movement dies down "two months afterward," he rescues the whiskey from its hiding place and goes into business, "very prosperously, too" (*Mark Twain's Satires and Burlesques* 149).

Clemens's most notable work of fiction to include temperance as part of its plot is *Adventures of Huckleberry Finn*. In this book, Pap, trying to hoodwink the new judge in St. Petersburg, signs the temperance pledge ("made his mark"). Pap's vow of abstinence lasted approximately four hours, whereupon he "got powerful thirsty and clumb out onto the porch-roof and slid down a stanchion and traded his new coat for a jug of forty-rod" (23). The second temperance mention comes some seventy pages later, with the introduction of the Duke and the Dauphin. The Dauphin informs the Duke that his latest scheme had involved, "a-runnin' a little temperance revival thar, 'bout a week, and was the pet of the women-folks, big and little, for I was makin' it mighty warm for the rummies . . . and business growing all the time; when somehow or another a little respect got around, last night, that I had a way of puttin' in my time with a private jug, on the sly" (99).

In these two excerpts, Clemens identifies and satirizes a real problem: many went through the motions of temperance reform, such as signing pledges and attending revivals, but how long-lasting and effective was this kind of action? Clemens, too, had given his pledge to his mother when he left home as a young man — a promise that evidently was soon broken. Did reformers create abstinence where there had been intemperance or, as Clemens remarked to Henry Ward Beecher in 1885, should "do-good" reformers be regarded as "enemies of the human race who go around enslaving God's free people with pledges — to quit drinking instead of to quit wanting to drink" (Paine, ed., *Mark Twain's Letters* 459). In these passages, Clemens also addresses a major point of contention regarding the gendered nature of leadership within the temperance movement: the involvement of male civic and religious leaders. Clemens had grave doubts regarding the intentions of those men who, in the act of placing themselves as the movement's social or moral leaders, marginalized the efforts made by women. In *Adventures of Huckleberry Finn*, Clemens portrays the pious judge as a simpleton, and the supposedly civic-minded Dauphin as a fraud.

Temperance and Beyond

As they worked for the temperance cause, white, middle-class church women were brought into close contact with Elmira's disenfranchised populations: namely, the laboring classes comprised of recent immigrants and African-Americans. In 1877 Elmira churchwomen, wishing to aid the families of individuals who had signed the pledge of temperance and to help ensure that the newly temperate would keep their resolution, founded an "Industrial School." The date of the school's official opening is remembered as July 13, 1878 (Gratto 1). The school's original function was to provide clothing and food for newly temperate families, and the school itself was regarded as "an annex to the temperance movement" (42). By the early 1880s, the mission of the school had slowly changed, and instead of concentrating only on those poor with temperance ties, all the poor of Elmira were included.[11]

Again, the Langdons and the Cranes were involved with this local missionary work. Charles Langdon was a member of the industrial school advisory board from 1884 until 1915, and was acting treasurer in 1894. In 1887, in *The Industrial School Appeal*, under the heading of donations for "City Missionary Work," Theodore Crane is listed as a contributor ("5 tons coal") along with Mrs. Charles Langdon ("27 pieces of second hand clothing") (*The Industrial School Appeal* 2). Susan Crane served as the acting president of the industrial school in 1894 (*Grand Concert* 2). Clara Clemens played with her cousin, Julie Langdon, in a concert benefiting the school in September 1893 (Wisbey, "One Hundred Years Ago," 6).

Diocletian Lewis's lecture in Fredonia at the end of 1873 had marked the onset of the temperance crusade and also provided the impetus for the formation of the Women's Christian Temperance Union (WCTU). The first chapter of the WCTU was begun in Fredonia just two days after Lewis's speech on December 13, 1873, and the first WCTU convention was held on October 14, 1874, in Syracuse (Crocker 55; Graham and Gardenier 18). In addition to being one of the original crusaders, Pamela Moffett, Clemens's sister, was an early WCTU member and also belonged to the Fredonia Political Equality Club, which elected her as its delegate to the National Convention for Suffragists, held in Washington, D.C. (Simpson and Simpson 14). Moffett was apparently one of the WCTU's first treasurers (Kirst 16). On April 11, 1874, Jane Clemens wrote to Olivia and Samuel Clemens from Fredonia, inquiring whether they would donate books to the Fredonia WCTU's reading room:

All the ladies in this village in favour of temperence [sic] for some time have been working very hard to stop the sale of all liquors. The ladies have done great good, but have not succeded [sic]. But they have worked hard to start a reading room to draw the ladies and gentlemen . . . from the saloons. . . . Livy it ocured [sic] to me that you and Sam would like to do good. You have many books that perhaps you can spare to give to them. (MTP*)

Clemens and Olivia sent sixteen volumes (Gribben, *Mark Twain's Library* 576).

The press frequently referred to the events occurring during the winter of 1873–74 as the "Woman's War," and indeed it was. With the formation of the WCTU, women now had a structured organization that enabled them to carry on what was to become a political battle.[12] While women were effectively barred from male gathering places that constituted the "cultural setting of formal politics," as Peiss explains, they created an alternative political culture "rooted in women's clubs, [and] voluntary associations. . . . By the end of the century, such female institutions as the Women's Christian Temperance Union . . . had become major players in national politics" (819).

Clemens must have been aware of these developments when he wrote "The Temperance Insurrection," for this essay stands as one of his strongest expressions of the suffrage cause:

> [The crusaders] find themselves voiceless in the making of laws and the election of officers to execute them. Born with brains, born in the country, educated, having large interests at stake, they find their tongues tied and their hands fettered, while every ignorant whiskey-drinking foreign-born savage in the land may hold office, help to make the laws, degrade the dignity of the former and break the latter at his own sweet will. (*Mark Twain: Collected Tales, Sketches, Speeches & Essays,* 1,015)

By the close of his essay, Clemens proclaims that "in extending the suffrage to women this country could lose absolutely nothing and might gain a great deal. . . . From the day that Adam ate of the apple and told on Eve . . . man, in a moral fight, has pretty uniformly shown himself to be an arrant coward" (30). For many individuals, the year 1874 marked the merging of two movements that would preoccupy women for the remainder of the nineteenth-century, and Clemens, kept well informed by his female family circle, sensed this.

Just a year later Clemens pursued this same line of thought in a speech given to the Hartford Monday Evening Club on February 15, 1875:

> Our marvelous latter-day statesmanship has invented universal suffrage. That
> is the finest feather in our cap. All that we require of a voter is that he shall be
> forked, wear pantaloons instead of petticoats, and bear more or less humorous
> resemblance to the reported image of God. . . . We brag of our universal,
> unrestricted suffrage; but we are shams after all, for we restrict when we come
> to the women. (Paine, *Mark Twain: A Biography* 541–42)

When Clemens pointed out the irony of America's "universal suffrage" as it
was being practiced, he was commenting on an issue that was being widely
debated. Guy Cardwell maintains that Clemens's reasoning "smack[s] of
Know-Nothingism" (*The Man Who Was Mark Twain* 109), and attacks
Clemens's call for female suffrage as "nativist." Yet Clemens here utilized the
same arguments that suffragist and African-American rights activist Frances
Harper would use in her 1894 address to the World's Congress of Representative Women entitled "Women's Political Future." Harper proclaimed:

> I do not believe in unrestricted and universal suffrage for either men or
> women. I believe in moral and educational tests. I do not believe that the most
> ignorant and brutal man is better prepared to add value to the strength and
> durability of the government than the most cultured, upright, and intelligent
> woman. (Lauter 120)

When Frances Willard was elected national president of the WCTU in
1879, she "proceeded to make it not only a temperance but also a suffrage
organization."[13] In 1883, the WCTU "endorsed an equal suffrage plank
without a vote in opposition" (148). Willard had long been supportive of
the suffragist cause, and at a WCTU camp meeting in 1876 she had made
this clear (Bordin, *Frances Willard,* 98–99). What Willard did, which up to
that point suffragists had not, was to assimilate two opposing nineteenth-
century notions of women's roles for the greater success of her organization.[14] When Willard was elected WCTU president, she adopted the slogan
"Do Everything," and indeed the WCTU of the 1880s and 1890s appears to
have taken on most of the social issues of the day. Willard's WCTU espoused such causes as dress reform, health reform (advocating hydropathy), prison reform, alcohol and tobacco reform, the free kindergarten
movement, labor reform, education for women, and animal rights.

According to Estelle Freedman, by the late 1860s women had "joined
other critics of American prisons in calling for change" (49). The formation
of the American Prison Association, in 1870 sparked renewed debate regarding penal methods in general. Individuals working toward American
prison reform were particularly impressed by the British model, which

endorsed "policies of commutation of sentences for good behavior, the merit marking-system, and progressive reentry into society" (Freedman 49). Elmira's WCTU members were also instrumental in reforming the local prison system. In 1869, New York State enacted a law authorizing the establishment of prison reformatories intended for first-time male offenders aged sixteen to thirty. Elmira was selected as the site for the first of these reformatories. Zebulon Brockway, an early American proponent of prison reform, was selected to serve as superintendent of the Elmira Reformatory. Brockway offered incentives for good behavior, and at Elmira the prisoners' actions determined, to a large degree, the date of their release (Freedman 49). Brockway instituted reforms that rewarded inmates for internalizing many of the controls formerly imposed by the external discipline of the penitentiary. The Elmira Reformatory opened in July of 1876, and by 1877 the total prison population stood at 164 (Byrne 548). (Frances Willard paid a visit to the Elmira Reformatory, most likely sometime in the summer of 1878, and approved of what she saw during her stay [Bordin, *Frances Willard,* 130].)

Clemens and Superintendent Brockway knew and liked each other, and Brockway evidently helped make Clemens a proponent of prison reform. Brockway believed entertainment had a positive influence on reformatory inmates, and he invited Clemens to come and lecture. Clemens performed there on three separate occasions: the first time on July 21, 1886, reading "German," "Whistling," "A Trying Situation," and "King Sollermun"; the second time on September 11, 1888; and the third in 1895 (Jerome and Wisbey 69, 72). In the decades Clemens spent visiting Elmira with his family, because he came there principally to write and rest, he gave only two public performances. In Elmira, then, Clemens had lectured more to convicts than to the free citizenry. Clemens enjoyed his prison performances: "The Elmira Reformatory contains 850 convicts, who are there for all manner of crimes. . . . It's the best audience in the world" (Jerome and Wisbey 71).[15]

The Elmira chapter of the WCTU was formed in 1885 with Helen Chapel Bullock elected as its president; by that time Frances Willard had been national president of the WCTU for six years.[16] The national WCTU was lobbying for female correctional facility reform and stricter laws governing alcohol and tobacco use. By the mid-1880s, it also began promoting industrial training schools for young women. Bullock and her WCTU members rose to meet both challenges. In the late 1880s members of the Elmira central chapter began to campaign for separate correctional institutions for women and for a police matron. In April 1889, Bullock and her WCTU members secured the appointment of the city's first police matron, Mrs. Esther D. Wilkins, the sister of Elmira's mayor (Edholm).[17] According to Bullock:

> The prison work of Elmira Central W.C.T.U. revealed the great need for a police matron to care for the women and girls who are brought to our police station. . . . So many of these thoughtless, wayward girls needed training in an industrial Christian home in order to save them that we found it necessary to organize the Anchorage, which was done April 1, 1890. ("Annual Report of the Anchorage," 1)

The Anchorage was mainly a place of refuge for unwed mothers. Bullock was the Anchorage's founder and president. Joan Brumberg explains in her informative article "'Ruined' Girls," that places "like the Anchorage, supported and staffed by evangelical Protestant women, were intended to reduce the chaos, insecurity, and brutality that illegitimacy could generate" (261). The institution provided food, shelter, educational and industrial training, and medical care. Brumberg reports that for the unwed mother staying at the Anchorage, "the imperative for adoption was strong and the institutional records confirm that fact: of 32 babies born alive at the Anchorage between 1890 and 1907, 69 percent were adopted; 31 percent were kept by their mothers" (260). Two of the Anchorage's staff of women physicians, Dr. Anna M. Stuart and Dr. Jessie L. Herrick, had been trained by Rachael Gleason at the Water Cure. Brumberg credits the Elmira WCTU as the "crucial linchpin in developing a local institution to serve girls in need" (252).

Another of the WCTU's contributions during the 1880s was its promotion of public kindergartens. In 1883, Willard endorsed the kindergarten movement, which was already widely supported by WCTU members (Bordin, *Frances Willard*, 131).[18] The industrial school founded by Elmira churchwomen in the late 1870s appears to have allied itself with the WCTU by the turn of the century. This is not particularly surprising, for the WCTU evidently had found a stronghold among the Elmira women. Susan Crane, president of the school in 1894, was herself a WCTU "white-ribboner."

The WCTU was also a staunch advocate of labor reform.[19] Historian Ruth Bordin credits the Knights of Labor, an organization formed in 1869 to protect the rights of workers, as early champions of women's rights: "In their first constitution (1878) they supported equal pay for equal work regardless of sex. Women were admitted to the order in 1882, sixty-four women's locals had been organized by 1885, and over 50,000 women were members by the next years" (Bordin, *Frances Willard*, 138). The same year the Reformatory was built (1876), the first Knights of Labor group was formed in Elmira. During the period 1876–1889, fifteen separate Knights of Labor local assemblies were formed in Elmira, and they included such laborers as shoemakers, carpenters, telegraph operators, cigarmakers, iron workers, and clerks. Although there appears to have been no solely female assemblies in Elmira, women may have taken part in assemblies that had a combined male and female membership. Extant membership rolls have yet to be unearthed, but considering the climate of reform in Elmira at the time, it seems very likely that there were mixed-sex assemblies of the Knights of Labor.

Clemens, too, advocated labor reform and took careful note of the changes that occurred among the Knights of Labor assemblies during the 1880s. When the Knights won a victory over railroad financier Jay Gould in 1885 (the Knights successfully unionized Gould's southwestern railroad line), Clemens "hailed it as a triumph for all who believed in democracy" (Foner 168). On March 22, 1886, while the Knights were being vilified privately by business leaders and publicly by newspapers with ties to business, Clemens delivered a speech to the Monday Evening Club in Hartford entitled "Knights of Labor—The New Dynasty" (Carter). Clemens later adapted his speech into an essay he sent to William Dean Howells; Howells apparently tried to get the essay published, but was unsuccessful. (Clemens would defend the unions again—this time in fiction—in *A Connecticut Yankee in King Arthur's Court* [1889].) Although the power and influence of the Knights had faded by the close of the 1880s, the union movement continued to grow, proving true Clemens's words in his 1886 speech, that the union man "is here; & the question is not—as it has been heretofore during a thousand ages—What shall we do with him? For the first time in history we are relieved of the necessity of managing his affair for him. He is not a broken dam this time—he is the Flood!" (Foner 173).

By the 1890s the WCTU's membership had grown to more than 150,000 women (a phenomenal increase from the 13,000 dues-paying members of 1876), and they campaigned regularly for women's suffrage. Under Frances Willard's direction, the WCTU joined forces with the suffragists and became official allies of the National Woman Suffrage Association. In part their development came about as a result of Willard's conversion to "Christian socialism" after reading Edward Bellamy's 1888 novel,

Looking Backward (Bordin, *Women and Temperance* 108). Bellamy espoused the belief that women would become the future leaders of the world and that the future was in their hands.

Olivia's connection with the women's movement began early in life and continued until her death. In 1900 Olivia happily accepted an invitation from Lillie Devereux Blake to come to a Pilgrim Mothers' Dinner. Blake was an accomplished lecturer and writer on women's issues in addition to serving as president of the New York State Woman Suffrage Association (1879–1890) and as president of the New York City Woman Suffrage League (1886–1900). For a time she was considered to be Anthony's successor to the National American Woman Suffrage Association; however, in 1900 she was forced to withdraw in favor of Carrie Chapman Catt. Blake was a contributor to Elizabeth Cady Stanton's *Woman's Bible*. Her best known novel was *Fettered for Life* (1874), which contains a great deal of information regarding nineteenth-century temperance and moral reform movements and, as Grace Farrell notes, "deals with issues of sexism: the novel is a female *bildungsroman*." Blake began the Pilgrim Mothers' Dinners, which were held annually at the Waldorf-Astoria Hotel, as an antidote to the universal reference to Our Pilgrim Fathers (White 52–53). Olivia was evidently considered by Blake to be part of the Pilgrim Mothers' group and, as Olivia's reply to Blake's invitation makes clear, she was happy to be invited:

> Dec. 13, 1900
> My dear Mrs. Blake,
> I am truly sorry to have missed you & your daughter yesterday. I accept with pleasure and great interest your kind invitation to the Pilgrim Mothers' Dinner on Dec. 22nd at 12:30 o'clock. (MHS)

Examining the tone and subjects of Clemens's speeches and essays on women and women's rights prior to 1870, one might conclude that prior to 1870 Clemens objected to women's suffrage. After his marriage, however, as Edgar Branch notes, Clemens "reversed his opinion," as indicated by his post-1870s writings (193). In 1901, before an audience at the annual meeting of the Hebrew Technical School, Clemens declared, "For twenty-five years I've been a woman's rights man" (*Mark Twain Speaking* 223).[20] Clearly, Clemens was open to and supportive of women's issues — issues with which, significantly, the women in his family circle were intimately involved. By 1909, suffragists considered Clemens such an avid supporter that Elizabeth Bacon, the president of Connecticut's Woman Suffrage Association, wrote to ask him to lend his name to their cause:

> Dec. 26, 1909
> The National Woman Suffrage Association at its recent annual Convention, voted to make a National Petition to Congress, asking the submission for a 16th Amendment to the National Constitution which shall enable women to vote, and the workers in this state are just entering upon our part of the work. A few names of national repute would be of great assistance and having just seen your photograph in the *Woman's Journal* with these words quoted underneath "I would like to see the ballot in the hand of every woman" I immediately thought "I will mail a petition to 'Mark Twain.'"

Clemens wrote on the back of the letter, "I am very glad to sign the petition but I am in terror lest I should be asked to do something, for I don't do anything now, but rest after 73 years of activity" (Bacon, MTP*).

Education Reform: A Female Student's Progress

After the establishment of the Water Cure in 1852 and the religious and social reforms introduced with the arrival of Thomas Beecher in 1854, the triptych of reform in Elmira was completed with the establishment of Elmira Female College on October 2, 1855. The establishment of women's colleges during the second half of the nineteenth century underscored the growing schism in American society between women's traditional roles within the private sphere and women's greater participation in the public sphere in the form of temperance and social reform movements and suffragist activities. Women's colleges became suspect because of their avowed purpose of educating the female, an idea considered by nineteenth-century allopathic practitioners (among many others) as unnatural and potentially health-threatening. Karen Blair observes that "like the demand for suffrage, job, property rights and the right of women to speak in public," women's colleges "were categorized as part of the threatening Woman Movement" (135). Before her death in Elmira in 1878, Catharine Beecher (then living with Julia and Thomas Beecher) confided to a close female friend that it was her desire to "reestablish the domestic department of the college." Catharine's unnamed friend ruefully noted that she feared "the opinion still holds at the college, in favor of the one-sided education" ("R").

The Elmira Female College claimed it would be the first in America to offer a bachelor of arts degree equal to that of male colleges. One of the college's bylaws provides a particularly instructive clue to the nature of the institution: "Act. VIII. This institution — while it shall be our aim to make it highly evangelical in its character, shall never assume a sectarian cast" (Meltzer 19). We can trace the path to the college's formation by following the trajectory of Olivia Louise Langdon's educational career. Olivia's educational background, we will see, was as well established as her church and social activist roots.

Olivia received both elementary and post-secondary school education. Her first formal educational experience took place at Miss Clarissa Thurston's Female Seminary (founded in 1848).[21] In her seminary catalog, Miss Thurston stated that the goal of her school was to "furnish young ladies with an opportunity to acquire a thorough scientific education, and at the same time to aid them in the formation of such a character as shall fit them for the active duties of life" (13). Before settling in Elmira and opening her seminary, Miss Thurston taught school in Maine, Georgia, New Jersey, and in Geneva and Brockport, New York. A dynamic figure, she wrote three books during her career as an educator; after her retirement at age seventy, she embarked on a tour of Europe (Palmer 1).

In the surviving school records, Olivia is registered at the seminary at the ages of six, ten, and twelve. The seminary had a Preparatory Department where children under twelve studied reading, spelling, penmanship, math, grammar, geography, and world and United States history. The junior, middle, and senior classes undertook a three-year course of study in algebra, geometry, trigonometry, ancient history, botany, physiology, astronomy, philosophy, theology, chemistry, modern history, logic, composition, vocal and instrumental music, painting, and French or Latin (Thurston 13–15). Susan Langdon attended school with Olivia and received her diploma in 1853 at the age of seventeen (Sharlow, "Cranes," 9). Had the Elmira Female College not been established, both girls' formal education in Elmira would have ended here.

When one traces the history of female education in Elmira, the name Simeon Benjamin repeatedly surfaces. Benjamin served on the board of the Elmira Misses Cleeves seminary and was instrumental in the founding of Elmira Female College. On November 29, 1851, Benjamin pledged a five-thousand-dollar endowment in order to secure the selection of Elmira as the site of the new college. This initial cash gift was followed by several more. In 1854, the official college stamp was chosen (a seal bearing the letters "F.U." for Female University), and the first president of the college, Dr. James R. Boyd, was selected (Meltzer 21).

Another indispensable individual during the college's formative years was Jervis Langdon. Langdon influenced the earliest affairs of the college before its 1853 charter and served on its board of trustees from 1862 until 1870 (Sharlow, *Glimpses,* 1). Rachael Gleason was also on the planning committee for the Elmira Female College, and both she and her husband, Silas, were among the earliest contributors to the fund for its establishment.

Both Olivia and Susan Langdon attended the Elmira Female College. Olivia entered as a student on September 1, 1858, "first academic class, preparatory" (*Register of the Elmira Female College, 1855–1859*). Upon her enrollment, Olivia was twelve years old. Classes at the college were small; the local paper counted a total of fifteen women in the graduating class of 1860. Olivia studied Latin, arithmetic, English, grammar, and U.S. history (*The Fourth Annual Catalogue and Circular of the Elmira Female College, 1858–1859*). She continued her studies during the second semester commencing in January 1859; her subjects included U.S. history, arithmetic B, grammar, and music.[22] The *Elmira Female College Cash Book, 1856–1879,* lists the dates and amounts of payment for her tuition: "February 1859, Olivia Langdon, ninety-five dollars"; "June 30, 1859 Tuition Account Cash of Olivia Langdon, eight dollars." Olivia boarded at the college her first year; it is likely that her roommate during the second semester was Ellen A. Park of Warsaw, New York (Wisbey 7).[23] Olivia is listed in the *Register, Elmira Female College, 1857* as "Olivia Langdon, age 13, Elmira, Congregationalist. Arith., Latin, Hist. Miscell." Olivia returned to school on September 1, 1859, again as a student in "first academic class, preparatory." In the college cash book for 1856–1879, her tuition payment of twelve dollars is dated November 28, 1859.

Olivia stopped attending the college when her health failed. But even though her formal education had ended, Olivia remained intellectually curious, as she would throughout her life, and continued to educate herself aided by tutors, study groups, and her own extensive reading. The archives at the Elmira College contain Olivia's geography text, *McNally's System of Geography,* with the date "August 1863," written in her hand on the flyleaf. By that date Olivia was being treated by the Taylors in New York City. The book stands as silent testimony to Olivia's determination to educate herself: even as she lay in the Taylors' Institute, Olivia continued to read and to learn.

In February 1867, Olivia was visited in Elmira by Alice Hooker, and the two embarked on home tutorials conducted by Professor Darius Ford, an instructor at Elmira Female College. In a letter written by Hooker to her mother, Isabella, on February 8, she reports their schedule of study:

> From ten to eleven study and twice a week from eleven to twelve recite to Prof. Ford, one of the college professors, who is a very fine man, (young, unmarried too!) and who makes the hour of recitation most interesting—Livy and I are wild with delight over Philosophy and Prof. Ford's teaching—we enjoy it so much, for he comes to the house and we have cosy chatty lessons. (SDF)

Alice Hooker was greatly impressed by Olivia's intelligence and occasionally complained to her mother about her own lack of education (ironically, years earlier Isabella had voiced this same regret about her father regarding her lack of formal schooling). Two weeks after her February 8 letter, Hooker wrote again to her mother, informing her that she and Olivia were currently reading "Young's Night Thoughts" and were enjoying it "exceedingly." Hooker confessed that "I never should have thought of reading them myself but as Livy proposed it I did and am very glad of it now." She closed her letter with this observation about her twenty-one-year-old friend: "[Livy] is so much more thoughtful, original, deep, than most girls and so is constantly making me go to the foundations of things. I feel very shallow sometimes by her but then am glad I am with her to get good from talking with her" (Feb. 24, 1867, SDF).

Even after Olivia met Clemens, and despite the amount of attention their courtship demanded, her devotion to her studies continued unabated. Eight months after Olivia and Clemens's initial introduction, Olivia wrote to Hooker to say that she had resumed her tutorials with Professor Ford and was studying "Natural Philosophy." Olivia added that both she and Susan Crane were being taught French by local nuns. Olivia asserted that she was enjoying her lessons and that she had just begun to read *A History of the Huguenots* by W. Carlos Martyn; she was careful to add, "I do not know yet whether I like it or not. I have not read far enough to judge" (Sep. 29, 1868, SDF).

Clemens was well aware of Olivia's determination to continue her education. On March 9, 1869, Clemens wrote to Susan Crane, humorously describing Olivia's Elmira home-chemistry course: "Livy and the Spaulding girls are taking Chemistry lessons, & we are all afraid to stay in the house from 11 till noon, because they are always cooking up some new-fangled gas or other & blowing everything endways with their experiments. It is dreadful to think of having a wife who will be always inventing new chemical horrors & experimenting on me with them" (*Mark Twain's Letters, 1869*, vol. 3: 181).

At the end of the month, Clemens wrote to Mary Fairbanks, again mentioning Olivia's foray into the hard sciences: "I am in exile here at the office, for an hour, while the girls take their chemistry lesson" (*Mark Twain's Letters, 1869*, vol. 3: 185). Far from feeling threatened by Olivia's education, Clemens often bragged of her intelligence and capacity for business. During their courtship he confided to his sister Pamela that "I take as much pride in her brains as I do in her beauty, & as much pride in her happy & equable disposition as I do in her brains" (*Mark Twain's Letters, 1869*, vol. 3: 189).

On November 1, 1869, nearly two years into her courtship with Clemens, Olivia wrote again to Alice Hooker Day (Alice had married John Calvin Day in June 1869), telling her that she had just organized a class to study English history. This group, consisting of Susan Crane, Emma Sayles, Mrs. Post, Mrs. Robert, and Mrs. Fred Hall, was to receive instruction from a Mr. Monks, a teacher from Elmira whom Olivia described as a "very finely educated and cultivated young man." Olivia informs Day that the group "began with the geography of England. Told us of the supposed derivation of Albion and Britania [sic], of the Celts and the Celtic language, of the Druids [illegible] the Goths of course." Olivia ends her letter on an extremely personal note, commenting on Day's observation regarding married life: "I wish we could have one good long visit, I think [illegible] with the reputation that women have, that any man who should chance to overhear us would be surprized [sic] — I am glad you 'have tried it and say "Verily it is good"' I hate to hear the whining of married women —" (SDF). Olivia, herself just three short months away from marriage, reveals her awareness of the sexual aspect of marriage and is frankly curious to know how her intimate friend had found the experience. Perhaps it is also possible to detect Olivia's sense of relief at receiving Alice's positive report. It is intriguing to note, too, Olivia's awareness of the male assumption that women knew little of, much less talked about, such frankly sexual matters.

Transition and Transformation

The three years between 1852 and 1855 encompassed an era of remarkable change in Elmira. A sizable number of reform-minded citizens were able to make their voices heard, but by no means did they represent the majority's views: one must remember that the Langdons left their church due to differences of opinion regarding abolition, and that the local newspaper frequently published pieces critical of women who participated in reform activities. Throughout the latter half of the nineteenth century, the Langdon women and their female relatives and friends continually and knowingly transgressed the boundaries delineating what was considered socially acceptable for women by becoming involved in educational, political, religious, dress, and medical reform.

It should come as no surprise, then, that Clemens looked forward to returning to Elmira, the site of this experiment in social reform. Clearly, the reforms that took place in Elmira during this time influenced not only Clemens's personal views, but his writing as well. By the 1880s, Elmira had established its own chapter of the WCTU; the Elmira Reformatory stood as a model of prison reform; and its industrial schools and labor unions thrived. Its population stood at more than thirty-thousand, and more than sixty passenger trains stopped in the town each day. Elmira had fully earned her nickname, "Queen of the Southern Tier."

Notes

1. Congregationalism is a liberal, activist denomination categorized within Protestantism.

2. The Beecher connection with Elmira began with Thomas Beecher's installation as minister. From that point on, Elmira became a frequent destination for visits by his brothers and sisters: half-brother Henry Ward Beecher, James Beecher, sister-in-law Annie Beecher, half-sister Catharine Esther Beecher, and Isabella Beecher Hooker. At the close of her life, Catharine Beecher retired to Elmira and spent her last days living with Thomas and Julia. Catharine Beecher died on May 7, 1878, and was buried in Elmira. Olivia Lewis Langdon attended her funeral. Her last days in Elmira are chronicled in an unpublished handwritten manuscript, *Sketch of the Life of Miss Catherine Beecher,* by "R" (Beecher Family Papers, Williston Memorial Library).

3. Beecher changed location twice, the second time moving to rooms located above Jervis Langdon's office.

4. Dixon Wecter downplays the impact Thomas Beecher had on his Elmira congregation — and, by association, on the reform-minded Langdons — with the curious statement that despite "the 'radical' social implications of the Reverend Thomas Beecher's preaching," Olivia remained unaffected and maintained a "middle-of-the-road piety" (*The Love Letters of Mark Twain* 9). James Cox also passes over Thomas Beecher's influence and instead cites the treatises on faith of Beecher's famous half-brother, Henry Ward Beecher. Cox implies that Thomas Beecher's sermons were probably as tedious as his brother's writings. This does

Beecher a gross injustice; his views differed radically from those of other ministers of his time, and his ministry is still considered a model of innovation. When Thomas Beecher grew ready to retire he chose a female minister, Annis Ford Eastman, to succeed him, a move that would have mortified his conservative father, the Calvinist minister Lyman Beecher.

There is some controversy as to Beecher's views regarding slavery. In his book *The Beechers* (New York: Harper, 1981), Milton Rugoff reprints a portion of a letter published in the New York *Sun* after Beecher's death which quoted Beecher as having stated: "There are questions nearer home than slavery to occupy our attention. . . . I will make a five years' agreement with you. . . . During that period we will let the thing rest. If you can stand by my pro-slavery nonsense I can stand by your anti-slavery absurdities" (442). On the other hand, Beecher did enlist in the Union Army for duty in the Civil War (although his length of service was admittedly brief). When Beecher returned to Elmira, he ministered to the Confederate prisoners of war held in a camp on the outskirts of town (Taylor and Myers 16).

5. Toward the end of the Civil War, Elmira churchwomen worked together to aid families whose men had been killed in the conflict. The Ladies' Relief Association was founded in 1864 to relieve the suffering of widows and their children. The Association also helped injured and disabled soldiers who returned from the front to make the transition from wartime to peacetime lives. Due to the large number of Union men killed, many families were without their principal wage earner, and many widows and their children found themselves bereft of shelter and sustenance. On January 16, 1866, the Relief Association established a center where these impoverished families could live. The Association continued this early form of social aid by establishing the Southern Tier Orphans Home in 1868 and the Home for the Aged in 1874 (*Southern Tier Children's Home* [CCHS], 1; Catharine S. Connelly, "Women's Role Changed With New Frontiers" [Scrapbook, Chemung County Historical Association], 72: 26).

6. Jack S. Blocker, in *American Temperance Movements: Cycles of Reform* (Boston: Twayne Publishers, 1989), remarks that the crusade's effectiveness far surpassed anyone's expectations: "In all the Crusade appeared in at least 911 communities spread across thirty-one states and the District of Columbia" (77). In total, nearly "32,000 women in Ohio and nearly 60,000 nationwide" decided to take direct action in support of temperance (Hardesty 146). Blocker identifies Ohio as the leading crusade state, with the next most active states being Indiana, Illinois, Michigan, and New York (78).

7. Paine apparently later retitled the piece "The Temperance Crusade and Woman's Rights."

8. For a nineteenth-century account of the Elmira temperance movement see, "History of the Movement in Elmira," *Elmira Advertiser,* Apr. 4, 1874 (Steele Memorial Library, Elmira, New York).

9. This omission is not particularly surprising since the few purportedly inclusive histories of the area—Towner's *Our County and Its People: A History of the Valley and County of Chemung* (1892) and Byrne's *Chemung County, New York, History, 1890–1975* (1975) — are traditional works that focus on the life and culture of the prevailing white, patriarchal society. When women's social movements and

organizations receive mention at all in these works, it is decidedly brief. A more recent history is Michelle L. Cotton, Herbert Wisbey, Jr., and Robert D. Jerome's *Mark Twain's Elmira: 1870–1910* (Elmira, N.Y.: Chemung County Historical Society, 1985), which purports to include the very years during which the crusade took place, excludes *any* mention of women's participation in the town's affairs.

10. Olivia gave birth to her second daughter, Clara, approximately one month after the Clemenses' arrival at Quarry Farm, on June 8, 1874.

11. The industrial school underwent frequent name changes: "The Industrial Home became in 1894 the Elmira Industrial Association. In 1903 the name was changed to the Industrial School and Free Kindergarten. In 1922 the name was changed to the Elmira Industrial School and Free Kindergarten and also known as Neighborhood House" (Gratto 1).

Gretchen Sullivan Sorin explains in "The Black Community in Elmira" that "financial difficulties of the late nineteenth century, brought on by economic depression . . . created pockets of poverty within the community" (12–13). Elmira churchwomen vowed to eradicate such "pockets." The school adopted a daily program of providing hot meals, decent clothing, and large doses of religious instruction, as well as instructing children of both sexes in academics and the vocational skills. The school was racially integrated, although as Sorin points out, "the majority of children in attendance were not black" (13–14). While there was an obvious inequity in the racial make-up of the school, the attempt at integration is in itself noteworthy. At the time of the institution's founding, racial segregation in Elmira had long been established.

The school proved a successful undertaking, and by 1883 a new school was built to accommodate the growing student body. The industrial school can be viewed as an example of Progressive era reform. This was a period devoid of any form of state or federal aid; any assistance it received came from private sources. Reformers often accomplished more in terms of treating the symptoms of social injustice than in attempting to effect permanent cures. In an essay written for *The Industrial School Appeal of 1884,* Zebulon R. Brockway, superintendent of Elmira's State Reformatory, argued that "the Industrial School . . . is the best to be done now for gathering together the neglected children, giving them a taste of home life, if only for an hour a day, and teaching them to earn for themselves" ("Home, Work and Love," *Industrial School Appeal* 1.2 [CCHS, 1884]: 1).

12. Ruth Bordin claims that the WCTU was the first "mass organization of American Women and that it was their work in the temperance cause . . . that enabled women to move widely into public life by 1900" (*Women and Temperance,* xiii).

13. Bordin contests Hardesty's view of the immediate effect of Willard's election, arguing that one cannot view her election in 1879 as transforming a formerly passive "temperance praying society to an activist organization." Bordin attests that evidence of "political action and assertion of women's rights were present in this movement as early as the Crusade itself" (*Women and Temperance* 63).

14. Bordin defines these two opposing views: "the women's rights feminism, best exemplified by Elizabeth Cady Stanton, which was basically egalitarian and antagonistic to the idea of women's separate sphere; and the idea of a separate

women's culture, best exemplified by Catharine Beecher, which emphasized women's special mission in society." Bordin views Willard's greatest success as taking "cultural values . . . accepted as being women's special province — . . . the nurturant home — and transform[ing] them into a political arsenal to be used to advance women's rights and social and economic position" (Bordin, *Frances Willard* 103).

15. During the late 1870s and 1880s, the early days of the Elmira Reformatory, Thomas Beecher was a frequent visitor. Charles Langdon served as prison commissioner in 1892.

16. Mrs. Bullock was remembered in the December 1982 issue of the *Chemung Historical Journal* as an individual possessing a "strong moral character, [and who] became a leader in the temperance movement" (Elisabeth Carr Chapman, "Elmira's Anchorage" [Dec. 1982]: 3,225). Two years after Bullock's election, she was appointed to the post of superintendent of the state WCTU's newly formed department of "Narcotics." During her tenure as superintendent, Bullock authored a pamphlet entitled "The Tobacco Toboggan," and often lectured on the evils of alcohol and tobacco addiction. Frances Graham and Georgeanna Gardenier, authors of *1874–1894, Two Decades: A History of the First Twenty Years' Work of the Woman's Christian Temperance Union of the State of New York,* credits Bullock with securing passage of an 1889 law prohibiting tobacco use by children (48).

17. In the nine years following her appointment, Mrs. Wilkins reportedly had under her care "one thousand and seventy-two women and girls . . . one-third of these being under twenty years of age, also three hundred and fourteen boys under fourteen years of age" (Edholm).

18. In 1903 the board of managers of the Elmira industrial school announced that a "new branch of work [had] been added. . . . The kindergarten will be a potent factor in elevating the degraded classes here, as it has proven to be elsewhere" (*Industrial School and Free Kindergarten* [CCHS]).

19. The first serious attempt to build a national labor organization came during the early 1880s. The Knights of Labor was founded in 1869, and by 1881 had shed much of their early ritualistic secretiveness and invited women to join their membership. The years between 1881 and 1886 marked the Knights' most rapid period of growth, and during this time one hundred and thirteen assemblies consisting solely of women were chartered. It has been estimated that by 1886 the Knights of Labor had approximately 50,000 members; women members represented 8 to 9 percent of this total (Philip Foner, *History of the Labor Movement in the United States,* vol. 2 [New York: International Publishers, 1955], 61).

The WCTU made overtures to the Knights in May 1886. A delegation of WCTU members was sent to the Knights' national convention and evidently was warmly received, as Willard was eventually made an honorary member of the order (Bordin, *Frances Willard,* 137).

20. In *Mark Twain: Social Critic,* Philip S. Foner places Clemens's conversion to the women's suffrage cause as occurring sometime in the early 1870s. In his discussion of Clemens's involvement with suffrage, however, Foner omits mention of Olivia and instead credits Isabella Beecher Hooker with changing his mind (Clemens's views must have began to change around the time of his first meeting with Olivia.)

Clemens's post-1870 writings certainly appear to contradict Emmanuel Diel's contention in "Mark Twain's Failure: Sexual Women Characters" (*San Jose Studies* 5 [Feb. 1979]: 55) that "Twain's articles and speeches about such social topics as women's suffrage—he opposed it—reflect the prevailing male views of the day." Clemens's work also calls into question Joyce Warren's ambiguous remark that "Twain believed that it was 'just' that women should vote, and he advocated equality of the sexes. But he did not think that it was 'right'" (167).

21. Karen Blair views the female seminary as an outgrowth of church reform movements: "Just as efforts to embody ladydom through church work developed into reform movements, the drive to study ladydom in the schools generated a higher education for women" (17). Some famous early seminaries were Emma Willard's Troy Female Academy (established 1819) and Catharine Beecher's Hartford Female Academy (established 1821).

22. In a 1979 article about Olivia's education, Herbert Wisbey, Jr., mistakenly states that Olivia did not enter Elmira Female College until the second semester of 1859. In fact, Olivia entered in the fall of 1858.

23. Park was a member of the sophomore class of 1858–59. The handwritten *Register of the Elmira Female College, 1855–1859* lists the following information about her: "age 17, Warsaw Epis. Eng. Lit., Virgil, Chemistry, French."

6. "I am woman's rights": Olivia Langdon Clemens's Feminist Intimates

> We easily perceive that the peoples furtherest from civilization are the ones where equality between man and woman are furthest apart — and we consider this one of the signs of savagery. But we are so stupid that we can't see that we thus plainly admit that no civilization can be perfect until exact equality between man and woman is included.
>
> —*Mark Twain's Notebook* (1895)

Several fallacies regarding the upbringing, personality, and politics of Olivia Langdon Clemens can now be laid to rest. Olivia was not a "pampered darling" of a wealthy family whose education consisted of sporadic private instruction. Neither was she a hysterical hypochondriac who insisted on manipulating her parents and, eventually, controlling her husband and emotionally crippling her children. Upon her marriage, Olivia was hardly willing to give up her personality to become the archetype of the idealized, asexual, obedient Victorian wife. Olivia was very much an active participant in the events that shaped her society, and she was hardly a victim of Clemens's alleged misogyny.

At an early age, Olivia become close to such radical suffragists as Isabella Beecher Hooker and Anna Dickinson. Dickinson proved so influential in Olivia's development that at one point Olivia agonized whether she, too, should join the public ranks of the women's movement. In a letter to Mary Fairbanks, co-written by Olivia and Clemens shortly after their marriage, Olivia defiantly proclaimed: "I am woman's rights" (*Mark Twain to Mrs. Fairbanks* 127). Throughout her life Olivia was close to women who were dynamic, intelligent, and unapologetic as well as committed feminists — women who had rejected the purely domestic sphere in favor of participation in the world outside. In this chapter I will discuss the personalities and accomplishments of these women, and how they influenced Olivia and, ultimately, Samuel Clemens.

Julia Beecher: The Teacher as Role Model

In 1857, three years after accepting the Elmira ministry and suffering the death of his first wife, Olivia Beecher, Thomas Beecher married Julia Jones (1826–1905). Julia Jones Beecher was a renowned beauty and amateur sculptor, and was considered brilliant as well as outspoken. One of her grandfathers was Noah Webster, and she was formerly known in Connecticut as "the Belle of Bridgeport" (Taylor and Myers 15).

Apparently this was a match of some convenience; Julia Jones had been Beecher's first wife's best friend, and she had long been an admirer of his. After their wedding she was disappointed to realize that no one could replace Olivia Beecher in her husband's affections. Still, despite their personal difficulties, the pair were united in mutual caring for Beecher's parishioners. Before their marriage, Thomas had been living at Gleason's Water Cure, and afterward he saw no reason to change residences. Julia gamely followed suit, although she expressed her longing for a home in a letter to Mrs. Lyman Beecher: "She [Annie Beecher, her sister-in-law,] too would be of our household if we had one, as I more & more wish we had" (Jan. 21, 1860, SDF). The Beechers remained as boarders at the Cure for three years before building their own home across the street from the Cure late in 1860. In late November 1861, a gleeful Julia described to her sister-in-law, Isabella Beecher Hooker, the simple pleasures of living in her own home. Although their residence was, at that juncture, far from finished (only the pantry had been completed, and Thomas and Julia were sleeping in the "girls" room over the kitchen), Julia reports that "Tom is better & happier & more hopeful than when we were at the Cure" (Nov. 19, SDF).

Julia Beecher was a dynamic woman, an individual who always retained her sense of independence from the dictates of fashion and polite society. Thomas Beecher, describing what married life with such a dynamo was like, remarked, "Life with her was like being harnessed to a steam-engine" (Langdon, *Some Childhood Memories* 7). In her memoir of Julia Beecher, *A Flower of Puritanism,* the Reverend Annis Ford Eastman recounts that in 1857, to free herself from the hours she spent dressing, Julia bobbed her waist-length hair (pre-dating the short haircuts of the twenties by sixty years), and took to wearing men's Congress boots (heavy work boots) (40). As far as the Reverend Eastman was concerned, cutting her hair was "one of [Julia's] mistakes. . . . The saving of time became almost a passion with her toward the last, and one sometimes felt that more precious

5. Photograph of Julia Beecher, 1889. (Courtesy of the Chemung County Historical Society)

things were sacrificed in the effort" (40). Not everyone shared the Reverend Eastman's opinion; Ida Langdon, daughter of Olivia's brother Charles, reminisced that Julia's was the first bobbed hair she had ever seen and she found it "very pretty" (*Some Childhood Memories* 8). Determined to remain her own person despite any outside pressure to conform, Julia also decided that she would dress in terms of comfort, not fashion, and thus happily proceeded to free herself from the confines of the corset.

As well as being an intimate family friend of the Langdons, Julia was also Olivia's Sunday school teacher and proved an integral role model in her development. The Reverend Eastman, who succeeded Thomas Beecher at Park Church, recounted Julia Beecher's involvement with the Sunday school:

> Of the many directions in which her [Julia's] genius for improvement found exercise, perhaps the most pre-eminent was the Sunday School which grew under her hand from the small unorganized institution which she found it, until it became one of the most thoroughly organized and splendidly drilled bodies in the country, a forerunner of the modern, graded Sunday School. (52)

In the Park Church archives there survives a handwritten document listing the twenty-three verses chosen by Thomas and Julia Beecher for the Park Church Sunday School liturgy for use during the years 1873 to 1902 (*Park Church Sunday School Liturgy*). Ida Langdon, Olivia's niece, attended Park Church Sunday School during the mid-1880s, and remembered the school as the "joint creation of Mr. and Mrs. Beecher." She recalled that the school offered a six-year course of study and was organized extremely well (*Some Childhood Memories* 10). Each child was provided with a study schedule containing passages that comprised the liturgy. Every student was expected to memorize the liturgy and recite it before class, and each was graded on a scale ranging from "perfect" to "satisfactory" to "imperfect." At the end of six years, students could choose between a Bible dictionary or a concordance to the Bible. During the 1880s over seven hundred children were enrolled in the Beecher's Sunday school (*Mark Twain's Elmira* 18).

Thomas Beecher considered his wife a full partner in their ministry. He once remarked that "nine-tenths of the achievement of our long life in Elmira" was due to Julia's efforts (Taylor and Myers 15). Much of Julia's energy was devoted to raising money for charity: she created what came to be known as the "Beecher doll" and fashioned birds and animals out of roots that Clemens called "Jabberwocks." On one occasion, Julia was successful in having Clemens auction off some of her creations. Clemens and Julia enjoyed a close friendship, and, as with Susan Crane, Clemens frequently debated with her over the validity of religious belief. Indeed, the two made a bet that if they met in heaven a million years in the future Clemens would admit that he was wrong (Jerome and Wisbey 17).

Another cause to which Julia was devoted was the Women's Christian Temperance Union (WCTU); she was a long-time member and proud WCTU "white-ribbon" wearer. It is significant that a woman so beloved by the Langdons and who had such great influence on Olivia belonged to this overtly politicized movement. Ida Langdon recalled that when she was approximately ten years old, Mrs. Beecher organized a parlor game in which each child had to choose to be a particular kind of food. Rebellious Ida chose "red claret wine." When Ida whispered her choice to Julia, Julia rose and "swift as lightning gave me the choice of signing up for something else, or leaving the game. It was indicated that something more on the order of a baked potato would do. . . . But I couldn't be a baked potato . . . and I stepped out of the circle" (*Some Childhood Memories* 15). After concluding her days as Julia Beecher's Sunday school student, Olivia continued her relationships with strong female personalities.[1]

Isabella Beecher Hooker: "All her splendid energies"

Isabella Beecher Hooker (1822–1907) was a family friend of the Langdons since Olivia's girlhood as well as Mrs. Langdon's confidante. Her daughter, Alice Hooker Day, was Olivia's intimate friend. The earliest recorded contact between Olivia and Isabella Hooker occurred when Isabella came to Elmira to rest at Gleason's Water Cure. In 1860, a few months before she came to Elmira, Isabella had written her first pro-suffrage document, "Shall Women Vote? A Matrimonial Dialogue," which addressed the issue of equal rights and justice for men and women and its political expediency. Isabella Hooker was disheartened by the opinion expressed by her mentor, *Atlantic* editor Thomas Wentworth Higginson, that the piece was probably too radical to see print; despite his support (or possibly owing to the lack of it), the piece was never published during her lifetime.[2]

After this rejection, Isabella established herself at Gleason's Water Cure and remained there from April through August. Olivia Langdon was her roommate during the month of July. Isabella needed a new roommate because she was making her former one ill. Isabella wrote her husband that she was being moved to another room because:

> I am too strong & wide awake & stimulating for her — Mrs. Gleason has always said, that she needed to be utterly brought down as to nervous power — so as to be stupid — sleepy — uninterested in any person or thing — & she seems to be approaching that state now (which is a favorable thing) & so we must do everything to help on — that can be thought of. Againe [sic] — I cannot be in the room with her, when her week of suffering comes on — especially now that I am so much confined to *our* room. . . . I am going in about a week — to take a large airy room, on the *second* floor — with some new room-

6. Photograph of Isabella Beecher Hooker (1850s). (Courtesy of the
Stowe-Day Foundation, Hartford, Conn.)

mate the best I can find. This room will be nine dolls. per week. My present
one in *third* story being 7.50 — but I do not hesitate. . . . That room — is directly
opposite the parlor . . . it is the largest in the house. (May 29, 1860, SDF)

Evidently fourteen-year-old Olivia and her parents did not consider Isabella
quite so life-threatening.

While the two boarded together, the youthful Olivia became well-
versed in Isabella's views regarding women's rights. Isabella went on to
become a pivotal figure in the women's rights movement, publishing po-

lemical tracts and a book entitled *Womanhood: Its Sanctities and Fidelities* (1873). Isabella also sponsored and organized Hartford's first women's suffrage convention in 1869, and encouraged her husband to write a bill, eventually passed by the Connecticut State Legislature, that granted tax-paying women their voting rights (Margolis 39–40).[3]

The link between Clemens and Isabella Hooker is a curious one, with both literary and business implications. After disembarking from the *Quaker City* in 1867, Clemens found a letter waiting for him from Elisha Bliss. Bliss, secretary and managing director of the American Publishing Company of Hartford, was interested in the letters Clemens had been sending to the *Alta California*. He invited Clemens to compile them into a book manuscript and submit it for publication. Clemens expressed his interest in this venture. Six weeks later, on New Year's Eve, Clemens met Olivia Langdon. Clemens visited her the next day at Mrs. Anna E. Berry's salon, where Olivia, Alice Hooker, and quite likely Isabella Beecher Hooker and Mr. and Mrs. Langdon were in attendance. Clemens wrote to his mother and sister on January 8, 1868, reporting that during his visit he had "sent the old folks home early" (*Mark Twain's Letters, 1867–1868*, vol. 2: 144). Earlier that week, on Sunday, January 5, Clemens had dined with Henry Ward Beecher, Harriet Beecher Stowe, Catharine Beecher, Eunice Beecher (Henry Ward Beecher's wife), Emeline Beach, and Isabella Beecher Hooker. Clemens noted that not only was he planning to "spend a few days with the Langdons in Elmira," but he was going to stay a "few days at Mrs. Hooker's in Hartford . . . shortly" (*Mark Twain's Letters, 1867–1868*, vol. 2: 144). Clemens saw Olivia again, with her parents and Alice Hooker, on January 18, 1868, in New York City, where he was invited to dinner (Alice Hooker to Isabella Beecher Hooker, Jan. 19, 1868, SDF).

Clemens's first visit to Hartford, where he stayed with the Hooker family, came less than a week later, on January 24, 1868. During this same period, Clemens also had his first meeting with Bliss. Clemens wrote Mary Fairbanks on the same day that "I am the guest of Mr. Hooker's . . . family here for a few days, & I tell you I have to walk mighty straight. I desire to have the respect of this sterling old Puritan community." Clemens also told Fairbanks that he had "promised to be Mrs. Hooker's special Washington correspondent" upon his return to Washington (*Mark Twain's Letters, 1867–1868*, vol. 2: 166). (Clemens was then living in Washington, D.C.) Isabella wanted to be kept informed about Elizabeth Cady Stanton's and Susan B. Anthony's efforts to lobby for a federal suffrage amendment; Clemens's favor was particularly important to Isabella as the suffrage movement at the time was in a state of turmoil. After much infighting on both sides, Isabella had decided to join the newly formed New York faction, the National Woman Suffrage Association (NWSA), which had broken away from the Boston-based main organization, the American Women Suffrage Association (AWSA).[4] Perhaps laying the groundwork for the siblings' later feud, Isabella's brother, Henry Ward Beecher, agreed to act as president of the Boston group in late 1869, with Isabella deciding to take on the role of director of the 1869 NWSA Convention held in Washington (Boydston et al. 187, 295).[5]

Clemens was still under contract to the *Alta California,* and on March 3, 1868, the newspaper published this report about his time spent with the Hookers: "At the hospitable mansion where I am a guest, I have to smoke surreptitiously when all are in bed, to save my reputation, and then draw suspicion upon the cat when the family detect the unfamiliar odor. . . . So far, I am safe; but I am sorry to say that the cat has lost caste" (*Mark Twain's Letters, 1867–1868,* vol. 2: 164).

Evidently, so did Clemens. Despite his best efforts, something occurred during his stay which, as he told Olivia over a year later, humiliated him. In a letter dated March 6, 1869, Clemens gave Olivia his opinion regarding the Hookers:

> I am afraid I never shall feel right in that house, though. I let my trust & confidence go out to them as I seldom do with new acquaintances, & they responded by misunderstanding me. If I had given them *all* of my trust & confidence, they never *could* have humiliated me by any ordinary slight, because then, not expecting such things, I would have been stupidly blind to them. . . . I like them pretty well, but I believe it is more because you like them than for any other reason. And for the same reason I shall choke down my gorge & do the *very best* I can to like them well — always provided, that they will give me a chance — can't *seek* it, though, Livy darling. (*Mark Twain's Letters, 1869,* vol. 3: 140–41)

Clemens went on to compare his connection with the Hookers to his friendship with Mary Fairbanks:

> [It just occurs to me that maybe Mrs. Fairbanks has slighted me fifty times, but I never thought of it before — I suppose she would have to knock me down to make me understand it — & even then I guess I wouldn't give her up till she told me *why*] — But it is different with the Hookers. . . .
> You see I don't care much about *acquaintances.* When I can come & go, & not be misunderstood, & can be at liberty & unweighed, uncriticized, unsuspected, as part of the very household, as at your house & Mrs. Fairbanks's

my "friendship" (as we term it) really comes nearer being *worship* than anything else I can liken it to—but to be a ceremonious visitor; a person of set hours & seasons; a foreigner in the household, without naturalization papers; an alien from whose ears the language of the fireside is withheld; an effigy to poke *p o l i t e n e s s e s* at & offend with affabilities that are hollow, invitations that are not meant, & complementary lies that are as thin & perishable as the air they are made of—*this* is Acquaintanceship, & a very little of it goes a great way with *me*. (*Mark Twain's Letters, 1869*, vol. 3: 141)

Whatever the incident, perhaps it contributed to Olivia's later tendency to watch over Clemens in case he made a remark that might offend one of their guests.

The person with whom Clemens undoubtedly came into conflict was the tempestuous Isabella. Isabella possessed a forceful personality. As well as being a committed suffragist, she was also known as a spiritualist. Isabella would freely voice her opinions regarding both subjects, overriding or ignoring other people's objections. It was Isabella's belief that a global matriarchal government would eventually replace the current patriarchal system, and that the new government would merge with Christ's kingdom in an epochal, millennial period (Taylor, *Gender* 39).

The two intense personalities of Isabella Hooker and Clemens obviously made for an explosive duo; yet in Katy Leary's memoirs, she remembered Clemens as being a respectful audience: "Mr. Clemens admired her [Isabella] very much, I guess, 'cause he always listened to everything she said—quiet as a lamb" (Lawton 210). Perhaps in his dealings with Isabella, Clemens learned that a defensive silence was a better social strategy than an active offense.

Despite the difficulties in Clemens and Isabella's relationship, the Clemenses always remained supportive of Isabella's activities. Isabella regarded Clemens as an advocate of women's rights, and her confidence in him was great enough to provoke an 1883 letter asking for his assistance in financing a suffragist conference:

I enclose notice of our Convention next week. I am sorry you are all probably going to the seaside [Olivia was ill]. I hoped you would say a few words on some subject of the woman question. . . . But at least I will ask you to help me pay expenses of other speakers from New York & Boston & the hall—all which I have assumed in order to make the sessions free. (May 3, 1883, MTP*)

A year later, Clemens wrote a letter to Isabella which appears to pledge his and Olivia's support for her feminist cause:

> Mrs. Clemens & I have conferred together, & decided that if you can get the necessary subscriptions you may hold us responsible for fifty-dollars a year toward your proposed salary. We should be very glad to make it more, but are forced to go according to our ability, not our inclinations. . . . P.S. I write in Livy's place because I am idle for the moment & she is very busy. (May 27, 1884, SDF, MTP*)

A business panic in 1884 had significantly depressed the nation's businesses and banks, and this may have been the reason Clemens could not send more aid.

If Clemens and Olivia were, indeed, contributing money so that Isabella could continue to fight for women's rights, any acrimony generated by the Tilton-Beecher sex scandal had evidently been forgotten.[6] The Tilton-Beecher scandal began when the famous and well-respected Reverend Henry Ward Beecher was publicly accused by feminist Victoria Woodhull of having an affair with Mrs. Elizabeth Tilton, one of his parishioners. The imbroglio was front-page news and continued to be so for three years, until the case was brought to trial. Theodore Tilton, Elizabeth Tilton's husband, sued Beecher for alienation of his wife's affection. However, Beecher was let off by a hung jury in 1875. Isabella Hooker sided with her feminist colleagues in denouncing her brother's alleged affair. Because of this, relations between Clemens and Isabella Hooker were at one point so poor that Mollie Clemens, the wife of Clemens's brother Orion, wrote to Jane Clemens that "Sam says Livy shall not cross Mrs Hookers threshold and if he talks to Mrs H he will tell her in plain words the reason" (Nov. 26, 1872, MTP*). (What makes this ultimatum by Clemens superbly ironic is that at the time of Mollie's letter he was leasing Isabella's house at Nook Farm.)[7]

Clemens's opposition to Isabella's position regarding the Tilton-Beecher scandal should be viewed with the understanding that, at the time, Clemens was new to Nook Farm and was acting in accord with the rest of the community, including Isabella's immediate family.[8] The acrimony eventually became so strong within the Beecher family that Mary Beecher Perkins, Isabella's half-sister, told John Hooker that none of them would have Isabella in their homes and that the community of Nook Farm would not forgive her unless she stopped "all intercourse with Mrs. Stanton and Miss Anthony and all that set" (Boydston et al. 298). During this period, it was Isabella against friends, family, and the press, and although her husband was supportive, even he at times expressed frustration at Isabella's refusal to reconsider Henry Ward's possible innocence. Clemens's injunction to Olivia may have sounded unforgiving after Isabella had returned from a year's absence in Europe to escape the strain caused by the scandal, but Olivia was among the women who officially welcomed her back to Hartford at a luncheon held in her honor in December 1876.

After Isabella died (on January 26, 1907), Clemens paid her this tribute in the *Autobiography:*

> The Beecher talent is all gone now; the last concentration of it went out of the world with Isabella Beecher Hooker. . . . Isabella Beecher Hooker threw herself into the women's rights movement among the earliest, some sixty years ago, and she labored with all her splendid energies in that great cause all the rest of her life; as an able and efficient worker she ranks immediately after those great chiefs, Susan B. Anthony, Elizabeth Cady Stanton, and Mrs. Livermore. . . . These brave women besieged the legislatures of the land . . . [and] achieved a revolution. . . . They broke the chains of their sex and set it free. (March 1, 1907, Autobiographical Dictation, No. 68, MTP*)

Anna Elizabeth Dickinson: The Lecture Circuit's Joan of Arc

One person responsible for Isabella's (and, ultimately, the Clemenses') development of and commitment to a pro-suffrage stance was Anna Elizabeth Dickinson (1842–1932). When the twenty-one-year-old Dickinson lectured in Hartford on March 24, 1863, at an enormous Republican election-eve rally (making her the first women to give a public address in Hartford), Isabella and her husband John were in attendance. Deeply impressed by the speech, they left with Dickinson in tow, having invited her to stay at their home for the night (Chester 51–52).[9] Dickinson introduced Isabella to Harriet Taylor Mill's essay "Enfranchisement of Women" (1851); this work, which argued that women should have equal status with men as well as the right to attain gainful employment, would be considered far more radical in content than John Stuart Mill's 1869 treatise, "The Subjection of Women" (Margolis 20).[10]

Anna Dickinson was born in Philadelphia on October 28, 1842. She was reared a Quaker and, consistent with her family's beliefs, was a staunch abolitionist. (The Dickinsons, like the Langdons, were active in the Underground Railroad.) Dickinson was an active campaigner against slavery and for women's rights, although she never became a member of any of the various factions. She began her career as a lecturer in 1860. Her first public speech was on January 29, 1860, and her first paid address came on February 27, 1861, in Philadelphia, where her talk was entitled "The Rights and Wrongs of Women" (Chester 23).[11]

7. Anna Elizabeth Dickinson, "the juvenile Joan of Arc." (Courtesy of the Library of Congress)

Dickinson was a shrewd, tough, and fearless orator, and she quickly learned how to hold her audience's attention. During the early 1860s, she lectured in Kansas, where the legislator later passed a referendum supporting women's rights. In the spring of 1863, Dickinson began giving political speeches. These speeches proved so popular that she earned the same amount of money for each lecture as Henry Ward Beecher, the top draw on the lecture circuit, did (Chester 73). Dickinson became well known enough that she was invited to speak before the Congress, and on January 16, 1864, she lectured on the war before the House of Representatives and President Abraham Lincoln. The Washington address made Dickinson nationally famous. She traveled extensively throughout the West and spoke again on suffragist matters. She was well received in Cheyenne, Wyoming, in 1869 (Myres 219–220). In her memoir, *A Ragged Register,* Dickinson writes about her extensive travels and includes a remark uttered by her friend Thomas Beecher after she had made a frantic trip in terrible weather in order to speak before a packed New York City audience. Beecher commented that no man would have been so foolish as to keep the engagement; Dickinson retorted that Beecher "should remember that the world . . . demands of a woman that she do twice as much as a man to prove that she can equal him" (18).

What distinguished Dickinson from other popular speakers of the day (and what helped earn her generous fees) was that, compared to other female lecturers, she adopted a radically different approach to abolition. Departing from more typical rhetorical avenues, such as speaking from a mother's perspective or that of a moral reformer, Dickinson argued against slavery from a political point of view. Dickinson did not try to play on emotions; instead she employed reason. Dickinson represented the second wave of suffrage activity, inheriting a political consciousness initiated by Susan B. Anthony's generation ten years earlier.[12] Thomas Wentworth Higginson recalled that Dickinson possessed "a remarkably clear head for political questions" and that her personality was so forceful she could travel to mining regions in Pennsylvania where "almost any man of like opinions would have been mobbed into silence." Higginson concluded that Dickinson "was probably the most effective orator sent out by the Republican Committees during that election, and certainly earned the right to pass from that theme [abolitionism] to her present one, the enfranchisement of her sex" (54).

Olivia came into contact with Dickinson long before Elmirans had ever heard of Mark Twain. It is unknown exactly when the two women met, but it is likely that Isabella Hooker was the intermediary. Olivia and Dickinson were contemporaries, though Anna was three years older. It is clear from Olivia's letters that she liked and admired Dickinson. The earliest evidence of a connection between the two is found in a letter Thomas Beecher wrote to Dickinson on February 9, 1864, inviting her to Elmira for a "Sanitary Fair" to help raise funds for the Union Army (Anna Dickinson Papers, Library of Congress). Just two months later, in April 1864, Dickinson had a private interview with President Lincoln to discuss his politics, and to determine whether she would lend him her support in the upcoming election. After twice reversing herself, and drawing much negative criticism, Dickinson decided affirmatively (Chester 80).

Dickinson traveled to Elmira to lecture on December 8, 1864, where she was a guest of the Langdons for at least two nights. The subject of her talk was equal rights for women, and she delivered her lecture before the Young Men's Christian Association. The local Elmira paper questioned the propriety of such a subject before an audience comprised primarily of young men: "We know that Miss Dickinson was actuated in all she said by the highest and purest motives, and possibly men and women ought to learn to discuss such questions in drawing room conversation . . . and perhaps not. We think not" ("Anna Dickinson," *Elmira Advertiser,* December 9, 1864). This comment provoked a rebuttal, printed in the paper three days later: "Thank God! there are some noble women who are not troubled with this false modesty. . . . You must admit that there is a great and crying need of discussion somewhere" ("C," *Elmira Advertiser,* December 12, 1864).

In September 1866, between stops on the lecture circuit, Dickinson joined Theodore Tilton, editor of the *Independent,* and Frederick Douglass on the platform at the National Loyalists' Convention held in Philadelphia. During the convention the three co-wrote a proposition that would "prohibit disfranchisement of any person on account of race, sex, color, or previous condition of servitude" (Chester 94). This proposal was eventually adopted (in modified form — the word "sex" was omitted) by the Republican Party, and the Fifteenth Amendment was thereafter added to the Constitution. Susan B. Anthony and Elizabeth Cady Stanton both credited Dickinson with being the originator of the document. Frederick Douglass wrote to Stanton praising his two friends: "To . . . Anna E. Dickinson and . . . Theodore Tilton belongs the credit of forcing that amendment upon the attention of the nation at the right moment and in the right way to make it successful" (Chester 94).[13]

The Langdons warmly received Anna Dickinson in March 1867, when she again lectured in Elmira. This time her talk was entitled "Something To Do, or Work for Women." Reflecting how local attitudes had changed, the *Elmira Advertiser* this time printed Dickinson's lecture in its entirety. Below is a brief excerpt:

> I stand to-night the mouth-piece of many women who toil all day long for a loaf of bread and a bed of straw. . . . Women who do the same work as that man beside them, and receive but a portion of his pay. . . . Women who desire to know many things, and are told that ignorance is their lot. . . . There may be a great many women not married to-day who will be married some time in the future, and to some of those present I shall in advance tender my most hearty and sincere commiseration. . . . There are women who will not be married at all, and to some of these I will tender my congratulations. ("Lecture Last Night," *Elmira Advertiser,* March 30, 1867: 1)

Two days after Anna's lecture, on March 31, Olivia's mother recorded in her diary, "Mrs Julia Beecher came after ch. [church] + staid [sic] till evening to see Anna. My heart was solaced by an earnest + intimate talk with Anna—" (MTM). A year after her fourth visit to Elmira to lecture, in 1873, Anna had this to say about the Langdon family: they were "full of simplicity, large heartedness [sic], generosity" (Young 40–41).

It appears that in 1867 Dickinson was using Elmira as her base for a series of lectures in the area. Dickinson's sister Susan wrote three letters to her in Elmira during March (March 22, 27, 30, 1867, Library of Congress). On March 27, Susan wrote Dickinson thanking her for two letters, a telegram from Syracuse, and one additional letter from Oswego. In the same letter Susan expresses her relief that Dickinson was apparently recuperating from an unspecified illness. Olivia's mother recorded Dickinson's departure the morning of April 1; her visit had lasted four days. On April 4, 1867, Mrs. Langdon wrote to Isabella Hooker that she had "enjoyed greatly Anna Dickinson's cheerful visit here. She was never more agreeable or charming" (SDF). One final letter from Susan to Dickinson mentions a person of particular importance whom Anna met in Rochester while lecturing there: "As I wrote to Jamestown thine from Elmira enclosing a check . . . came safely to hand. . . . I had a letter this morning from Susan Anthony telling me about her going into Rochester to meet thee, and having such a nice time" (Apr. 6, 1867, Library of Congress).

Judging from all this activity and this letter it appears as though Olivia was certainly in touch with the progress of the women's movement—and its very leaders. A few months later, Dickinson's name reappears in a letter Olivia wrote to Alice Hooker. In the letter, Olivia wishes that Dickinson could visit the family again that summer and asks Hooker to extend an invitation to her (July 29, 1867, SDF). In September, Hooker wrote to her mother describing Olivia's stay in Hartford and mentions that they had a surprise visit from Dickinson. Alice reported that everyone was "glad to see her, Livy because she knew her already and the others because they *didn't*. She looked as gorgeous and beautiful as ever — and seemed to enjoy her stay here very well" (Sep. 28, 1867, SDF).

Clemens's introduction to Anna Dickinson came on February 23, 1867 — ten months before he met Olivia. Clemens was in the audience when Dickinson lectured in New York City, giving the same speech ("Something To Do") she would deliver less than a month later in Elmira. Clemens commented:

> The aim of her speech was to call the attention of the people to the meagre number of avenues to an honest livelihood that are permitted to women, and the drudging, unintellectual character of those employments, and to demand, as simple justice to her sex, that those avenues be multiplied till women may earn their bread elsewhere than in kitchens and factories without unsexing themselves. She did her work well. She made a speech worth listening to. (*Mark Twain's Travels with Mr. Brown* 105–6)

Guy Cardwell comments on Clemens's reaction to Dickinson's speech and asserts that while Clemens very likely "thought that she commanded respect," what "may have been responsible for this favorable opinion" was Clemens's "personal liking for Miss Dickinson" (*Man Who Was Mark Twain* 109). But Cardwell seems to be selling Dickinson's oratorical gifts short; in fact Dickinson and Clemens shared a mutual dislike for each other that intensified with the passing years. In the letter excerpted below, Clemens coyly explains to Olivia how he managed to ride on the same train with Dickinson, yet not exchange a word.

> At Utica, this morning, I saw Miss Anna Dickinson pass along & enter the drawing-room car, & I *wanted* to follow & talk with her a while, but I was unshaven & very shabby in dress in consequence of early rising, & so I just sat still & we traveled many miles together & yet *not* together. Scold me, Livy, dear. I suppose I deserve it. And yet see the sacrifice I made — & all for *you:* I *wouldn't* go there & tell her that such a looking object as I was, was regarded with respect & esteem by *you* & your family. Shucks, I am *always* making sacrifices. (*Mark Twain's Letters, 1869,* vol. 3: 334)

When Clemens approved of Dickinson's speech, then, it was scarcely due to any discernible "personal liking." Obviously Clemens was relieved that he would not share the miles in conversation with Anna, and what is also made clear here is Clemens's awareness regarding his personal appearance. Three years later, Dickinson's sister Susan wrote to Dickinson affirming Dickinson's disapproval of Clemens's "personal appearance, tone, or manner" (Young 41). Clemens was always appreciative of quality in an oral performance — the exercise of a voice was what drove him to perfect his own platform style; it is thus likely that Dickinson's oral performance, rather than her personality, earned Clemens's approval.

In 1870 Dickinson introduced what quickly became her most famous lecture, a speech in praise of Joan of Arc; indeed, she became popularly known as the "juvenile Joan of Arc" (James 475–76). During 1871 and 1872, Clemens and Dickinson were on James Redpath's lyceum circuit together, and one cannot help but wonder to what degree Clemens might have been influenced by Dickinson's topic, and if the impetus for his eventual historical novel on Joan of Arc was in part fueled by the audience's warm reception to Dickinson's subject.

Clemens claimed that his interest in Joan of Arc was first kindled when he was a boy of thirteen working for his brother as a printer's apprentice. While Clemens was walking down a Hannibal street, an errant gust of wind blew a page from a history book into his path. The page contained a portion of Joan of Arc's biography. After reading the page, Clemens went to his younger brother Henry and discovered that Joan of Arc had actually existed. The verity of Clemens's account concerning his discovery of Joan of Arc has been the subject of some debate by Twain scholars, and the tale of the errant page does strain credulity.[14] Clemens may have located the genesis of his interest in Joan of Arc in his childhood in order to excuse his own belatedness in writing about her, for Joan of Arc was a favorite topic among writers during the 1870s. This disassociation would also free Clemens from having to recognize that Dickinson, a woman he probably did not particularly care for, might have influenced him to write on Joan of Arc. (Dickinson actually managed to beat Clemens to the inkwell and started to write her own novel about Joan of Arc, but she never completed it.)

One Twain character who may have been modeled after Dickinson herself was Laura Hawkins in *The Gilded Age*. Clemens might have been venting a bit of professional jealousy over Dickinson's enormous success and popularity when he depicts a desperate Laura trying her hand at lecturing. The audience's reaction to her oratory is to boo her off the stage, from whence, heartbroken, Laura makes her way to her hotel room to die.

While lecturing with Clemens, Dickinson was at the height of her fame, earning vast sums from her personal appearances. Clemens, in dictations for his autobiography, remembered Dickinson as a "compelling attraction," and that her "price was four hundred dollars a night" (Oct. 12, 1907, No. 69, MTP*). Clemens was exaggerating somewhat in citing Dickinson's lecture fees. A review of her 1870, 1871, and 1872 "Route Books" reveals that Dickinson usually received between one hundred fifty and one hundred seventy-five dollars a night. She made her large (on average, twenty-thousand-dollar) yearly salary by touring constantly. Her tour books show that she lectured practically every day, resting only on holidays. She did, however, earn four hundred dollars when she lectured in Philadelphia, and she was paid three hundred dollars in Chicago. Dickinson lectured in Hartford on November 18, 1870, and December 20, 1871 (she was paid two hundred dollars), and in Elmira on April 17, 1871, and March 1, 1872 (when she earned one hundred and seventy-five dollars) (Dickinson, "Route Books" nos. 22–23 [22]). In 1872 alone Dickinson grossed the fabulous sum of twenty-three thousand and ninety dollars—at the time an immense amount of money for a man or woman.

Due to her decidedly iconoclastic behavior, Dickinson was an object of fascination for the public. She fought against nineteenth-century social dictates inhibiting the ambitions and actions of women, and she lived her life in flagrant violation of these dictates: she sported bobbed hair, she never married (although her name was periodically linked with that of Whitelaw Reid, whom Clemens detested for a time), she supported herself and her family members, she traveled wherever she liked, and she dressed as unconventionally as she chose. She regularly horrified proper Boston by riding through the city park astride her horse "Topsy" (Chester 86).

The Langdons clearly were well acquainted with Dickinson's polemics, and as a result of both Dickinson's and Isabella Hooker's influence Olivia eventually became concerned about what her role should be within the women's movement. In a revealing letter written on January 22, 1869, Clemens responded to Olivia's worries regarding what action she should take to support the suffragists. In the letter he recognizes that the success of the women's movement is an important matter to his fiancée, and he reiterates that he is a defender of Anna Dickinson. At the same time, he tries to persuade Olivia that, although she is not an active participant like

Dickinson (her health might enter into the equation here), the life and the role she has chosen is just as vital.

> *Don't* grieve, Livy, that you cannot march up & down the troubled ways of life *fighting* wrong & unfettering right, with strong fierce words & dazzling actions, for *that* work is set apart for women of a different formation to do, & being designed for that work, God, who always knows His affairs & how to appoint His instruments, has *qualified* them for the work — & He has qualified you for *your* work, & nobly are you performing it. Therefore, be content. Do that which God has given you to do, & do not seek to improve upon His judgement. You cannot do Anna Dickinson's work, & I can freely stake my life upon it, she cannot do yours. Livy you might as well reproach yourself for not being able to win bloody victories in battle, like Joan of Arc. In your sphere you are as great, & as noble, & as efficient as any Joan of Arc that ever lived. Be content with the strength that God has given you, & the station He has given into your charge — & don't be discouraged & unsettled by Anna Dickinson's incendiary words. I like Anna Dickinson, & admire her grand character, & have often & over again made her detractors feel ashamed of themselves; but I am thankful that you are not the sort of woman that is her ideal, & grateful that you never *can* be, Livy, darling. (*Mark Twain's Letters, 1869,* vol. 3: 63)

It might be tempting to construe this letter as that of a chauvinist. This would be done so in error. Clemens's reply to Olivia is practically identical to the advice Dickinson dispensed to young women coming to her with much the same question: What could they do to aid the cause? In *A Ragged Register,* Dickinson relates a short vignette about a young bride-to-be who, after reading tracts concerning women's rights and hearing feminist speakers, came to Dickinson for advice on the nature of her own role in this struggle. Dickinson responded that she could help "all women — and all men — who come near you, and help the cause . . . by showing what a woman can *be* in the world. If you want a 'mission,' I find there are plenty of house-keepers, but very few *home-makers. There* is something to do and an example to set" (129).

Although Olivia never spoke from the platform, she did participate and support the suffrage movement by providing a place for lecturers such as Dickinson to stay, and, at times, as with Isabella Beecher Hooker, by providing financial assistance. Olivia often referred to women's rights in her correspondence. Six weeks after their marriage, in a whimsical letter to Mary Fairbanks, Clemens played the misogynist, with Olivia acting the part of the staunch suffragist: "SILENCE WOMAN — That is to Livy — not you, Mother dear — she is carrying on here, at a dreadful rate. . . . Already, though, I have got her trained so that she tones down & [almost] stops

talking at the word of command. (I deny it, I am woman's rights. Livy)"
(*Mark Twain to Mrs. Fairbanks* 127).

Dickinson visited the Clemenses periodically when they were living in
Hartford, and these visits must have been tinged with tension since by this
time Dickinson and Clemens shared a healthy dislike for each other. Toward
Clemens's character, Dickinson was, like Lilian Aldrich, decidedly disap-
proving. She viewed the match between Olivia and Clemens with marked
animosity. After visiting the Langdon's in Elmira in 1873, Dickinson remarked to her mother:

> Each time I see them [Mrs. and Mrs. Langdon], I have a fresh wonder how
> the flower of their house, Olivia, as frail in body as she is clear of mind & lovely
> of soul ever married the vulgar boor to whom she gave herself. — I hear him all
> about the country at wine suppers, & late orgies, — dirty, smoking, drinking —
> with brains no doubt, but —. (Young 41)

Anna also mocked Clemens's features, poking fun at what she called his
"bird-of-prey-beak" (Young 41). Hattie Lewis Paff observed during one
visit to the Clemenses: "Anna Dickinson came before she had the insane
idea that she was a tragedian. She and Mr. C. did not get along well
together. They seemed to be always trying to test each others [sic] right to
being famous" (7). Dickinson stayed with the Clemenses while she was still
lecturing on women's rights (she later tried playwriting and acting, both
unsuccessfully), and Olivia must have watched Dickinson openly challenge
Clemens. Clemens was, indeed, critical of Dickinson, but he also respected
her tenacity and intelligence from their days together on the lecture circuit.

Grace King: A Southern Woman of Letters

Isabella Hooker, a feminist convert of Anna's, made a suffragist of her own
out of another contemporary of Olivia's, the Southern writer Grace King
(1852–1932). King, an avowed supporter of the Confederacy, made her
first trip to New England as a guest of Charles Dudley Warner of Hartford
in June 1887. There, at Nook Farm, she first met Isabella Hooker and
Olivia. Of Hooker, King had this to say in her autobiography: "Isabella
Hooker [was] . . . a tall, handsome woman, who talked to me about
'Woman's Rights' and converted me to her point of view" (*Memories of a
Southern Woman of Letters* 77). During her stay in Hartford, King managed
a second interview with Hooker, to the consternation of the Warners,

"where they discussed at length women's rights, spiritualism, and family troubles" (Taylor, *Gender* 39). While King found Hooker's views on free love and spiritualism unpalatable, she was convinced by her feminist arguments. Helen Taylor makes the claim in *Gender, Race, and Region in the Writings of Grace King, Ruth McEnery Stuart, and Kate Chopin* that after her meeting with Hooker, King "appears to have gone on to meet and actively seek out strong female friends, to read women's writing, and to focus closely on women authors" (40). King met and became friendly with Annie Fields, Sarah Orne Jewett, and Ruth McEnery Stuart.

King never married. She traveled widely, and was a respected author of realist fiction and biographical and historical studies.[15] At one point in her career, she functioned as a literary agent for French writers who wanted to publish in America. Most of King's fiction centered on women's experiences; Taylor cites King as "one of the very few American women writers who have confronted the problems of race and gender in relation to regional political and social concerns" (28). King was a protegée of Charles Warner, who helped her gain entrée into *Harper's Magazine* and the *Century*. Clemens had high praise for her work and called her novella "Earthlings" a "masterpiece": "I cannot find a flaw in the art of it—I mean the art which the intellect put there" (Bush 41–42). Ironically, King held a poor opinion of Clemens's fiction, commenting in her manuscript, "Mark Twain—Second Impression," that "[Clemens] has the great mind of a great humorist—not the great mind of a great philosopher or moralist. He is not critical—nor picturesque—if he were he would be a great novelist—He ought to be a great realistic novelist—but he is not" (4).

Clemens, a transplanted Southerner who had adopted Northern beliefs, and King, a proud Louisianian who never lost her Southern sympathies, made an interesting combination, particularly so on June 19, 1887, when a dinner was given by the Clemenses for King and General Lucius Fairchild, a Union army hero. King detested Fairchild and wrote to her sister May King McDowell that the Clemenses "admire[d] Fairchild immensely and only object[ed] to the sentiments being expressed before me" (Bush 37).

Of the man himself, King commented in her manuscript that

[Clemens's] frankness is startling. He simply doesn't care; he cannot stop to apologise or explain, and beg you not to consider him egotistical. And the absence of this uneasiness about the opinion of others, is perhaps the pleasantest trait in his intercourse, for it puts you also at your ease. . . . He takes you at the moment for what you want to be taken. . . . He treats ladies generally as if

they were nice clever boys — like himself — If they need his advice or protec-
tions — he treats them as if they were nice, good sort of sisters — without any
sentiment, or exaggeration of his services. ("Mark Twain — Second Impression," 3)

King stayed in Hartford during the fall of 1887 as a guest of the
Clemenses and returned for a second, month-long visit in October 1888. In
1892 King and her sister, Annie (Nan) King, visited the Clemens family in
Florence, Italy. King became a family intimate, and both Susy and Clara
regarded her as a confidante. The correspondence between Olivia and King
began in 1888 and continued until 1901. It was to King that Olivia wrote in
1899, asking for her opinion as to whether the family should return to
Farmington Avenue. King wrote back on December 26, 1899, encouraging
their return and, at the same time, commenting negatively on the "American Philistinism" rampant in Hartford. Again it was to King that Olivia
confided her misgivings about Clara's singing career in 1901.

It must be understood that although Olivia elected to marry, run a
household, and bear children, her interaction with these prominent women
and her involvement with Clemens's fiction-writing belies past interpretations that she was a typical upper-class, nineteenth-century women who,
limited her interests and concerns to the confines of hearth and home.
Clemens did not dominate Olivia, and he supported her political beliefs,
both publicly and privately. Clemens married a woman who had a distinct
sense of self, who was well educated, and who, since her pre-teen years, had
been an avid believer and supporter of the suffrage movement.

Notes

1. Olivia continued to attend Sunday school until her marriage. In a letter
dated November 13, 1869, Olivia tells Clemens that she "would like to write on but
I must close this and get ready for Sunday school" (*Mark Twain's Letters, 1869,* vol. 3:
394).

2. This pattern was repeated when Higginson functioned as Emily Dickinson's mentor and her poetry remained unpublished until after her death. Clemens
and Higginson were acquainted with one another, and Clemens corresponded with
him in 1905.

3. Boydston et al.'s *The Limits of Sisterhood* (1988) examines in detail Hooker's
involvement with the women's movement, although it is deficient in its discussion
of other areas related to her biography.

4. A good source of information on the political and philosophical differences between the NWSA and the AWSA is Mari Jo and Paul Buhle, eds., *The Concise History of Woman Suffrage* (Urbana: University of Illinois Press, 1979), 22.

5. In 1903, Hooker, responding to a letter sent by an admirer, complained that she had never received proper recognition for her role in forming the NWSA, "although in the earlier days I carried the Convention for them one year [1869] when they [Stanton and Anthony] dared not have their names used because of Boston" (Boydston et al. 331–32).

6. Diana Royce, Librarian for the Stowe-Day Library in Hartford, Connecticut, explains that, while she cannot give a definitive answer about the content of Clemens's May 27 letter, she can speculate that "during the late 1870s and 1880s Isabella's financial difficulties impeded her suffrage work, particularly her desire to work full-time in Washington, D.C. She may have been soliciting money [i.e., a salary] by subscription from those she knew to be sympathetic to suffrage" (letter to the author, Oct. 3, 1989).

7. In the fall of 1871 Olivia and Clemens rented the Hookers' house at Nook Farm while they began making arrangements for building their own home, which was completed in the fall of 1874.

8. Guy Cardwell cites as proof of Clemens's opposition to women's rights a letter to Olivia written a month earlier, in which Clemens applauds Hooker's decision to retire from politics. But Cardwell misreads the circumstances surrounding Clemens's letter (*Man Who Was Mark Twain* 110). Clemens's expressed pleasure about "Mrs. Hookers solemn retirement from public life" had nothing to do with his anti-suffrage sentiments; rather, Clemens was happy that Hooker was leaving the public eye because he thought this might put an end to her very public quarrel with her brother (*The Love Letters of Mark Twain* 180).

9. Kenneth Andrews, in *Nook Farm: Mark Twain's Hartford Circle* (Seattle: University of Washington Press, 1969), mistakenly gives 1861 as the date Dickinson first lectured in Hartford. In an article Isabella wrote on her eighty-third birthday, she also mistakenly remembered the date as 1861 ("The Last of the Beechers," *The Connecticut Magazine Co.* 2 [Spring 1905]: 291–95). Giraud Chester, in his biography, *Embattled Maiden: The Life of Anna Dickinson* (1951), provides the correct date: March 24, 1863.

10. Kenneth Andrews claims that Hooker did not "begin to ponder action" in regard to the suffrage movement until she read John Stuart Mill's essay (135); actually, it was Harriet Mill's work, "Enfranchisement of Women" (1851), that gave her the initial impetus. Hooker became committed to the suffrage movement in 1864, but it was not until 1868 that she became publicly active.

11. The date of Dickinson's first public address comes from research cards compiled by her biographer, Giraud Chester (no. 25 [29], ms., ts. Microfilm, Library of Congress).

12. According to Kathleen Barry in *Susan B. Anthony: A Biography of a Singular Feminist* (New York: New York University Press, 1988), Dickinson was so effective as a speaker in part because of "the groundwork laid by Anthony, Stanton, and the woman's rights movement during the preceding decade" (157).

13. Florence Willard first heard Dickinson speak in 1866 at the Opera House

in Chicago. Dickinson's topic that night was the assassination of Abraham Lincoln, a subject that would find immediate empathy among her audience; while Willard found her "a splendid woman and can afford to let people praise or blame her as they listen," she also thought Dickinson "too radical" (Bordin, *Frances Willard* 84). Willard would eventually change her opinion concerning Dickinson, and in her personal papers there is a list she composed of "the significant events in her march toward support of woman suffrage"; Willard began her list with her Chicago meeting with Dickinson in January 1875 (Bordin, *Frances Willard* 101).

14. Both Paine, in his *Mark Twain: A Biography,* and Dixon Wecter, in *Sam Clemens of Hannibal,* provide Clemens's account, although Wecter mentions Isabel Lyon's recollection that Clemens had consulted his mother as to Joan of Arc's identity, not Henry. John Gerber, in his 1988 biography of Clemens, repeats Paine's anecdote without mentioning Lyon's version (*Mark Twain* [Boston: Twayne Publishers, 1980]). Foremost among the unbelievers is James Cox, who in 1966 dismissed the entire story as "a fabrication, not a tall tale." Cox asserts that as there is "no direct evidence" to prove that the episode actually happened, "there is no reason to believe in it any more than in any of the other dubious memories of Mark Twain" (248). The reasoning for concocting such a "fabrication," Cox maintains, was so that "the tall tale of Mark Twain" would be transformed "into the invention of the boy-author Samuel Clemens"; that Clemens's purpose was "to present the emergence of literary ambition in the untutored but sensitive boy," making *Personal Recollections of Joan of Arc* the fruit of a seed planted over forty years earlier.

John Cooley argues that Clemens wrote *Personal Recollections of Joan of Arc* in part as an expression of love for his eldest daughter Susy, but that he was "also riding on a surge of public interest in Joan of Arc during the last two decades of the nineteenth century" (xxiv). In his unfinished "Memorial" to Susy, Clemens was careful to point out that, apart from his daughter, he had received no other inspiration for the physical description of Joan of Arc, while historical texts provided his only other source material: "Secretly, I drew Joan's physical portrait from the Susy of that age. . . . I had no formally-appointed model for Joan but her own historical self" (MTP* 46 1/2).

Albert Stone Jr., in *The Innocent Eye: Childhood in Mark Twain's Imagination,* provides an extended discussion of Joan of Arc's enormous popularity during the latter half of the nineteenth century (New Haven: Yale University Press, 1961), 202–8.

15. Helen Taylor views King as possessing several characteristics nineteenth-century women writers shared: "[Women writers] have tended to be unmarried and/or childless; they have often begun to write after family misfortunes . . . they have tacitly acknowledged their abnormal, even freakish role as writers by a retreat into anonymity, pseudonymity, or . . . covert codes" ("The Case of Grace King," *Southern Review* 18, no. 4 [1982]: 687).

7. The Circle Dissolves

> In talking with Mrs. Clemens one day, just before she was smitten with
> the illness which was to take her from me, we spoke of this curious &
> pathetic fact of life: that when parents are old & their children grown
> up, the grown-up children are *not the persons* they formerly were; that
> their former selves have wandered away, never to return again, save in
> dream-glimpses of their young forms that tarry a moment & gladden
> the eye, then vanish & break the heart.
> — Mark Twain, "Memorial to Olivia Susan Clemens" (MTP*)

For Clemens the ability to create fiction was a tenuous one. Clearly he
possessed this ability, but he could only manifest it under particular circumstances. A crucial element, and one that enabled Clemens to create extended
written works, was his link to childhood. This link was strengthened by
Clemens's experience of his daughters' youth. When Clemens completed
The Adventures of Tom Sawyer, Susy was three and Clara one. When he
completed *The Prince and the Pauper* and *A Tramp Abroad,* Susy was eight
and Clara was six. During *Life on the Mississippi,* Susy was eleven, Clara was
nine, and Jean was three. During *Adventures of Huckleberry Finn,* Susy was
twelve, Clara was ten, and Jean four. Clemens completed *A Connecticut
Yankee in King Arthur's Court* when Susy was seventeen, Clara was fifteen,
and Jean was nine. Here, then, was Clemens's perfect children's audience;
when the circumstances subsequently changed, his longer works of fiction
ceased. Indeed, the first signs that his creative voice was ebbing coincided
with the maturation of his daughters. In an unpublished autobiography
dictation dated April 17, 1908, Clemens bemoaned the loss of his little girls:

> One day at Riverdale-on-Hudson Mrs. Clemens and I were mourning for our
> lost little ones. Not that they were dead, but lost to us all the same. Gone out of
> our lives forever — *as little children.* They were still with us, but they were
> become women, and they walked with us upon our own level. There was a
> wide gulf, a gulf as wide as the horizons, between *these* children and *those.* We
> were always having vague dream-glimpses of them as they had used to be in
> the long-vanished years — glimpses of them playing and romping, with short
> frocks on, and spindle legs, and hair-tails down their backs — and always they

were far and dim, and we could not hear their shouts and their laughter. How
we longed to gather them to our arms! but they were only dainty and darling
specters, and they faded away and vanished, and left us desolate. (No. 69,
MTP*)

Clemens's rueful admission of the chasm between the children of his
memory and the women of his present is evocative of the struggles he had
with his writing in his later period. He was unable to bridge the gulf
between the fiction of his golden Farmington Avenue–Quarry Farm period
and his writings after 1890. The year 1890 is of particular significance in that
it marks Susy's first separation from the family when she left for college at
Bryn Mawr.[1] Clemens's sense of loss over Susy's departure can be attributed
not merely to the physical absence of his daughter, but also to the absence of
an integral source of his inspiration.

The Author as Humorist

By the time of *Personal Recollections of Joan of Arc*, written when Susy was
twenty-three, Clemens had lost the leader of his trio of little girls to young
adulthood. Susy had assumed Olivia's mantle as didactic monitor. She
feared that her father would be known only as a "humorist," a label she
violently disliked. Indeed, Susy expressed her loathing for her father's
pseudonym to Grace King: "How I hate that name! . . . My father should
not be satisfied with it! . . . He should show himself the great writer that he
is, not merely a funny man. Funny! That's all the people see in him — a
maker of funny speeches!" (King, *Memories of a Southern Woman of Letters*
173–74).

This concern of Susy's had surfaced much earlier in the biography she
wrote about her father when she was just thirteen. In an excerpt from her
biography, Susy praises *The Prince and the Pauper* and views this work as a
welcome departure from his style in *Adventures of Huckleberry Finn:*

> One of papa's latest books is "*The Prince and the Pauper*" and it is unquestiona-
> bly the best book he has ever written, some people want him to keep to his old
> style. . . . That enoyed [sic] me greatly, because it trobles [sic] me . . . to have
> so few people know papa, I mean realy [sic] know him, they think of Mark
> Twain as a humorist joking at everything. (Feb. 9, 1906, Autobiographical
> Dictation, No. 64, MTP*)

Susy desperately wanted her father to use his writing for a more serious
purpose than what she regarded as mere entertainment. Critics have ob-

8. Clemens dancing with Susy in 1890. (Courtesy of The Mark Twain Project, The Bancroft Library)

served that Clemens modeled *Personal Recollections of Joan of Arc* after Susy, which Clemens openly admitted: "Susy at 17 — Joan of Arc at 17. Secretly, I drew Joan's physical portrait from the Susy of that age, when I came to write that book. Apart from that, I had no formally-appointed model for Joan but her own historical self. Yet there were several points of resemblance between the girls: such as vivacity, enthusiasm, precocious wisdom, wit, eloquence, penetration, nobility of character" ("Memorial to Olivia Susan Clemens," 46½, MTP*).

More importantly, though, Clemens wrote *Personal Recollections of Joan of Arc* because of Susy and because of his and his family's reformist beliefs. Indeed, the work was intended originally as a companion piece to *The Prince and the Pauper.* Clemens's adored daughter had urged him to engage his talents for a higher, moral purpose, and he followed her wishes. He had trusted her literary instincts since she could first respond to his writing; he had no reason to doubt her now.

Susy's discontent with her father's limited reputation appears to have echoed her mother's opinion. In writing *Personal Recollections of Joan of Arc,* Clemens also can be seen working in accord with Olivia's wishes. He dedicated the book to her, the only title he singled out for this honor, in "recognition of her twenty-five years of valued service as my literary adviser and editor" (Paine, *Mark Twain: A Biography* 1,033). Even as early as their courtship, Olivia influenced the direction Clemens's writing would take. Henry Nash Smith noted that at the time Clemens had already finished the first draft of *The Innocents Abroad,* but his revision was "dictated" to a large degree by his wanting "to become the kind of writer he thought she [Olivia] wanted him to be" (*Mark Twain-Howells Letters* 63).

Before their marriage Clemens wrote to Mary Fairbanks about Olivia's alleged misgivings regarding his career as a humorist: "Poor girl, anybody who could convince her that I was not a humorist would secure her eternal gratitude! She thinks a humorist is something perfectly awful" (*Mark Twain's Letters, 1869,* vol. 3: 8). It should be noted, however, that this statement may be Clemens's projection onto Olivia of his own insecurity about his future. This view is supported by the following letter, written by Clemens to his brother Orion in late 1865, in which his insecurity about being perceived as just a humorist is evident:

> I *have* had a "call" to literature, of a low order — *i.e.* humorous. It is nothing to be proud of, but it is my strongest suit. . . . Poor, pitiful business! Though the Almighty did His part by me — for the talent is a mighty engine when supplied with the steam of *education* — which I have not got, & so its pistons . . .

move feebly & for a holiday show & are useless for any good purpose. (*My Dear Bro* 6–7)

In the surviving correspondence between Clemens and Olivia, Olivia's primary objection to Clemens's following the lecture circuit is the prolonged absences away from home it entailed, not the humorous nature of his speeches. In 1895, Olivia accompanied Clemens on his global tour where she heard a year's worth of vintage Mark Twain, humorist, without complaint. Still, it appears that Clemens's reputation as a serious writer was important to Olivia, as is clear in a note she wrote admonishing him for his poor behavior toward the young novelist Marie van Vorst: "Where is the mind that wrote the *Prince & P. Jeanne d' Arc, The Yankee,* &c. &c. &c. Bring it back!" (*The Love Letters of Mark Twain* 333). Whether this humorist/writer conflict was a projection on Clemens's part, or was diagnosed first by Olivia, then Susy, and subsequently Clemens, it was obviously a concern shared by members of the family.

Personal Recollections, Fictional and Factual

Late in life, Clemens asked William Dana Orcutt which of his (Clemens's) books he liked best. Clemens was pleased when Orcutt cited *Personal Recollections of Joan of Arc*. Clemens's response appears to echo Olivia's and Susy's earlier points:

> I hope others feel the same way, I don't want to go down to posterity simply as a court jester. There is no lasting quality to humor unless it's based on real substance. Being funny doesn't amount to anything unless there is an underlying human note. That is what I've always tried to sound; but people don't realize that this required the same powers of observation, analysis, and understanding as in serious writing. (Orcutt 147)

Interestingly, modern critics have preferred Clemens's humorous writing, and have had considerable difficulty trying to fit *Personal Recollections of Joan of Arc* within the contours of Clemens's work.[2] But Clemens consistently maintained that *Personal Recollections of Joan of Arc* was his finest work, and Paine, presumably echoing Clemens, called the book "Mark Twain's supreme literary expression" (*Mark Twain: A Biography* 1,029).

Nonetheless, the critical tide against *Personal Recollections of Joan of Arc* does seem to be turning. Two recent works provide new interpretations of

Clemens's purpose in writing the text and comment favorably on the text itself. John Cooley, in his *Mark Twain's Aquarium: The Samuel Clemens Angelfish Correspondence, 1905–1910,* views *Personal Recollections of Joan of Arc* as an extension of Clemens's increasing interest in female childhood experience. Childhood was always a feature of Clemens's best-known works in his younger years, but in these earlier works Clemens was preoccupied with male youth, whereas in his later period of writing, girls' life experiences eventually supplanted those of boys. Cooley connects Clemens's increasing fascination with young girls, the "Angelfish" of his aquarium, with the shift in Clemens's gender focus in his fiction, ultimately resulting in the composition of the *Personal Recollections of Joan of Arc* (xxiii, 282). Thomas Maik argues in his recent study, *A Reexamination of Mark Twain's Joan of Arc,* that while Clemens acknowledged that this book was a departure from his other works, he may have also been trying to attract two disparate audiences: "one aimed at women and girls his daughters' ages or younger who would find this book to 'fit' the tradition of nineteenth-century juvenile female fiction. The other audience, a more traditional one that had grown accustomed to the rebel and 'outlaw' characters of Twain's earlier fiction" (67). Perhaps it is possible to interpret *Personal Recollections of Joan of Arc* as another example of Clemens relying on female-authored sentimental novels to provide the structure and themes for his historical novel. Clemens, working within a genre created by women writers, constructed a text that has as its main character a young female heroine whose objective is to transgress defined social boundaries. In *Personal Recollections of Joan of Arc,* Clemens was continuing his long-established authorial stance of critiquing society while taking a stand on social issues. In the character of Joan, indeed, Clemens created the archetypal WCTU social reformer.

Clemens was thus catering to several primary interests when he wrote *Personal Recollections of Joan of Arc.* The first was that of his and his female family's avid support for reform. Clemens's character "Joan of Arc" has little in common with the historical figure, and critics have frequently objected to the work on this account. Yet what critics have not realized is that despite Clemens's statements regarding his copious research into the period, he was not writing a historical novel per se. More likely, he was hiding an allegory of nineteenth-century progressive concerns within the covers of a historical novel. Indeed, Clemens's Joan of Arc espouses all the "pet" causes of the WCTU: she is an adamant defender of children's rights, animal rights, dress reform, and temperance. Joan stops her troops from engaging in whoring, drinking, and swearing; at no time, even in the midst of battle, does Joan ever lose her feminine characteristics.

Clemens was careful always to include Joan's feminine traits because she was operating almost entirely within the public/masculine sphere. Joan's intellect and military ability could provide ample grounds for unsexing her — a fear female reformers often had to confront when they engaged in the public arena. Maik recognizes that in military matters Joan was a violator of tradition, and that she also defied convention in other areas: "Through La Hire, Twain suggests that no longer can the traditional approach be the order of the day. New ideas, new approaches, and change now become the norm . . . in perceptions of gender, Joan of Arc represents a different vision and ushers in a new order" (112). George Bernard Shaw's remark, quoted by Maik, regarding Joan of Arc's anomalous position among Clemens's works might not be far off the mark: "Had Joan not been one of those 'unwomanly women,' she might have been canonized sooner" (112).

Clemens's other interest in writing the novel, which should come as no surprise, was to produce a commercial success. When Clemens published *Personal Recollections of Joan of Arc* in 1895, he was trying to recoup financially after his 1894 bankruptcy (Clemens would not become financially solvent until shortly before the end of the century). By writing a novel incorporating WCTU interests, Clemens was hoping to attract a large audience and perhaps have the WCTU embrace his work, as they had Edward Bellamy's best seller *Looking Backward*.[3]

Clemens was well aware of Joan of Arc's popularity among female reformers and suffragists, and his attempt to target this potential audience appears to have met with some success. In 1910 Clemens was contacted by the New York Jeanne D'Arc Suffrage League, which thanked him for his "splendid history of our patron saint" and informed him that at their last meeting the members had "resolved 'to honor ourselves by honoring Dr Clemens.'" "With your generous permission" the League wished to proudly "enroll you as an honorary member" (Jan. 6, 1910, MTP*). This may help explain Clemens's decision to publish *Personal Recollections of Joan of Arc* anonymously. He may have hoped that his humorist mantle would not interfere with or color the progressive interests represented in the work.

Significantly, *Personal Recollections of Joan of Arc* was to be Susy's last assignment as her father's editor. In his memorial piece to Susy, Clemens remembered that she "took as deep & earnest an interest in the book as if it

were her own. The nightly readings and editings covered many months"
("Memorial to Olivia Susan Clemens," 30–31 MTP*). On his seventy-third
birthday, Clemens wrote: "I like the *Joan of Arc* best of all my books; & it *is*
the best; I know it perfectly well" (Paine 1,034). It should come as no
surprise that Clemens maintained that *Personal Recollections of Joan of Arc*
was his greatest work — it was the book Susy and his family had wanted him
to write. To deny it would have meant denying their importance.

Susy grew into an intelligent, sensitive, introspective young woman,
and Clemens entertained the hope that she might become a writer. Clemens
later reminisced about the plays she wrote and performed, and he sum-
marized the plots of two novels she had begun. Although Clemens recognized that Susy was a talented singer and writer, he believed her greatest gift
was that of "oral expression" ("Memorial to Olivia Susan Clemens," 26
MTP*). Small wonder that Clemens should recognize Susy's ability of
"oral expression" as her best attribute — this ability of hers had an enormous, positive influence on his writing. Clemens recalled that her verbal
ability was so extraordinary that she was regarded by the family as a
"prodigy," and as one who "had no equal of girls of her own age" ("Memorial to Olivia Susan Clemens," 71 MTP*; *Mark Twain's Notebook* 317).

After Susy entered her teens, she became well known for her moodiness, a trait her family learned to accept. Writing to Susan Crane after Susy's
death, Clemens stated: "you were good to Susy, she made it hard for
you. . . . You stood by her staunch and true like the loyal and loving
friend . . . you have always been" (Sep. 30, 1896, MTP*). Admitting that
Susy was subject to periods of depression, Clemens chose to remember that
in between these periods of unhappiness, "there were outbursts of happi-
ness . . . exaltations of it." Clemens summed up her troubled personality:
"In all things she was intense; in her this characteristic was not a mere glow,
dispensing warmth, but a consuming fire" ("A Family Sketch," 1906, No.
40, MTP*).

Perhaps the most accurate characterization of Clemens and Susy's
relationship would be one of "compatriots." Dr. Clarence Rice, the family's
New York physician, remembered that Susy was Clemens's "constant companion and chum"; and she possessed "such originality of thought that she
offered him valuable suggestions . . . in his writings when she was little
more that sixteen years old" (3). Just as Olivia had won the role of
Clemens's initial muse, Susy evolved into his second. Two recently discovered letters underscore the closeness of their relationship. The first
letter, lost for over seventy years, helps to illuminate the writerly and

emotional bond between father and daughter (Skandera). Clemens was at sea when he wrote Susy this anecdote on March 24, 1893.

> Susy dear, Professor [Charles Eliot] Norton of Harvard, aged toward 70, a ripe scholar & a beautiful character, has the sweetness and bonhommie & refinement of Howells, with the lofty purity & saintliness and divine gravity of Louise IX. He has a noble & impressive delivery, in public speaking, with a rare grace & felicity of construction & a most winning & gentle & persuasive manner. The lamented William [Morris] Hunt the artist was his dear & darling friend from little-boyhood all through life to the end. Richard [Morris] Hunt . . . (brother of William), came on to Boston a few months ago . . . & they were given a banquet by the Tavern Club. . . . Professor Norton is chairman now. . . . You will remember how often I have said that the gift of introducing a speaker at a banquet is a divine gift. . . . There are only two men in America to whom God has vouchsafed that great talent in a great degree — Professor Norton & [William Dean] Howells.
>
> On the hurricane deck a minute ago, Longfellow (nephew of the poet), said — "You remember Norton's introductions . . . & how beautiful & eloquent & poetical they were & how full of graciousness & dignity?" "Yes, I do." "And you remember how deliberately he speaks, putting pauses between the words?" "Yes, I do." "Well, then, you will be able to *see* Norton & *hear* him. Imagine it, now. He is standing before the big audience, who know that the man waiting near his elbow is the brother of his last friend, — so they wait, breathless, knowing that something touching & beautiful will come from his lips now. Norton's emotion was visible. He made one or two efforts to command his voice — succeeded & then went on["]: "One day, many years ago, I had come — back from — Italy, & I sat with — William Hunt talking — & I had in my — pocket — a little silver — box — a beautiful creation of — old Italian art — & I was impatient to know — if he would like it — for I had bought it — for him — & I took it out — & gave it to him — & watched his face — with eager solicitude — for the light I hoped would break there — & I said — 'Do you like it?' Ah, his eye flamed! — & he said — 'Do I *like* it? Norton — it is a God damned *ultimate* of art!' Gentlemen — here stands — before you — the brother — of that most noble genius — and he — too — is a God damned *ultimate* of art!"
>
> "The house came down with a storm — Norton's tears were already flowing."
>
> There, Susy, dear, that is the very loveliest anecdote I have ever heard in my life, & one of the most touching — for I can *see* Norton, & hear his voice grow unsteady & finally break down at the end. . . . Don't you lose this, dear. I wouldn't trust it to my notebook, for notebooks get lost. (MTP*)

In the second letter, written later that same year on December 27, it is clear Clemens regarded Susy as his intellectual and social equal (Susy was twenty-one at the time). In the letter Clemens denounces a woman whom he detests, Lilian Aldrich, after he has been forced to sit next to her at a holiday banquet:

> Lord, I loathe that woman so! She is an idiot — an absolute idiot — and does not know it. She is show, show, show — not a genuine fixture in her any-where — a manifest and transparent humbug — and her husband, the sincerest man that walks . . . tied for life to this vacant hellion, this clothes-rack, this twaddling, blethering, driveling blatherskite! (MTP*)

Here was no patriarchal upholder of Victorian parental propriety. This was the true Clemens venting the full extent of his anger to a sympathetic colleague.

". . . The deadness which invaded me"

Along with the loss of his daughters to young adulthood, Clemens's problems were compounded by his monetary difficulties and his removal from his favorite writing environment. The Hartford house, built in 1874 at a cost of approximately one hundred thousand dollars and known for its lavish entertainments and constant stream of visitors, combined with his failed investment in the Paige typesetter and the failure of his publishing house, proved to be Clemens's financial downfall.[4] In 1891, after living at Farmington Avenue for seventeen years, Clemens moved his family abroad in an attempt to cut expenses. In 1894, after years of bad investments, Clemens declared bankruptcy. The family was not to return to America until 1900. As early as 1891, removed from his preferred creative environment, Clemens sensed that the days of his sustained fiction writing were threatened. When he was sailing to France with his family, Clemens jotted down a note that was prophetic of the difficulties he was to have with future attempts at writing fiction: "Tom comes, at last, 60 from wandering the world & tends Huck & together they talk the old times; both are desolate, life has been a failure, all that was lovable, all that was beautiful is under the mould. They die together" (Notebook No. 30, MTP*).

During the decade spent as an expatriate American, Clemens made many overseas crossings to try to salvage what he could of his business affairs. In 1895, Clemens returned to the closed Hartford home. After his visit he wrote to Olivia describing his reaction: "it seemed as if I had burst awake out of a hellish dream, & had never been away, & that you would come drifting down . . . with the little children tagging after you" (*The Love Letters of Mark Twain* 312). Until his death, Clemens would continue to wish that the shattering of his idyll at Hartford and Quarry Farm was just a bad dream. Shortly afterward the "circle" of his female family was broken, and Clemens's great period of novel-writing began its decline around the time of Susy's death on August 18, 1896. Clemens's ability to maintain a narrative was then essentially reduced to the more constricted range of short story writing, yet it was still potent. With the death of Olivia, however, Clemens's ability to complete long narratives would disappear entirely. Clemens never recovered from his losses and, significantly, neither did the author Mark Twain.

Almost immediately after Susy's death, Clemens threw himself into writing his fifth and last travel book, *Following the Equator*. At the time, Clemens refused to admit that his ability to write novel-length fiction had been irreparably damaged. The impact Susy's death had on Clemens's writing is a critical matter. DeVoto attributes the difficulties Clemens had with his fiction, beginning in 1890, to a "series of catastrophes," with Susy's demise taking prominence. This is an accurate assessment, but DeVoto errs in claiming that the tragedies made Clemens that much more determined "to vindicate himself as a writer" (*Mark Twain at Work* 106, 110). Vindicate himself? For whom? Clemens already had a world-wide reputation. William R. Macnaughton concurs with DeVoto and argues that, while attention has been given to the "supposed effects" of Susy's death, in his opinion, Clemens "pick[ed] himself up again" (15). As proof of this he quotes a letter Clemens wrote to his friend and adviser H. H. Rogers: "I've got a new book in my head — 3 or 4 of them, for that matter. . . . I shall write *All* of them — a whole dam library" (17). Macnaughton interprets this to mean that Clemens was enjoying writing, and that Clemens's attempt to lose himself in his work is a positive sign.[5] Clemens elaborated on these thoughts to Joseph Twichell: "I am going to write with all my might on this book, and follow it with others as fast as I can, in the hope that within three years I can clear out the stuff that is in me waiting to be written, and that I shall then die in the promptest kind of way and no fooling around" (*Mark Twain-Howells Letters* 264–65).

The undefeated tone Clemens employed in his letters to Twichell and Rogers may have been intended to convince them that his fiction-writing ability was not diminished. But the desperation is unmistakable in a letter Clemens wrote to Howells on January 22, 1898, seventeen months after Susy's death:

> I couldn't get along without work now. I bury myself in it up to the ears. Long hours — 8 and 9 at a stretch, sometimes. All the days. . . . It isn't all for print . . . for much of it fails to suit me; 50,000 words of it in the past year. It was because of the deadness which invaded me when Susy died. (*Mark Twain-Howells Letters* 620)

DeVoto also quotes from this letter but, interestingly, he omits the lines beginning with, "It isn't all for print. . . ." Yet here is Clemens confessing to one of his dearest literary mentors that the loss of his writing prowess is due to his daughter's death. Clemens was not writing his thousands of manuscript pages, which he knew were of inferior quality, to prove that his travails had left him untouched — rather, his writing appears to have been a pathological grieving acted out in the form of compulsive activity. Clemens was not working to achieve artistic mastery; he was, as he explains, working "for the sake of work." It was all that was left for him. In a letter to Joseph Twichell, written five months after Susy's death, Clemens determinedly asserted:

> I am working, but it is for the sake of the *work* — the "surcease of sorrow" that is found there. I work all the days; & trouble vanishes away when I use that magic. This book will not long stand between it & me, now; but that is no matter, I have many unwritten books to fly to for my preservation. (Jan. 19, 1897, MTP*)

Clemens erred in his optimism; there were no more completed novels or travel narratives to come. In his *Mark Twain: A Biography* Albert Bigelow Paine recounts a conversation Clemens had with Paine's young daughter, Joy, when he was living at Stormfield. The three were taking a buggy ride when, while passing some woods, Clemens remarked: "Those are elephant woods." Joy replied: "They are fairy woods. The fairies are there, but you can't see them because they wear magic cloaks." Clemens's pathos-filled response was, "I wish I had one of those magic cloaks, sometimes. I had one once, but it is worn out now" (1,453). A young girl wrung from Clemens this admission about the loss of his craft; even in the letter to Twichell, one of his closest male friends, Clemens refused to admit that the "magic" was gone.

The progressive losses — the maturation of his daughters, the myriad financial difficulties, the removal from his favorite writing place, the discovery of Jean's epilepsy, the death of Susy — all had conspired to rob Clemens of his narrative gift. Yet, despite all this, Clemens continued against odds to produce: *The American Claimant* (1892), *Pudd'nhead Wilson* (1894), *Tom*

Sawyer Abroad (1894), *Personal Recollections of Joan of Arc* (1895), and *Following the Equator* (1897). While these works do not match the artistry of his earlier period, Clemens could at least complete their narratives. The reason this was so was that he still possessed his initial source of security and inspiration — Olivia.

On the first anniversary of Susy's death, Clemens wrote two pieces that addressed his loss. The first was a poem published in *Harper's New Monthly Magazine* entitled, "In Memoriam. Olivia Susan Clemens" (929–30). The poem itself is a fairly conventional eulogy, except for the two last lines which read, "Where stood the temple when the sun went down, / Was vacant desert when it rose again!" (929). Both the temple and a crucial source of Clemens's inspiration had disappeared. The desert imagery is analogous to Clemens's metaphor of the "tank" of inspiration — it, too, was beginning to "run dry." The second piece, "In My Bitterness," expresses Clemens's deep sense of anger and frustration at his helplessness in the face of Susy's death. Clemens rails at the vindictive God who trapped and stole his child: "He gives you a wife and children whom you adore, only that through the spectacle of the . . . miseries which He will inflict upon them He may tear the palpitating heart out of your breast and slap you in the face with it. . . . You are out of His reach forever; and I too. He can never hurt me anymore" (*Mark Twain's Fables of Man* 131–32).[6]

After Susy's death and upon their return to America, the family leased a house in New York City. They never returned to the Hartford home, which served only to remind them of Susy and of a way of life that had been extinguished. Clemens's summers of writing at Quarry Farm were also at an end. The last novel he had worked on there before leaving for Europe was *A Connecticut Yankee in King Arthur's Court*. In 1903, the last piece of writing he was to complete at the farm was a maudlin short story called "A Dog's Tale," which was a far cry in quality from the days of "A True Story." Clemens made only sporadic visits to Quarry Farm after 1890.[7] Elmira and, specifically, Quarry Farm, came to occupy the same place in Clemens's memory as the Hartford home — that is, as another sad reminder of an unrepeatable past.

Clemens could, it was proved, be hurt again. This occurred with Olivia's death eight years after Susy's. When Olivia died, on June 5, 1904, the one constant in Samuel Clemens's life for the past thirty-six years expired as well. Olivia's impact on Clemens was, in the end, incalculable. From the first, Clemens made Olivia the integral link in his circle of literary readers and advisors. Revealing the extent of Olivia's interaction with his writing, Clemens responded to a query of Archibald Henderson's regarding the "serious spirit that crept into . . . his humor":

> I never wrote a serious word until after I married Mrs. Clemens. She is solely responsible — to her should go the credit — for any . . . moral influence my subsequent work may exert. After my marriage, she edited everything I wrote. (Henderson 183)

In the years after 1904 Clemens produced mainly polemical writings; he attempted to write extended works of fiction many times, but left the manuscripts incomplete. Clemens was now a man bereft of his favorite audience and of his secure home life. Without his female circle Mark Twain the novel writer disappeared; what remained was merely the public persona.

By the time of Susy and Olivia's deaths, Clemens had weathered his share of loss: the deaths of his father and four siblings in his youth; his father-in-law's death during his first year of marriage; the deaths of his only son, Langdon in 1872, of Jervis Langdon's mother, Eunice Ford, in 1873, and of Clemens's and Olivia's mothers in 1890. Clemens was no stranger to death, but the deaths of Susy and Olivia had a palpably different effect on him. What separated these deaths from the others was that these latter two induced his personal and creative dysfunction.

Notes

1. Clemens's frequently quoted letter describing the pathos of the scene when he left Susy at Bryn Mawr was only one of numerous, similar departure letters. On October 12, 1890, Clemens wrote his sister Pamela about their leave-taking when he left Susy at college: "The last time I saw her was a week ago on the platform at Bryn Mawr. Our train was moving away, and she was drifting collegeward afoot, her figure blurred and dim in the rain and fog, and she was crying" (MTP*).

In an 1893 letter to Jean (discovered in 1987), Clemens comments on people he sees on the pier in Genoa: "The pier was crowded with people . . . poor and dirty people *crying* good-bye. . . . I have never seen so many tears shed, or found the view of it so hard to bear. If you and mamma and Susy were to cry me good-bye from a pier I could not endure it" (MTP*).

Finally, in another frequently quoted letter (dated July 14, 1895), Clemens wrote to Henry Robinson about the last time he saw Susy — when he, Olivia, and Clara were setting off on the world lecture tour and leaving Susy and Jean in Elmira. The letter describes the parting scene: "Susy stood on the platform in the blaze of the electric light waving her good-byes to us as the train glided away, her mother throwing back kisses and watching her through her tears" (Paine, ed., *Mark Twain's Notebook* 317).

The difficulties both Clemens and Susy had in dealing with her removal to college have been documented in Edith Salsbury's *Susy and Mark Twain: Family Dialogues* (New York: Harper, 1965); and Charles Neider's *Papa: An Intimate Biography of Mark Twain* (1985).

2. James Wilson's "In Quest of Redemptive Vision: Mark Twain's Joan of Arc" (*Texas Studies in Literature and Language* 20 [1978]: 181–98) remarks on scholars' rejection of *Personal Recollections of Joan of Arc*: "Though an anomaly among Mark Twain's novels, *Personal Recollections of Joan of Arc* nevertheless exists; thus most Mark Twain scholars feel compelled to give the book some consideration, usually hastily dismissing the book because of its archness and sentimentality" (195).

3. Clemens met with Bellamy in Hartford on January 3, 1890, and he might have had Bellamy's success in mind when deciding on the subject for his next novel. An undated letter from Susy Clemens to Grace King describes Bellamy's visit:

> Mr. Bellamy was here the other day for a few hours. He is very sweet . . . in appearance with a pleasant eye, and gentle smile. He and papa had some very interesting talk upon the subjects which he discusses in "Looking Backward." Papa's admiration for the book and it's [sic] views and purpose is very great. We liked Mr. Bellamy exceedingly. How strange thoe [sic] that the men who think such thoughts as his and plan great reforms, should carry such absolute calmness . . . in their faces! (Coxe Collection)

Twain scholars have commonly looked to *A Connecticut Yankee in King Arthur's Court* as the most likely work to reflect Bellamy's influence; yet another possible candidate might be *Personal Recollections of Joan of Arc*. Along with affecting the direction of the WCTU, the Bellamy influence may have extended to Clemens. Alan Gribben has established that although there are "obvious similarities between *Looking Backward* (1888) and *A Connecticut Yankee* (1889)," Clemens's notebook reveals that he did not begin reading Bellamy's work until November 5, 1889 (*Mark Twain's Library: A Reconstruction* 58). This careful marking of the date, Gribben says, makes it seem almost as though Clemens wanted to "frustrate later scholars" who would want to investigate Bellamy's influence on Clemens's writing. However, although Clemens evidently did not read Bellamy's text until after the writing of *A Connecticut Yankee* was completed, this does not necessarily mean that the other members of his family also waited.

4. For background information on the Hartford years see Resa Willis's *Mark and Livy* (1992).

5. In addition to negating the impact Susy's death had on Clemens's fiction, Macnaughton proceeds to cast doubt on the sincerity of Clemens's grief:

> Much of this [Clemens's expression of grief] seems patently contrived, false, and melodramatic. . . . It is almost as if he was torturing himself because he believed that this is how he should feel, if he hoped to be truly human. . . . It is also incontestable that [his] moods . . . led him into moments when his grief and guilt were excruciatingly, if evanescently, real. (23–24)

This tendency toward questioning Clemens's sincerity of expression began with Hill in 1972 and has been perpetuated by Robert Bray (1974) and Macnaughton (1979). Unfortunately, the result of this line of critical discourse is a gross distortion of Clemens's biography. One can ascertain the depth of Clemens's anguish over Susy's death in another letter written to Susan Crane: "Oh, Oh, Oh, Dear Sue, I cannot believe it, cannot realize it, cannot accept it! It is a dream, & will pass, & Susy will come again" (Sep. 30, 1896, MTP*). This letter indeed reveals inarticulate, visceral pain.

6. An article by Carroll R. Schoenewolf, "Susy Clemens and 'My Platonic Sweetheart'" (*Mark Twain Journal* 21 [Winter 1981–1982]: 11–13), suggests that Susy's death possibly inspired a third piece of writing. "My Platonic Sweetheart" was written two years after Susy's death in the month of August, and it is Schoenewolf's contention that "Sweetheart" is a second-year anniversary memorial (11). Schoenewolf's essay contests Howard Baetzhold's piece, "Found: Mark Twain's 'Lost Sweetheart'" (*American Literature* 44 [1972]: 414–29), where he makes the claim that the source of inspiration for "My Platonic Sweetheart" was none other than fifteen-year-old Laura M. Wright.

7. After Theodore Crane's death in 1889, Susan Crane lived in town with her adoptive mother from 1889 to 1890; she then returned to Quarry Farm. Clemens traveled to Elmira in 1901 as a pallbearer, and again in 1902 to attend a wedding. In 1904, he returned for the funeral service held for his wife, and he made a speech in 1907, at the dedication of the Thomas K. Beecher Organ in Park Church (Jerome and Wisbey 166). Isabel Lyon commented on Clemens's last visit to Elmira in her 1907 daily reminder: "Today the King started off for Elmira—a sense-of-duty visit, and he was sorry that he had to make it. He went up to hear the great new organ, and to make his last visit there. He hates the place now and all the people there too—except the Staunchfields and Mrs. Crane" (Apr. 2, 1907, MTP).

On April 5, 1907, Isabel made this observation regarding Clemens's state of mind upon his return: "Yes, the King is depressed and tonight at dinner said that he wouldn't go again to Elmira. He couldn't" (1907 Daily Reminder, MTP).

8. The Resurgence of Mark Twain

> He was not lying consciously; he believed what he was saying. To him, his initial statements were facts, and whenever he enlarged a statement, the enlargement became a fact too. He put his heart into his extravagant narrative, just as a poet puts his heart into a heroic fiction, and his earnestness disarmed criticism — disarmed it as far as he himself was concerned. Nobody believed his narrative, but all believed that he believed it.
>
> — Mark Twain, *Personal Recollections of Joan of Arc*

At the age of sixty-eight Clemens had outlived his wife and eldest daughter. Immediately following Olivia's death in Florence in June 1904, Clemens returned to America with Clara, Jean, Isabel Lyon, Lyon's mother, and Teresa, the family's Italian maid. On their first night back in New York, the grief-stricken remaining members of the family stayed at the Wolcott Hotel, with Isabel Lyon, Mrs. Lyon, and Teresa staying at the St. Dennis. The Clemens family next went to *Century* editor Richard Watson Gilder's home in Tyringham, Massachusetts, where they stayed the rest of the summer. On November 30, 1904, the family took up residence at 21 Fifth Avenue in Manhattan.[1]

Clemens, whose pessimism had been muted while his family circle was intact, now openly vented his bitterness and frustration toward life in his correspondence and in his writings. In a letter to Joseph Twichell on March 14, 1905, Clemens commented sardonically on the poor progress made by humankind during his lifetime:

> Well, the 19th century made progress — the first progress after "ages and ages" — colossal progress. In what? Materialities. . . . Money is the supreme ideal — all others take tenth place with the great bulk of the nations named. . . . Money-lust has always existed, but not in the history of the world was it ever a craze, a madness, until your time and mine. This lust has rotted these nations; it has made them hard, sordid, ungentle, dishonest, oppressive. . . . If there has been any progress toward righteousness since the early days of Creation — which, in my ineradicable honesty, I am obliged to doubt — I think we must confine it to ten per cent of the populations of Christendom. (*Mark Twain's Letters* 669–770)

For someone who had, arguably, always considered money his "supreme ideal," this letter is particularly ironic. Clemens is quick to decry the emphasis his century has placed on money, yet, typically, he exempted himself from censure. In a sense, however, Clemens was the ideal person to comment on the excesses and emptiness of crass materialism, for he knew intimately the perilous risks inherent in such behavior. And while Clemens had viewed his era critically before, most notably in *The Gilded Age,* by the time he was in his seventies and had lost his wife and part of his family, wealth and fame were really all that remained to him. He had lost his fiction-making voice.

Reflection and Regeneration

In his last period of writing, from 1904 until his death on April 21, 1910, Clemens's completed writings consisted of uneven diatribes about war and politics such as those in "The War Prayer" (1905) and "King Leopold's Soliloquy" (1905); a scathing but almost unreadable indictment against Mary Baker Eddy in *Christian Science* (1907); diversely meritorious treatments of biblical and philosophical affairs in "Eve's Diary" (1905) and "What Is Man?" (1906); and essays concerning literary affairs in "Is Shakespeare Dead?" (1909) and "The Turning Point of My Life" (1909). He also wrote Jean's tragic epitaph in "The Death of Jean" (1910), and the inferior short story entitled "A Horse's Tale" (1906). He completed the much superior "Captain Stormfield's Visit to Heaven" (1907), begun nearly thirty years earlier, and left three fragments, composed over a period of eleven years (from 1897 to 1908), that comprised *The Mysterious Stranger* manuscript.

However, the work to which Clemens devoted the majority of his time and effort in the final years of his life was the *Autobiography.* Begun in the early 1870s, with one of the first installments concerning his family's Tennessee property, the work received Clemens's sporadic attention until the watershed years of 1897–98. This period marked some of Clemens's most evocative reminiscences: "Early Days," "Old Lecture Days," "Beauties of the German Language," and "Jim Wolf and the Cats," a total of nine separate pieces. It was not until 1904 that Clemens equaled this volume of work when he wrote approximately eight entries, among them the tedious "Villa Quarto," the minimally interesting "Notes on 'Innocents Abroad'" and the admiring "Henry H. Rogers." There is an obvious correspondence between the dates of these bursts of autobiographical writings and those marking Susy's death and Olivia's final illness. With each diminishment of his circle, Clemens reacted by turning inward and retracing his beginnings. The observation can be made that the form Clemens's grieving took was immersion in the past, for he attempted to relive happier times through the writing of his projected autobiography. Michael Kiskis, in his edifying article, "Susy Clemens as the Fire for Mark Twain's Autobiography," asserts that when Clemens wrote "Early Days," he painted an elegiac picture that

> enhanced and preserved his impressions of those formative times and places, but it was a false picture. It presented an ideal which existed only in Mark Twain's memories as he attempted to restore balance to his own life after the trauma of Susy's death. Susy was not part of the story, though she was the reason for its telling. (45)

In 1906, Clemens began a series of dictations that would continue until 1909.[2] During this period, Clemens cited his daughter Susy as acting not only as a major source of inspiration for his autobiography, but also as his literary advisor. Susy began her biography in 1885, when she was thirteen and her father was fifty.[3] According to Kiskis, Clemens recorded in his notebook an entry indicating that Susy "not only spurred her father's autobiographical impulse but also suggested dictating as a new method":

> Which reminds me that Susie, aged 13, has begun to write my biography — solely of her own motion — a thing about which I feel proud & gratified. At breakfast this morning I intimated that if I seemed to be talking on a pretty high key, in the way of style, it must be remembered that my biographer was present. Whereupon Susie struck upon the unique idea of having me sit up & purposely *talk* for the biography! (*Mark Twain's Notebooks and Journals* 112)

Clemens ultimately took Susy's advice about dictating his autobiography and hired Josephine Hobby, a stenographer, who worked for him from 1906 until August 12, 1908 (*Mark Twain-Howells Letters* 833). During the 1906 dictations, Clemens interpolated his autobiographical reminiscences with Susy's biography. Clemens's text becomes, in places, self-reflexive. Clemens quoted a section of Susy's biography where she wrote about how her father used to make up tales for her and Clara: "He does tell perfectly delightful stories. Clara and I used to sit on each arm of his chair and listen while he told us stories about the pictures on the wall" (quoted in Neider, *Papa: An Intimate Biography of Mark Twain* 203). Clemens then regaled his audience (consisting of Hobby, Paine, and Lyon) with a charming vignette about the rules and regulations the children would always impose on him before he would be permitted to tell a narrative. Thus, in the *Autobiography,* Clemens was again utilizing a female child's creativity as the impetus for his own text. And by incorporating Susy's biography into his work, Clemens made her live again — if only in his writing. Susy's biography had thus become her legacy to her father.

Clemens extended his dependence on Susy's writing by publishing chapters of the *Autobiography* (the chapters in which he had incorporated Susy's biography) in twenty-five installments in *The North American Review* in 1906 and 1907. Although initially Clemens planned that the *Autobiography* would not be published in his lifetime, he eventually submitted these extracts for print. This was the public's introduction to Clemens's *Autobiography,* and, with the work's mixture of Susy's contributions and his own, Clemens was confident of the *Autobiography*'s literary and commercial success.

In my view, Clemens's incorporation of Susy's biography into his own work emerges as a frustrated attempt to revive his charmed circle.[4] In the past, Susy's comments and feedback had enabled Clemens to create his finest works of fiction, and within his autobiography he attempted to work the same magic. In effect, Clemens was trying simultaneously to resurrect his deceased daughter and his fiction-writing ability. This act of weaving his daughter's ideas and comments into his writing can be seen as an extension of the stories Clemens created about the *objets d'art* on his mantelpiece.

While ostensibly the *Autobiography* was meant to relate as factually as possible the details of Clemens's life, Clemens himself admitted that the "truth" meant very little to him. As Kiskis comments,

> Mark Twain's goal was not history. Except for dates of singular importance, such as Susy's, Livy's, and Jean's deaths, accurate dates and precise times eventually held little interest for him within the context of his life's story. The autobiography was rarely, if ever, meant to be a source for historical research and Mark Twain was rarely, if ever, interested in providing an unimpeachable record of his life. . . . Neatly ordered and learnable, static and impersonal history was alien to his idea for his autobiography. (47)

Kiskis observes that Clemens's method in writing his autobiography was childlike, because of its "freedom from the order of chronological time and its dismissal of logical connection" (5). Clemens was far more concerned with delving into the rosy, beloved past, while simultaneously endeavoring to regain his fictional prowess. In explaining his philosophy for composing an autobiography, Clemens advised that it was best to begin "at no particular time in your life; wander at your free will all over your life; talk only about the thing which interests you for the moment; drop it the moment its interest threatens to pale" (*The Autobiography of Mark Twain* 193).

Clearly Clemens was doing more than merely reminiscing in the *Autobiography;* he was trying to regenerate the creative ferment of his earlier period and match the greatness of his past writing.[5] There was a purpose to this kind of seeming disorderliness: Clemens required the free ebb and flow of ideas because ultimately these random thoughts might coalesce and form the impetus for his fiction-writing. Using Susy's biography was just one of the ways in which Clemens attempted to recreate the charmed circle. For the remainder of his life, Clemens obsessively tried to replace what had been taken from him.

Redrawing the Circle

After Olivia's death, Isabel Lyon assumed an increasingly larger role within the family. Before he dismissed her in 1909, Clemens had given Lyon the power to organize his household, regulate his finances, edit his writing, and oversee the lives of Clara and Jean. Lyon was also kept busy as Clemens's social secretary, sending letters in his name and deciding just who would have access to her "King." In addition, Lyon managed the construction and interior decoration of Clemens's Redding, Connecticut, residence (named "Stormfield," appropriately enough, by Clara), a task which ultimately proved to be her downfall. Upon being informed by Clara of some purported embezzlement by Lyon, Clemens angrily dismissed her.[6]

While Lyon was with Clemens she functioned as a replacement of sorts for Olivia, but this arrangement was doomed. One critic has noted that the lack of a more intimate relationship between the two was lamentable, but it appears that there was really no possibility of the two becoming closer companions.[7] While Lyon was successful for a time in supplying Clemens with needed companionship, she was a failure at providing a critical audience for Clemens's fiction. Clemens informed her (and Lyon repeated in her daily reminder) that "for himself there are only Mr. Howells and Mr. Aldrich, and he [told] . . . me that he hasn't had much of a literary friendship with me, and he hasn't" (July 4, 1905, Daily Reminder, vol. 2, MTP). Indeed it is debatable whether, by this time, Clemens could have received useful feedback from any woman.

Pragmatically speaking, the social status Clemens had achieved was too great for him to enter into an ultimate relationship with a social inferior, and his veneration of Olivia and the sentiments of his daughters combined with class-prejudice to keep him from any possible liaison. In fact, the most likely explanation for Clara's ending Clemens and Lyon's relationship was that it was beginning to resemble, much too closely for her comfort, a type of permanent union.

Clara was probably accurate in her suspicions regarding Lyon's intentions. Indeed, early in Lyon's tenure in the Clemens's household, Clara gave her a thinly veiled warning, but Lyon failed to heed her advice. On July 27, 1905, approximately seven weeks after Olivia's death, Lyon recorded the following odd exchange with Clara:

> Santissima [Lyon's pet name for Clara] has given me a creed. No — a watchword, "Never take anything for granted." Kipling has given me another in his story "An Habitation Enforced," or rather he has forcefully put into two words what I say often to myself in many words — "Wayte A. Whyle." It's the only true way to live. When you're lying at night with weary wakeful eyes waiting for the dawn just say "Wayte A. Whyle." (Daily Reminder, vol. 2, MTP)

Evidently in October of that year, Clara repeated her warning: " 'Never take anything for granted —' A pretty good watch word, and when [Clara] reminded me that it *was* a good one, she didn't know that I'd learned it when I was a . . . 'Freshman.' . . . I'm nothing but a rusty 'Soph' now" (Oct. 17, Daily Reminder, vol. 2, MTP).

Lyon's greatest period of control came when Stormfield was being built. At the time she was in charge of handling large sums of money and was also involved in deciding which personal family papers Clemens's biographer, Albert Bigelow Paine, would be allowed to view. (Paine would later seek revenge for Lyon's limiting his access by accusing her of drug and alcohol abuse.) Yet her power proved ephemeral, and ultimately Lyon's possessiveness of Clemens contributed to her downfall. Apparently, Clara began to resent Lyon's intrusions into her personal life and disliked how decisions were being made without her consultation.

There had been periodic reports in the press about the nature of Clemens and Lyon's relationship. While on vacation with Clara in Nova Scotia, Lyon fielded reporters' queries and recorded the exchange in her 1907 daily reminder:

> another reporter — from the *Halifax Herald* too, but he really wanted to see me [not Clara], for a telegram had come from the *N.Y. Herald* linking the name of

the King with that of his secretary. I told him the King would be as pained as his secretary to hear of any such report. (July 1, MTP)

Lyon denied all rumors to the press, although she finally did seek shelter from speculation and married, but not Clemens. Instead, she married Ralph W. Ashcroft, Clemens's business manager. In a 1950 interview, Lyon claimed that she had never loved Ashcroft, and that the only reason she married him was so she could squelch rumors that she was Clemens's mistress. Lyon claimed that Clemens became upset when she told him of her plan: "He was still very angry (and never really forgave her) but said he would come [to the wedding]" (Webster Interview, Jan. 5, 1950, MTP). Lyon and Ashcroft married on March 18, 1909, in New York City with Clemens in attendance. Shortly thereafter, Clemens gave Lyon this cryptic warning: "remember, whatever I do is because of a promise I have made to Clara" (Webster Interview, Jan. 5, 1950, MTP). Evidently Clemens's promise meant destroying Lyon.

Clara had managed to set off what had always been Clemens's flash point — money — and accused Lyon of embezzlement. Clemens very likely was unconvinced by Clara's claims; however, unfortunately for Lyon, she became the unwitting lamb sacrificed to assuage Clemens's overwhelming sense of guilt about neglecting his daughters. Lyon's inconsistencies with record keeping gave Clara her chance, and, encouraged by his daughters, who were only too glad to rid themselves of someone whom they viewed as their mother's usurper, Clemens would make the most of it. Clemens finally dismissed Lyon on April 15, 1909, yet his vindictiveness did not end with her leaving. After cutting off her salary, Clemens repossessed the cottage he had given her on the Redding property (named the "Lobster Pot"), placed an attachment on her family's property in Farmington, and then tried to ruin her reputation and standing in the community. The scandal became public, and for a time charges and counter-charges appeared on the front pages of New York newspapers.

Clemens's reaction to the revelations of Lyon's purported misconduct, recorded in the "Ashcroft-Lyon Manuscript," strangely resemble those of a lover scorned. In the manuscript, written over a period of six months (May 2 to October 21, 1909), Clemens charged Lyon with drunkenness, thievery, and licentiousness. Clemens claimed that Lyon had attempted to seduce him; however, he was quick to reassure William Dean Howells, to whom the manuscript was addressed, that he had refused to succumb to her wiles:

And dear, dear, what a luxurious mandicant [sic] she was! She would get herself up in sensuous oriental silken flimseys of dainty dyes, & stretch herself out on her bepillowed lounge in her bedroom, in studied enticing attitudes, with an arm under her head & a cigarette between her lips, & imagine herself the Star of the Harem waiting for the eunuchs to fetch the Sultan & there she would lie by the hour enjoying the imaginary probabilities. ("Ashcroft-Lyon Manuscript," n.p., MTP*)[8]

These allegations would be almost laughable if the situation were not so harmful for both Clemens and Lyon. The "Ashcroft-Lyon Manuscript" is indeed an odd document. As a letter to Howells, it was rendered moot since it was never sent; as a legal document, it is ineffectual. In the manuscript, Clemens entertained the idea that his household machinations might serve as fodder for his return to fiction-writing. Clemens crowed to Howells about his domestic drama:

Doesn't it sound like print? Isn't it exactly the way it would happen in a book? Howells, this whole great long Lyon-Ashcroft episode is just as booky as it can be; so booky that sometimes its facts & realities seem . . . as if they hadn't ever happened, but had straggled into my half-asleep consciousness out of some . . . old-time novel of that hallowed ancient day when . . . when . . . well, you see, yourself, how dam [sic] *stagey* the whole thing is! ("Ashcroft-Lyon Manuscript," 54½, No. 34, MTP*)

One cannot help but wonder what Clemens meant by "when" — perhaps those bygone days when he could write extended works of fiction.

Clemens rambles on in the lengthy "Ashcroft-Lyon Manuscript," and the reader is finally struck by how terribly petty he sounds. The manuscript is also consistently contradictory, and for every accusation there is an admission of guilt by Clemens. In his defense of Clara's actions, Clemens finally condemns her. Supposedly when he was first informed by Clara of Ashcroft and Lyon's suspected duplicity, Clemens wrote back to Clara and insisted "that her [Clara's] mind had been poisoned by prejudiced people; that I knew this couple better than I knew anybody else in the world" (19, No. 34, MTP*).

The most unfair accusation leveled by Clemens was that Lyon had deliberately kept Jean away from home, in sanatoriums, because she wanted Clemens all to herself. But evidence suggests that this was a fabrication on Clemens's or Clara's part. In her 1907 diary, Jean duly records Clemens's infrequent visits. On September 30, after writing to her father of her unhappiness at a sanatorium in Katonah, New York, she bitterly noted her father's response to her entreaty: "No word of regret about my unhappiness [sic] nothing. Then a lot of *stuff* about the maids. . . . A truly sympathetic Father" (1907 Diary, HL).

By this time Jean had been away from home eleven months, and she felt as though both her father and her sister had forgotten her. On her twenty-seventh birthday, while at Katonah, a despondent Jean wrote, "I can't help feeling that my immediate family let the day go utterly" (1907 Diary, July 26, 1907, HL). Clemens heightened Jean's feelings of alienation by constantly complaining about her expenses. To Jean's indignation, Clemens begrudged the extra sixteen dollars it cost to board her dog. (This was the same year Clemens sailed to England to accept his honorary degree from Oxford and Clara and Isabel Lyon vacationed in Nova Scotia so that Clara could recuperate from her singing tour.) On August 12, 1907, when Clemens came to discuss this additional expense with Jean, he told her that he "tho't the dog of no value—no dog had even been of value that he had known. He ought to be destroyed." Jean "squelched the idea" by retorting that "Prosper [le Gai]" had been one of Olivia's last gifts to her (1907 Diary, HL). By November of that year, the rift between Clemens and his youngest daughter had become so wide that Jean failed to recognize his distinctive drawl in a telephone exchange:

> I telephoned home & after Clara spoke a moment, she said: "wait a minute, some one wants to speak to you." In an instant, a deep voice said "Do you know me Jean?" I was puzzled. I knew the voice, but I couldn't place it. I answered, in a queer tone: "I know your voice but I don't know who it belongs to." Then he said: "Some one who plays the piano." And I "Is it *you*, Mark?!" "That's right" & there he went on to say very cordially he wished he could see me. I *wish* a meeting could be arranged. (Nov. 3, 1907, 1907 Diary, HL)

What a curious passage this is. It is highly unlikely that Jean could not have known her father's voice; what is also odd is that Jean asked if this were "Mark" with whom she was speaking. In the rest of her diary, Jean refers to Clemens as "Father." She replaces "Father" with "Mark" only in this singular instance. One possible explanation is that by this time Clemens was no longer the father Jean knew from the past; he had become what Jean preferred not to recognize, his persona, Mark Twain. Jean was sensitive enough to know that it was a relief to her family to have her safely ensconced in suitable sanitariums, and she summed up the tragic state of her familial relations in her diary:

9. Clemens with Prosper le Gai. (Courtesy of the Mark Twain Memorial, Hartford, Conn.)

> While I know that neither one of them would admit being glad to have me
> away & therefore relived of the presence of an ill person, I am sure that they
> must feel so. . . . I am sure [Clemens] is fond of me but I don't believe that he
> any more than Clara, really misses me. . . . I don't really miss either of them.
> (Jan. 14, 1907, 1906–1907 Diary, HL)

After reading the Ashcroft-Lyon manuscript in its monotonous entirety,
one can only conclude that Clemens, in composing it, was attempting to
reconcile with his daughters. By ousting Lyon, Clemens tried to prove to
Clara and Jean that he still loved them.

What Lyon had done best was to serve as Clemens's sympathetic but
platonic companion. By accusing Lyon of treachery, Clara ultimately condemned her father to spending the rest of his life alone, pathetically search-
ing for comparable companionship. Indeed, the last section of Paine's *Mark
Twain's Letters* as well as the second volume of the *Mark Twain-Howells
Letters* provide an image of a lonely Clemens repeatedly asking friends to
visit him at Redding—Clara was certainly not willing to devote herself to
keeping her father company. (The confrontation between Clara and Lyon
turned out to be fortunate for Jean, because Lyon's banishment meant her
reinstatement to her father's home. Lyon was dismissed on April 15, 1909,
and Jean returned to Redding on April 26, 1909—the closeness of the dates
is no small coincidence.)

Ultimately, Lyon was just one of the links in the circle Clemens was
trying so desperately to reforge. Another link Clemens sought to reinstate
was that of his audience of children. To that end, he filled what he termed
"the Aquarium" with "Angelfish," a club made up of a coterie of young girls
between the ages of eleven and seventeen. Clemens selected approximately
sixteen girls as members of "the Aquarium." Hamlin Hill has charged that
Clemens's search for the lost childhood of his daughters was an exercise in
"latent sexuality" and, although Hill recognizes the possibility that these
children functioned merely as surrogate daughters, he more than hinted
that Clemens's interest was implicitly sexual, and that Clemens eventually
acted on his sexual interests (*Mark Twain: God's Fool,* xxvii).[9] Hill views
Clemens's fascination with prepubescent girls as an unhealthy obsession.

Aside from Clemens's affectionate letters to the girls, Hill's sole proof
of any impropriety on Clemens's part is a letter sent to Paine by Julian
Street. Street reported that a former employee of Robert Collier (of *Collier's
Magazine*) knew "something very terrible that happened in Bermuda
shortly before M.T.'s death. . . . It is something unprintable" (Hill 261).
Further examination of the letter makes it apparent that Hill too readily

reads into this ambiguous reference a substantive statement: First, Street remarks that the former employee, Albert Lee, was "beheaded by Mr. Collier some time since"; thus it is possible that Lee might have held a grudge against his former employer. Second, Street writes that Lee never actually told him this supposedly horrific tale; instead Lee wrote Street a letter stating that he would write about the incident in a second letter (of which there is no record). At the close of the section dealing with Lee, Street remarks, "I cannot imagine what it is, but think it something unprintable, from what Lee wrote. He says he will write it for me. So you see I *am* getting on" (Jan. 2, 1912, MTP). From the body of the letter, it appears that Street is preparing a personal scrapbook on Clemens, for he tells Paine he has already received a letter from Howells, and he is waiting for responses to letters he sent to Colonel Harvey, Robert Collier, and Joseph Twitchell. From this vague evidence, Hill surmises that the young Helen Allen was the victim of Clemens's improper behavior.

John Cooley, in his 1991 edition of the "Angelfish" letters, has greatly furthered our understanding of Clemens's relationship with these young girls. Thanks to Cooley's work, one can finally read the extant correspondence between Clemens and his Angelfish, instead of the bits and pieces that have been excerpted in various articles. In an autobiographical dictation dated April 17, 1909, Clemens discusses the genesis of the Angelfish. According to Clemens, after Olivia's death he became terribly lonely and believed he was now bereft of family. His daughters had retreated from him into their own lives, and he was left alone. As Clemens convincingly if hyperbolically recounts,

> I was washing about on a forlorn sea of banquets and speechmaking in high and holy causes — industries which furnished me intellectual cheer and entertainment, but got at my heart for an evening only, then let it dry and dusty. I had reached the grandpapa stage of life; and what I lacked and what I needed, was grandchildren, but I didn't know it. . . . My heart has never been empty of grandchildren since. No, it is a treasure-palace of little people whom I worship, and whose degraded and willing slave I am. In grandchildren I am the richest man that lives to-day: for I *select* my grandchildren, whereas all other grandfathers have to take them as they come, good, bad and indifferent. (No. 69, MTP*)

I would offer a less sensational interpretation of Clemens's fascination with young girls than Hill's allegations. It appears that Clemens's meetings and correspondence with his bevy of Angelfish were an attempt to form another chorus of substitute daughters for whom he could spin tales.

Ideally, Clemens could then go and write his fiction and return to read his efforts aloud to them, reenacting those halcyon days of Quarry Farm and Farmington Avenue. Cooley offers the thought that Clemens may have been trying to relive his youth: "His Angelfish behavior was certainly unusual, even obsessive, but it was also the final expression of a lifelong love affair with his teenage years" (282). Whatever Clemens's reasons for establishing the Angelfish, sexuality, latent or active, was probably not prominent among them.[10]

Clemens's attempt to recreate his family circle was futile, and he was reduced to cajoling and flattering in order to gain a few moments of attention from others. Years later, one of the Angelfish, Carlotta Welles, who had made Clemens's acquaintance on board a ship traveling to England, remembered: "I used to get restless and chafed at times at being expected to sit quietly with him when my inclination was to race around." At time, Welles purposely avoided Clemens's smothering attentions: "I remember that on one of our last days on board, I failed to show up in his stateroom where he had invited our whole party to hear him read. . . . (We had had one or two readings already)." Welles was perceptive enough to realize that she was in a sense functioning as a Susy replacement: "I felt, in Mr. Clemens's attitude toward me, something tender and very sad. He talked quite a bit about 'Susy.'" Apparently there was even a passing physical resemblance between the two: "A gentleman in Paris who had known the Clemens family told me, about a year later, that I looked somewhat like Susy, and that may have explained why he seemed to cling to me as he did." This was not the only similarity between the two girls; Welles was returning to France after having attended boarding school at the "Baldwin School in Bryn Mawr where I had spent that year" (Briggs, November 4, 1947, MTP*).

It was children's honesty that had always attracted Clemens, and now this capacity was proving to be his sorrow. These girls did not want to spend their time having to be quiet in the company of an old man in ill health and often ill temper. Clemens held no particular attraction for many of them; instead, he was simply an adult for whom they had to behave. (And it can be supposed that considerable parental pressure would have persuaded these girls to be cordial to the eminent Samuel L. Clemens.) Clemens, no longer the beloved patriarch of a close-knit family, was a lonely, aged, cantankerous celebrity. By the time the Angelfish were old enough to appreciate and understand Clemens's importance, Clemens had no need for them — they had been lost to young adulthood.

There were, however, a few girls among the Angelfish who would form lasting bonds with Clemens and who, unlike Carlotta Welles, would allow themselves to be joyfully singled out by Clemens as his "Susy surrogates." Dorothy Quick was one of these. Of all the Angelfish, she was one with whom Clemens had one of his closest relationships. Over a period of three years, Clemens would write seventy letters to her, the last one sent the day he died.

In the youthful Quick, Clemens doubtlessly saw his precious Susy. Dark-haired and brown-eyed, Quick had aspirations to be a writer, a goal Clemens greatly encouraged. A particularly telling incident, which Quick related in her memoir, *Enchantment: A Little Girl's Friendship with Mark Twain,* occurred one afternoon while Quick was visiting and Clemens happened upon her while she was listening to Clara sing. Informed by Quick that she wished to be a singer like Clara, Clemens angrily responded that she would be a "writer" and that the matter was settled.

A second Susy substitute was Mary Rogers, Henry H. Rogers's daughter-in-law. Mary was young, wild, and intelligent; Clemens greatly admired her and sent her scores of letters. All but one of the letters were written during the last four years of Clemens's life. In the fall of 1907, Clemens wrote Mary a teasing note pleading for a little "butter," his name for affection.

Butter Wanted
Any Kind:
New; Old;
Salted; Unsalted;
Odorless; Fragrant;
Real preferred, but
Oleomargarine not turned away.
Apply at the old stand,
21 Fifth Ave.,
at the
Sign of the Butterfly. (*Mark Twain's Letters to Mary* 106–7)

On September 9, 1906, Mary wrote him a teasing note about his enormous need for affection: "Your abnormal hunger for Butter is perfectly shocking! 'I'm perishing for Butter —' you write" (*Mark Twain's Letters to Mary* 56). In a dictation on May 19, 1907, Clemens candidly admitted his need for affection: "I like compliments, praises, flatteries; I cordially enjoy all such things, and am grieved and disappointed when what I call a 'barren mail' arrives — a mail that hasn't any compliments in it" (No. 68, MTP*).

These letters to Mary are reminiscent of the exchanges between Susy and Clemens. Clemens had regarded Susy as his confidante, and now Mary stepped in to fill that role. Indeed, Clemens occasionally complained to Mary about the indifferent treatment he claimed he had suffered at Clara's hands. In a letter dated September 21, 1906, Clemens made an illuminating comment, which he quickly covered with a joke, betraying the strained relationship he was having with his daughters:

> When I was taking leave of Clara I asked her to let me lead her out before her audience. She said, no — "You'll get all the welcome, and I none." But on the way to the station she told Katy she had changed her mind and she would like to be led out by her father! Mariechen, it's butter from the butterless! and very gratifying. Next, there'll be butter from Jean — yes, and even from you; I am not despairing. (*Mark Twain's Letters to Mary* 62–63)

But despairing Clemens unquestionably was. During her father's last years, Clara acted more as an impersonal guest than as a dutiful daughter. Frequently absent, either for singing engagements or prolonged stays in sanatoriums due to poor health, Clara would sweep in for occasional abbreviated visits. Lyon made a remark concerning an exchange between Clara and Clemens in a daily reminder entry dated March 24, 1906:

> This is the wretched day when Mr. Clemens went down to the living room, and there wasn't anyone there. For a half hour he waited for a human being, and none came to stay. C.C. [Clara] looked in upon him as she passed out of the house, and then a blast of cold & bedevilled loneliness swept over him and made him hate his life. C.C. was late for luncheon, and Mr. Clemens loathed the meal. He dropped his 2 hard water biscuits with a bang on the mahogany table, in a cursing wave of bitterness. These are the agony days when he knows Mrs. Clemens is gone. (1906 Daily Reminder, Original Copy, MTP)

Just as abruptly as she arrived, Clara would leave to return to her friends and the life she was attempting to create apart from her father. According to Lyon, Clemens confided in her that "he didn't get much good out of Clara. When she is in N.Y. he never sees anything of her and when he goes to her rooms he feels like a stranger making an untimely and unwelcome visit" (Sep. 1, 1907 Daily Reminder, MTP). Throughout her journals, Lyon would document Clemens's arrivals and Clara's immediate departures; this pattern was not to be broken for the remainder of Clemens's life.

By the time Clemens was installed in his Redding, Connecticut, home his ersatz charmed circle was eerily complete.[11] Stormfield itself appears to be an attempted replication of the "charmed circle" days, for Clemens's treatment of it was reminiscent of that time long ago, when, after embarking on his honeymoon with Olivia, he discovered that what he thought was a prohibitively expensive boarding house was actually to be their new home. He refused to have any participation in Stormfield's planning and construction, wanting it instead to be a surprise to him. In *Mark Twain: A Biography,* Paine described at length the scene when Clemens was shown his new home:

> [Clemens] was taken through the rooms; the great living-room at one end of the hall . . . and at the other end of the hall, the splendid, glowing billiard-room, where hung all the ["Angelfish"] pictures in which he took delight. . . . When he had seen it all. . . . He said, as a final verdict: "It is a perfect house — perfect, so far as I can see, in every detail." (1,450)[12]

Indeed it was so perfect in every detail that, following Clemens's instructions, the mantel from the Hartford home was installed in the living room, and the carriage Jervis Langdon gave the young couple on their wedding day was housed under the porte cochere. The only presence missing on Clemens's first night in his new house, Paine noted, was that of his daughters. Bereft of family members, Clemens was left to celebrate with acquaintances and hired employees. Most poignant is a photograph in Paine's biography showing Clemens on the terrace of Stormfield playing cards with three young girls. The photograph is captioned "The First Week in Redding, 1908" (1,454). Inside the house, Lyon waited. Stormfield also hosted a continual stream of guests, which for Clemens must have been reminiscent of the distinguished visitors and elegant meals served at Farmington Avenue.

In Redding, Clemens also tried to create an atmosphere of support for literary endeavors. He founded and was chosen president of the town's first lending library, which served as a tribute to the library his father began in Hannibal, the Young Men's Christian Association's library to which Jervis Langdon contributed five hundred dollars in 1868, and the library the Langdon family donated funds and books to in Thomas Beecher's Park Church in 1875. Clemens also made his return to lecturing at a benefit for his library, resurrecting what he told Howells was the "same old string of yarns" (*Mark Twain-Howells Letters* 838). Paine elected to overlook Clemens's blunt admission about the quality of his material, and instead viewed the lecture and library as an "important benefit . . . conferred upon the community, and there was a feeling that Redding, besides having a literary

10. Clemens playing cards at Stormfield, 1908. (Courtesy of The Mark Twain Project, The Bancroft Library)

colony, was to be literary in fact" (1,473). In making this statement Paine was exhibiting either extraordinary kindness or overt self-interest. Paine's benefactor hoped that a literary colony at Redding would resemble the one that existed so long ago at Nook Farm.

The "Real" Mark Twain

Clemens had succeeded in fashioning a duplicate of his charmed circle, but it was only a façade; the happiest days and most productive times of his life were over, and on a deeper level — not always consciously — Clemens knew it. For the rest of his life, Clemens was condemned to try to recreate the past. What he managed to construct with Isabel Lyon and the Angelfish was only a poor imitation. Clemens was tragically morose, and his bitterness arose from his keen awareness that his efforts to bring back the earlier days were doomed to frustration. Instead of confronting the agony of his present, Clemens deliberately chose, as Paine delicately phrased it,

> [to] retreat from the actualities of life. Dwelling mainly among his philosophies and speculations, he observed vaguely, or minutely, what went on about him; but in either case the fact took a place, not in the actual world, but in a world within his consciousness, or subconsciousness, a place where facts were likely to assume new and altogether different relations from those they had borne in the physical occurrence. . . . Insubstantial and deceptive as was this inner world of his, to him it must have been much more real than the world of flitting physical shapes about him. (*Mark Twain: A Biography* 1,519–20)

Isabel Lyon also noted this change in Clemens in her daily reminder: "His [Clemens's] moods have been quite at variance with his former self. He is none the less great, but he is living in a world apart" (June 16, 1906, Daily Reminder, MTP). Clemens had no desire to see his existence as it really was. To avoid this, he created his own reality, one that was far more congenial — at Stormfield he could again return to the peaceful days of Quarry Farm.

Along with trying more and more to reclaim the past, Clemens strategized to attract the attention he so desperately craved, often allowing his "Mark Twain" persona to dominate — hence, in part, the donning of the white suit. Whether it was to infuriate Mrs. Aldrich or to trumpet the presence of Mark Twain, Clemens was very much aware of the power of the image.[13] Contrary to what some critics have believed, Clemens always possessed an integrated self-awareness. The adoption of the Twain persona was a strategy, not a symptom, and, in the six years before his death, Clemens relied on his persona to alleviate his loneliness and to provide him, in the guise of adulation, what he had received earlier in the form of familial love. Yet Clemens always remained aware of this, as can be seen in his overwhelming bitterness toward the world. He was bitter because he had to resort to such tactics in order to receive the affection he needed. Clemens was acutely aware of what had befallen him; and the awareness only intensified his pain, because he knew that he had become what he, Olivia, and Susy had always feared — the caricature of a humorist.

The transition from writer to figurehead was facilitated by the fact that so many of Clemens's contemporaries, namely, all of Clemens's siblings and most of his oldest friends, had predeceased him: Ward Cheney, Thomas Beecher, Theodore Crane, Zebulon R. Brockway, Mary Fairbanks, Charles Dudley Warner, Sir Henry Stanley, Julia Jones Beecher, Joe Jefferson, Patrick McAleer, Isabella Beecher Hooker, Thomas Bailey Aldrich, Sam Moffet, Mary E. (Mollie) Clemens, Silas Gleason, Grover Cleveland, Edmund Clarence Stedman, Henry Rogers, Murat Halstead, Edward Everett Hale, Rachael Brooks Gleason, Richard Watson Gilder, and William M. Laffan. As time passed, fewer and fewer people remembered the person Clemens; those who remained were familiar only with Mark Twain. Significantly, both Paine and Lyon had become acquainted with Clemens after the end of his successful fiction-writing days and at the beginning of his career as "American Spokesman." Lyon had been hired by Olivia as a personal secretary in the summer of 1902. Clemens's last work of note was the travelogue *Following the Equator,* published in 1897. Paine met Clemens at his seventieth birthday party, held December 5, 1905, at Delmonico's where Clemens was heralded by America's most eminent literati. Paine beheld a "Mark Twain" applauded by dozens of cheering admirers. (Among those in attendance at the banquet were authors Willa Cather, Mary E. Wilkins Freeman, Kate Douglas Riggs, William Dean Howells, Carolyn Wells, Richard Watson Gilder, and Elizabeth Jordan.)[14] After such a sensational introduction to Clemens, Paine, perhaps inevitably, was not predisposed to discover any dark revelations concerning his subject.

The persona was fairly easy for Clemens to uphold. Clara and Jean were practically the only people left who intimately knew and remembered the middle age of the man Samuel Clemens, but they had been rejected and replaced, and Clara ultimately also supported the "Mark Twain" persona. Two close friends of Clemens who knew him before 1900, William Dana

Orcutt and William Dean Howells, readily recognized Clemens's habit of playing up "Mark Twain," though they seemed powerless to change the situation. Orcutt recalled that he had

> learned to recognize the signs when he [Clemens] felt that people around him expected him to be humorous. Then he would assume a professional attitude, and good-naturedly give them what they wanted; but his efforts lacked that spontaneous expression which came from his instinctive approach to any given situation. (141)

Indeed, Clemens's efforts to give the public what he thought it wanted were far from impromptu. This was apparent to Howells, who, upon receiving Clemens's invitation for a lecture to benefit the town library in front of "100 of the sterlingest farmers and their families encounterable anywhere," perceptively responded: "I should like mightily to meet your farmers, but, poor fellow, I thought you went to Redding to get rid of Mark Twain" (*Mark Twain-Howells Letters* 838–39). Howells declined to state openly the fact that Mark Twain was basically all that Clemens had left from his earlier existence.

Critics have noted a wide discrepancy between the "real" Clemens and the image of him as depicted by Clara and Paine.[15] Hamlin Hill, in the introduction to his biography, states his premise that Paine

> was also the officially chosen guardian of an image which Clara Clemens . . . believed the public expected of Mark Twain. Exactly the extent to which Clara, and Paine, nourished that image for material advantage, or the extent to which they both believed in it, is irrelevant here. Whatever their reasons, they managed to impart a representation of Mark Twain, "the Belle of New York," the beautiful aging spokesman for the oppressed, the "King" of a devoted family and world, the playlike cynic whose twinkling eye betrayed his warm underlying sympathy and essential humanity. (xv–xvi)

The extent to which Paine and particularly Clara believed in the "image" of Mark Twain *is* actually quite relevant. Without an understanding of the underlying motivation for their "whitewashing" of Clemens, an accurate picture of Clemens's last decade cannot emerge. For by the end of his life, the persona Mark Twain was the only acceptable side of Clemens's character that remained to him. He was no longer husband or father — he was primarily a celebrity, and the personal side of Clemens was anathema to those closest to him. Clara wanted to remember solely the positive aspects of her father. In the last ten years of his life, the father she had known while growing up had rejected her; it is thus understandable that Clara would choose to ignore the antagonism of his last decade and instead direct attention to his beloved public side.

As for Paine, the only Clemens he had ever known was that of the personage, "the King," not the man. Paine also may have been influenced by Isabel Lyon's expressions of intense devotion toward Clemens, and by Clara, who, still wounded by her father's treatment, discouraged Paine from focusing on the negative by threatening to limit his access to primary materials. Thus Paine, the biographer, focused on Mark Twain, the positive icon, rather than on Samuel Clemens, the complex man. In a letter dated January 28, 1908, Paine argued his case for full access to Clemens's personal letters to a dubious Isabel Lyon:

> Nowhere is a man's life and nature so revealed as in his letters; and it is the King's life and . . . nature that I am to preserve as well as the story of his progress. I do not care to prepare what would be a mere resemblance, or even to paint an accurate portrait of him — or a dozen of them. My purpose is to *present* the man *himself,* with all his colossal genius, his strength, and his triumphs; with all his weaknesses and his failures. . . . I have no desire to parade the things he would wish forgotten — to hold them up to the world saying, "See how weak a strong man may be," but it is *absolutely necessary* that I should know all there is to know, whatever it may be, in order that I may build a personality so impregnable that those who, in years to come, may endeavor to discredit and belittle will find themselves so forestalled at every point that the man we know . . . will remain known as *we* know him, loved and honored through all time. (MTP*)

The Mark Twain Paine describes above was all he ever knew, and the father of twenty years earlier was all Clara could bear to remember. Clara, faced with revealing the rift between her father and herself, may have chosen, as a defense, to portray the Clemens the public craved. However it should be remembered that the creation of the public Mark Twain originated not with Clara or Paine, but with Clemens, for Clemens could not deal with his dual feelings of personal and professional loss. (Louis Budd, in *Our Mark Twain: The Making of His Public Personality,* discusses the crafting and evolution of Samuel Clemens's public persona.) Clemens was not insensitive; rather, he felt so injured that he could not recover and go on with his life, choosing instead to hide his vulnerability under the facade of "Mark Twain."

It seems that Clara never recovered from this phase of denial, and in her remembrances of him a striking ambivalence emerges. For Clara, her

father had been lost to her a decade before he died. In 1937, after the death
of her first husband, Ossip Gabrilowitsch, Clara contacted Elmira sculptor
Enfred Anderson about constructing a memorial to her spouse.[16] Anderson
suggested that she incorporate her father into her husband's memorial, and
Clara agreed. Before that time, Clara had not erected any memorial in her
father's honor, and, while all gravestones in the Langdon-Clemens plot
have inscriptions on them, Clemens's remains blank.

Anderson designed at least two models for the monument: The first
was a marker designed to be two fathoms high ("mark twain"). On top was
a bust of Clemens, with his birth name underneath, and below that was one
of Olivia in left profile, perhaps suggestive of the miniature Clemens had
glimpsed so long ago. Under Olivia's profile was her maiden name, and at
the bottom was a sculpture of a kneeling Huckleberry Finn. The other
monument Anderson designed was again two fathoms high, with Clemens
in right profile and his pseudonym below, and underneath that Ossip
Gabrilowitsch in right profile with his birth name underneath. At the
bottom was inscribed:

Death is the starlit strip between the
companionship of yesterday and the
reunion of tomorrow. To the loving
memory of my father and my husband.
CCG [Clara Clemens Gabrilowitsch] 1937

Significantly, Clara chose the latter monument, and in doing so, she made
the statement that the person she wished to memorialize was the public
Mark Twain, and not her father. A kinder memorial of imitation was the
small study Clara had built on her Hollywood property. Set approximately
three hundred yards away from the house, Italianate in style, was a small
structure, tucked into the hillside overlooking the Los Angeles basin. This
memorial—on a more human scale—was supposedly a place where Clara
retreated to write.

Unfortunately, the repercussions of Clemens's treatment of Clara continued in her relationship with her own daughter. Nina Clemens Gabrilowitsch was born on August 18, 1910, four months after Clemens's death on
April 21, 1910; her father, Ossip Gabrilowitsch, was internationally famous
as a pianist and conductor. Reared primarily by nannies, Nina was in her
teens before her mother informed her of her grandfather's identity.[17] Nina
was a beautiful little girl who grew up without much sense of purpose. By
the time Nina grew to adulthood she suffered from drug and alcohol

addiction and mental illness. For a time she was a patient at the California State Psychiatric Hospital in Camarillo. Clara, unable to deal with the severity of her daughter's medical and mental problems, entrusted her faithful secretary, Phyllis Harrington, with Nina's care. By the end of Clara's life, daughter and mother were irreconcilably estranged. Nina committed suicide in 1966 in a hotel room off Sunset Boulevard in Hollywood, California, four years after her mother's death.

Notes

1. This information appears in Isabel Lyon's 1903–6 Journal (MTP).
2. In *The Authentic Mark Twain: A Literary Biography of Samuel L. Clemens,* Everett Emerson provides a record of the dates when Clemens dictated his autobiography:

> Beginning with twelve dictations in January [1906], Mark Twain continued for three years. Until June in the first year, there were each month from seven to seventeen sessions; then there was a short break. . . .
> After another break in late June and July, he continued throughout 1906, when a total of 134 dictations were recorded. In 1907 as interest cooled there were fewer, seventy in all, with only four during November and December. In 1908 there were just thirty-four. The last dictations were made in early 1909, the very last being dated April 16. Dictations averaged about 1,500 words each, making the total (including undated dictations) about 450,000 words, to which should be added some 60,000 words written or dictated before 1906. (262)

3. Susy stopped writing her biography when she was fourteen. The last entry is dated July 4, 1886. Clemens states in his "Memorial" to Susy that she made her last entry "in Paris two years ago when she was twenty-two," although no such entry is extant ("Memorial to Olivia Susan Clemens," 39).
4. Charles Neider suggests that the combining of Susy's and Clemens's writing bespoke a "wonderful relationship, a sort of love affair, between a father and daughter," and that upon reading the sections where Susy is quoted, one "sense[s] that the book may be larger than an intimate portrait of the two chief actors, that just possibly it's an unusual . . . portrait of other father-daughter relationships" (*Papa: An Intimate Biography of Mark Twain* 6).
5. In contrast, Neider sees Clemens's method of writing for the autobiography simply as an effort to keep boredom at bay: "Mark Twain was trying to amuse himself: that was his chief aim during the dictations. . . . He had produced his share of work in the world. . . . And so he reminisced, and by so doing he amused himself — reminisced on his own terms, not on the world's, not according to some theory of autobiographical composition" (*Papa: An Intimate Biography of Mark Twain* xv).

6. Hamlin Hill gives an extensive and valuable account of the events leading to Lyon's dismissal and the subsequent legal wrangling on both sides in his *Mark Twain: God's Fool.*

7. Laurie Lentz, in her article, "Mark Twain in 1906: An Edition of Selected Extracts From Isabel V. Lyon's Journal" (*Resources for American Literary Study* 11 [Spring 1981]: 1–36), states that it was "regrettable that Clemens, who desperately needed a replacement for Livy, and Miss Lyon . . . maintained their professional distance" (8).

8. Apparently dressing in harem garb was a common activity in Clemens's household. Dorothy Quick recalled that, after having read a story about an Indian princess, Clemens asked her if she would like to dress as one. Dorothy replied affirmatively, and she retired with Lyon to make some prodigious preparations:

> I had a tan linen dress with heavy red embroidery about the neck and short sleeves. . . . Then a long length of mirror-embroidered material was wrapped around me for a skirt in true Balinese fashion, fastened at the waist with a jeweled girdle. My long braids were wound around my head in a very grown-up manner and fastened so that the red hair ribbons I wore on their ends made bows over each ear that looked like flaming red poppies. Then a headband that matched the jeweled girdle was put across my forehead, and rows and rows of bright colored beads were hung around my neck. Long turquoise chiffon veils were draped over all this and allowed to trail yards after me on the ground, until I looked like a veritable rani of old India. (88–89)

According to Quick, Clemens was not adverse to dressing the part of the Indian raj himself: "SLC wound a marvelous yellow scarf turban-fashion around his head and draped a large piece of Indian embroidery over his shoulders" (191).

9. This sensational accusation has been propagated in articles by Gershon Legman, "Another Side of Twain," *Bookletter* 3.8 (Dec. 1976): 11; Robert Bray, "Mark Twain Biography: Entering a New Phase," *The Midwest Quarterly* (1974): 286–301; and Emmanuel Diel, "Mark Twain's Failure: Sexual Women Characters," *San Jose Studies* 5 (Feb. 1979): 46–59.

10. Annette Ducey has researched Clemens's visits to Bermuda and his time spent with the Allen family. According to Ducey, who has read several manuscripts by Helen Allen's mother which recount Clemens's visits, she has found no evidence of any kind to support Hill's allegations. (Information from an interview with Annette Ducey on January 30, 1989.)

11. Clemens moved into his Redding residence on June 18, 1908.

12. Howells, in *My Mark Twain: Reminiscences and Criticisms,* reported that Clemens's "daughter [unspecified] has told me he loved [Stormfield] best of all his houses and hoped to make it his home for long years" (85). Clemens's allowing Lyon to take charge of Stormfield's construction was not without precedent. In the case of their Hartford home, Olivia handled the bulk of the plans for the house and its construction as Clemens was frequently absent on Redpath's lyceum circuit. Lyon remarked in her daily reminder,

Mr. Clemens refuses to discuss the [house]. He won't allow himself to be informed or consulted; he will pay the bills and that's all he will do, but when the house is finished then he will go to it. It astounds his questioning friends to hear him answer, "I don't know" to every question they ask about the house or the property. He doesn't want to see it, or hear anything about it. He leaves all the affairs now with John Howells [the architect] and me. (Apr. 9, 1907, Daily Reminder, MTP)

Jean noted this peculiarity of her father's:

The grounds in Redding consist of 210 acres, but Father doesn't know whether the building has been begun or not. He said he signed the contract yesterday, but also that he told Clara & [Lyon] to tell him nothing until the house was built & furnished. Then he would go & see it. (May 21, 1907, 1907 Diary, HL)

13. Regarding Clemens's awareness of dress, Isabel Lyon recorded this entry in her daily reminder: "The King is filled with the idea of defying conventionalities and wearing his suitable white clothing all winter, so he has bidden me order 5 new suits from his tailor" (Oct. 8, 1906, Daily Reminder, MTP).

14. A copy of Clemens's seventieth birthday party seating chart and information about Henry James's and Edith Wharton's declinations were provided in correspondence from Terry L. Gellin.

15. John S. Tuckey, in his review of Hill's biography, commented about the degree of speculation concerning this issue: "The public Clemens is not absent from Mr. Hill's pages; but there is often the suggestion that he is something of a sham, a public image built up by Albert Paine . . . and Clemens's daughter Clara" (175).

16. Information about the memorial that currently stands is from Jerome and Wisbey (160, 163). The other model for the memorial was discovered at the Elmira Historical Society, located in New York State.

17. Information regarding Nina's childhood comes from Marianne J. Curling, Curator at the Mark Twain Memorial in Hartford, Connecticut.

Epilogue

In writing this study my purpose has been threefold: First, to identify and trace the dichotomy present within Twain scholarship owing to the schools of Brooksian "dualism" and DeVotoian "integration" and their subsequent critical offshoots; second, after rejecting the dichotomous structure, to examine the social and cultural influences of the women closest to Clemens and the effect they had on his life and literature; and, third, to investigate the background and feminist influences of the one person who inarguably had the greatest effect on Clemens, his partner Olivia.

When Clemens wrote to Frederick Duneka at *Harper's Magazine* in 1902, "My wife being ill, I have been — in literary matters — helpless all these weeks. I have no editor — no censor," he was identifying a very real and, for him, frightening situation (MTP*). Various critics have erred in viewing such comments as gross exaggerations. Clemens, like Huckleberry Finn, had found his sense of self in his identity as a writer, and with the loss of his female circle, this identity, this selfhood, was threatened. Clemens accepted, in DeVoto's words, "tuition" when he came East and he possessed, as Edward Wagenknecht proclaimed, too much "vitality" to be diverted from what he deemed important. Yet the "tuition" and "vitality" to which critics have often alluded were most importantly the signals of Clemens's openness to the world of the female. Clemens realized early on that his fictional powers were enhanced — more than enhanced, empowered — by his interactions with women. As is evident from the time of his letter to Ann E. Taylor to the era of the "Angelfish," Clemens relied on female audiences for his creative inspiration. To conjure up his greatest works of fiction, Clemens abandoned the realm of the purely male and investigated — indeed ultimately incorporated — the world of the female.

Bibliography

PRIMARY WORKS CITED

Alcott, Louisa May. "Unwritten Romance." *Independent,* Dec. 18, 1873.
"An Appeal to Dealers in Intoxicating Drinks." *Elmira Advertiser,* April 4, 1874. Steele Memorial Library. Elmira, New York.
"Anna Dickinson." *Elmira Advertiser,* December 9, 1864. Steele Memorial Library. Elmira, New York.
"Annual Report of the Anchorage." Anchorage Clipping File. CCHS.
"Authoresses to the Rescue." *Independent,* December 24, 1869: 1.
Bacon, Elizabeth D. Letter to Samuel Clemens, December 26, 1909. MTP.
Beecher, Julia. Letter to Isabella Hooker, November 19, 1860. SDF.
———. Letter to Isabella Hooker, November 19, 1861. SDF.
———. Letter to Isabella Hooker, June 6, 1862. SDF.
———. Letter to Mrs. Lyman Beecher, January 21, 1869. SDF.
———. Letter to Olivia Lewis Langdon, May 5, 1870. SDF.
Beecher, Thomas Kennicut. *Jervis Langdon Eulogy Memorial Pamphlet.* August 1870. CCHS.
———. Letter to Anna Dickinson, February 9, 1864. The Anna Dickinson Papers. Library of Congress.
———. *Olivia Lewis Langdon Eulogy Memorial Pamphlet.* November 1890. CCHS.
Book review of *The Gilded Age. Independent,* January 1, 1874.
Briggs, Carlotta (Welles). Letter to Dixon Wecter, November 4, 1947. MTP.
Brockway, Zebulon R. "Home, Work and Love." *Industrial School Appeal* 1.2 (1884). CCHS.
"W.H. Burleigh." Temperance Clipping File. CCHS.
Bush, Ada Gleason. Letter to Cornell University Library, April 6, 1945. John M. Olin Library. Cornell University, Ithaca, New York.
"C." *Elmira Advertiser,* December 12, 1864. Steele Memorial Library. Elmira, New York.
Chemung County Censuses, Elmira. 1860, 1865, 1870, 1880, 1890, 1900. Steele Memorial Library. Elmira, New York.
Chronology of Clemens's Locations, ts. MTP.
Clemens, Jane Lampton. Letter to Olivia and Samuel Clemens, April 11, 1874. MTP.
Clemens, Jean Lampton. 1906–1907 Diary: December 1–February 28, 1907. HL.
———. 1907 Diary. HL.
Clemens, Mary E. (Mollie). Letter to Jane Clemens, November 26, 1872. MTP.
Clemens, Olivia Langdon. Commonplace Book, ms. DV161. MTP.

——. Letter to Lillie Devereux Blake, December 13, 1900. MHS.

——. Letter to Alice Hooker, July 29, 1867. SDF.

——. Letter to Alice Hooker, April 22, 1868. SDF.

——. Letter to Alice Hooker, September 29, 1868. SDF.

——. Letter to Alice Hooker, November 1, 1869. SDF.

——. Letter to Olivia Langdon, November 30, 1879. MTM.

Clemens, Olivia Susan ("Susy"). Letter to Grace King, n.d. John M. Coxe Private Collection. New Orleans, Louisiana.

Clemens, Samuel Langhorne. "A Family Sketch." 1906, No. 40, ms. MTP. Microfilm.

——. "Ashcroft-Lyon Manuscript." No. 34, ms. MTP. Microfilm.

——. Autobiographical Dictation, January 11, 1906. No. 64 [53], ts. MTP. Microfilm.

——. Autobiographical Dictation, February 1, 1906. No. 64 [53], ts. MTP. Microfilm.

——. Autobiographical Dictation, February 9, 1906. No. 64 [53], ts. MTP. Microfilm.

——. Autobiographical Dictation, February 13, 1906. No. 64 [53], ts. MTP. Microfilm.

——. Autobiographical Dictation, March 1, 1907. No. 68 [57], ts. MTP. Microfilm.

——. Autobiographical Dictation, May 19, 1907. No. 68 [57], ts. MTP. Microfilm.

——. Autobiographical Dictation, October 12, 1907. No. 69 [58], ts. MTP. Microfilm.

——. Autobiographical Dictation, April 17, 1908. No. 69 [58], ts. MTP. Microfilm.

——. Autobiographical Dictation, April 17, 1909. No. 69 [58], ts. MTP. Microfilm.

——. Letter to Elizabeth Jordan, March 10, 1905. New York Public Library. MTP.

——. Letter to Frederick Duneka, September 15, 1902. MTP.

——. Letter to Isabella Beecher Hooker, May 27, 1884. SDF, MTP.

——. Letter to Jean Clemens, March 22, 1893. MTP.

——. Letter to Dr. John Brown, September 4, 1879. MTP.

——. Letter to Rev. Joseph Twichell, January 19, 1897. MTP.

——. Letter to Mary E. (Mollie) Clemens, July 20–21, 1872. MTP.

——. Letter to Pamela Moffett, October 12, 1890. MTP.

——. Letter to Susan Crane, September 30, 1896. MTP.

——. Letter to Susan Crane, July 25, 1904. MTP.

——. Letter to "Susy" Clemens, March 24, 1893. MTP.

——. Letter to "Susy" Clemens, December 27, 1893. MTP.

——. "Memorial to Olivia Susan Clemens." Ms., unpublished essay. MTP.

——. Notebook No. 30 [25]: August 1890–June 1891, ms. MTP. Microfilm.

Connelly, Catharine S. "Women's Role Changed with New Frontiers." Scrapbook. Chemung County Historical Association 72.

Conway, Moncure. Review of London performance of "Bucking Horse." *Independent,* January 29, 1874.

Cooke, Rose Terry. "Now." *Independent,* January 8, 1874.

——. "Thanksgiving." *Independent,* December 4, 1873.

——. "Thanksgiving Then: Remembered for Polly." *Independent,* November 27, 1873.

——. "Willow." *Independent,* December 4, 1873.

Crane, Susan. Letter to Samuel Clemens, January 1910. MTP.

Cuyler, Rev. Theodore L. "In Christ, or Not!" *Independent,* December 31, 1868.

Dickinson, Anna. *A Ragged Register.* New York: Harper & Brothers, 1879.

——. "Route Books." Nos. 22–23 [22], ms. The Anna Dickinson Papers. Library of Congress. Microfilm.

Dickinson, Susan. Letter to Anna Dickinson, March 27, 1867. The Anna Dickinson Papers. Library of Congress.

——. Letter to Anna Dickinson, April 6, 1867. The Anna Dickinson Papers. Library of Congress.

Dodge, Augusta, ed. *Gail Hamilton's Life in Letters.* Vol. 2. Boston: Lee and Shepard, 1901.

Douglass, Frederick. Letter to Olivia Lewis Langdon, November 9, 1870. MTM.

"Drs." Advertisements from the *Elmira Advertiser,* December 1, 1864. Steele Memorial Library. Elmira, New York.

Eastman, Annis Ford. *A Flower of Puritanism: Julia Jones Beecher.* Elmira, N.Y.: n.p., n.d.

Edholm, Charlton. *Traffic in Girls and Work of Rescue Missions.* Oakland, Calif.: Sierra Printing Co., 1900.

"Elmira Bank." *Elmira Advertiser,* January 14, 1860: 5. Steele Memorial Library. Elmira, New York.

Elmira Female College Cash Book, 1856–1879, ms. Center for Mark Twain Studies, Elmira, New York.

Eskuche, Mrs. Erna. Documents File, 1901. MTP.

Facts: By a Woman. Oakland: Pacific Press Publishing House, 1881.

The Fourth Annual Catalogue and Circular of the Elmira Female College, 1858–1859. Elmira, N.Y., 1859. Center for Mark Twain Studies, Elmira, New York.

Gleason, Orsemus. Biographical and professional material obtained from a typescript of clippings collected by Ada Gleason Bush. Document nos. 14, 15, and 22, Gleason file. CCHS.

Gleason, Rachael Brooks. Biographical and professional material obtained from a typescript of clippings collected by Ada Gleason Bush. Document nos. 14, 15, and 22, Gleason file. CCHS.

Gleason, Mrs. Rachael Brooks, M.D. "Letter to Ladies." *The Herald of Health and Journal of Physical Culture* 10 (July 1867): 11–14.

——. *Talks to My Patients.* New York: Wood & Holbrook, 1870.

Gleason Water Cure. Information about the Gleason Water Cure and patients obtained from a typescript of clippings collected by Ada Gleason Bush. Document nos. 14, 15, and 22, Gleason file. CCHS.

Graham, Frances W., and Georgeanna M. Gardenier. *1874–1894: Two Decades — A History of the First Twenty Years' Work of the Woman's Christian Temperance Union of the State of New York.* Oswego, 1894.

Grand Concert for the Benefit of the Industrial School. March 26, 1894. CCHS.

Hamilton, Gail. "The Gentleman of Genesis." *Independent,* November 13, 1873.

——. "A Soul Saved." *Independent,* January 1, 1874.

Higginson, Thomas Wentworth. "The American Lecture System." *Macmillan's Magazine* 18 (May): 48–56.

"History of the Movement in Elmira." *Elmira Advertiser,* April 4, 1874. Steele Memorial Library. Elmira, New York.

Hooker, Alice. Letter to Isabella Beecher Hooker, February 8, 1867. SDF.

——. Letter to Isabella Beecher Hooker, February 24, 1867. SDF.

——. Letter to Isabella Beecher Hooker, April 14, 1867. SDF.

——. Letter to Isabella Beecher Hooker, September 28, 1867. SDF.

——. Letter to Isabella Beecher Hooker, January 19, 1868. SDF.

Hooker, Isabella Beecher. Letter to Samuel Clemens, May 3, 1883. MTP.

——. Letter to Alice Hooker, December 2, 1866. SDF.

——. Letter to Hon. Edwin Stanton, April 1863. SDF.

——. Letter to John Hooker, May 29, 1860. SDF.

——. Letter to John Hooker, July 15 and 16, 1860. SDF.

——. Letter to John Hooker, January 28, 1863. SDF.

——. Letter to John Hooker, March 7, 1863. SDF.

——. Letter to John Hooker, October 16, 1864. SDF.

"How To Be Happy." *The Water Cure Journal,* New York (March 1857): 55.

Industrial School and Free Kindergarten (1903). Pamphlet, CCHS.

Industrial School Appeal 1.2 (1884). Pamphlet, CCHS.

——. 4.3 (1887): 2. Pamphlet, CCHS.

Jeanne D'Arc Suffrage League. Letter to Samuel Clemens, January 6, 1910. MTP.

Jewett, Sarah Orne. "The Turtle Club." *Independent,* November 27, 1873.

"John B. Gough." *Elmira Advertiser,* April 1, 1874. Steele Memorial Library. Elmira, New York.

King, Grace. Letter to Olivia Langdon Clemens, December 26, 1899. John M. Coxe Private Collection. New Orleans, Louisiana.

——. "Mark Twain—Second Impression," ts. Department of Archives, Louisiana State University.

Langdon, Olivia Lewis. Diaries, January 1, 1865 and September 9, 1867. MTM.

——. Letter to Isabella Beecher Hooker, April 4, 1867. SDF.

Larned, Augusta. "Parson Fielder's Christmas Visit." *Independent,* December 24, 1868.

"Lecture Last Night." *Elmira Advertiser,* March 30, 1867. Steele Memorial Library. Elmira, New York.

Lewis, Mary Anne. Letter to Olivia Lewis Langdon, August 23, 1841. CCHS.

List of W.C.T.U. Crusaders, December 15, 1873, ts. Reed Library. Fredonia, New York.

Lyon, Isabel Van Kleek. Annotated copy of *Mark Twain's Autobiography.* MTP.

——. 1905 Daily Reminder. Vol. 2. MTP.

——. 1906 Daily Reminder. Original Copy. MTP.

——. 1907 Daily Reminder. MTP.

——. 1908 Daily Reminder. MTP.

——. 1903–6 Journal. MTP.

———. 1906–8 Notebook. MTP.

Mott, Lucretia, Susan B. Anthony, and Henry Blackwell. "First Anniversary." *Elmira Advertiser,* March 23, 1867. Steele Memorial Library. Elmira, New York.

Newton, J. R. *Elmira Advertiser,* November 26, 1864. Steele Memorial Library. Elmira, New York.

———. *The Modern Bethesda, or The Gift of Healing Restored.* Ed. A. E. Newton. New York: Newton Publishing Company, 1879.

New York Courier and Enquirer, July 14, 1849.

Nichols, Mary Gove. *Experience in Water-Cure.* New York: Fowler & Wells, 1850.

"Noble Donation." *Elmira Advertiser,* November 30, 1864. Steele Memorial Library. Elmira, New York.

Paff, Hattie Lewis. "What I Know About Mark Twain," ts. MTP.

Paine, Albert Bigelow. Letter to Isabel Lyon, January 28, 1908. MTP.

Palmer, Mrs. George Archibald. Ts., CCHS.

The Park Church Sunday School Liturgy. N.d., ms. The Park Church Library Archives, Elmira, New York.

Parker, Jenny Marsh. "The Culture of Pauperism." *Independent,* November 6, 1873.

Phelps, Elizabeth Stuart. "The Female Education of Women." *Independent,* November 13, 1873.

———. "A Word for the Silent." *Independent,* January 1, 1874.

"R." Ms., Beecher Family Papers. Williston Memorial Library. Mt. Holyoke College.

Register, Elmira Female College, 1857, ms. Center for Mark Twain Studies, Elmira, New York.

Register of the Elmira Female College, 1855–1859, ms. Center for Mark Twain Studies, Elmira, New York.

"Report of Finance Committee of Soldier's Relief Association." *Elmira Advertiser,* December 7, 1864. Steele Memorial Library. Elmira, New York.

Sanderson, Kenneth. Personal copy, prospectus: *Personal Memoirs of U.S. Grant.*

Schwinn, Walter K. "The House That Mark Built," ts. MTM.

Southern Tier Children's Home. Pamphlet, CCHS.

Street, Julian. Letter to Albert Bigelow Paine, January 2, 1912. MTP.

Taylor, Charles Fayette. "Kinesipathy, or the Movement Cure." *The Water-Cure Journal* (March 1857): 53–55.

———. *The Mechanical Treatment of Angular Curvature, or, Pott's Diseases of the Spine.* New York: Bailliere Brothers, 1865.

"Temperance." *Elmira Advertiser,* April 3, 1874. Steele Memorial Library. Elmira, New York.

"Temperance Headquarters." *Elmira Advertiser,* May 11, 1877. Steele Memorial Library. Elmira, New York.

"Temperance Lecture." *Elmira Advertiser,* December 5, 1864. Steele Memorial Library. Elmira, New York.

"Temperance Rally." *Elmira Advertiser,* February 23, 1880. Steele Memorial Library. Elmira, New York.

Thurston, Clarissa. *Elmira Seminary.* CCHS.

Towner, Ausburn. *Our County and Its People: A History of the Valley and County of Chemung.* Syracuse, N.Y.: D. Mason & Co., 1892.

Twain, Mark. *Adventures of Huckleberry Finn.* [1885]. Ed. Sculley Bradley. New York: W.W. Norton, 1977.

——. *The Autobiography of Mark Twain.* Ed. Charles Neider. London: Chatto & Windus, 1960.

——. "Boy's Manuscript." In *The Adventures of Tom Sawyer.* [1876]. Ed. John C. Gerber, Paul Baender, and Terry Firkins. Berkeley: University of California Press, 1980.

——. *The Complete Humorous Sketches and Tales of Mark Twain.* Ed. Charles Neider. New York: Doubleday, 1961.

——. *Europe and Elsewhere.* New York: Harper & Brothers, 1923.

——. "In Memoriam. Olivia Susan Clemens." *Harper's New Monthly Magazine* 95 (Nov. 1897): 929–30.

——. "Jane Lampton Clemens." *Huck Finn and Tom Sawyer Among the Indians and Other Unfinished Stories.* Berkeley: University of California Press, 1989.

——. *The Love Letters of Mark Twain.* Ed. Dixon Wecter. New York: Harper and Brothers, 1949.

——. *Mark Twain: Collected Tales, Sketches, Speeches, & Essays.* Ed. Louis J. Budd. New York: The Library of America, 1992.

——. *Mark Twain to Mrs. Fairbanks.* Ed. Dixon Wecter. San Marino, Calif.: Huntington Library, 1949.

——. *Mark Twain Speaking.* Ed. Paul Fatout. Iowa City: University of Iowa Press, 1976.

——. *Mark Twain's Autobiography.* Ed. Albert Bigelow Paine. 2 vols. New York: Harper and Brothers, 1924.

——. *Mark Twain's Correspondence with Henry Huttleston Rogers, 1893–1909.* Ed. Lewis Leary. Berkeley: University of California Press, 1969.

——. *Mark Twain's Fables of Man.* Ed. John S. Tuckey. Berkeley: University of California Press, 1972.

——. *Mark Twain-Howells Letters.* Ed. Henry Nash Smith and William M. Gibson. Cambridge, Mass.: Harvard University Press, 1960.

——. *Mark Twain in Eruption.* Ed. Bernard DeVoto. New York: Harper and Brothers, 1940.

——. *Mark Twain's Letters.* Ed. Albert Bigelow Paine. 2 vols. New York: Harper and Brothers, 1917.

——. *Mark Twain's Letters, 1853–1866.* Ed. Edgar Branch, Michael Frank and Kenneth Sanderson. Vol. 1. Berkeley: University of California Press, 1988.

——. *Mark Twain's Letters, 1867–1868.* Ed. Harriet Smith and Richard Bucci. Vol. 2. Berkeley: University of California Press, 1990.

——. *Mark Twain's Letters, 1869.* Ed. Victor Fischer and Michael Frank. Vol. 3. Berkeley: University of California Press, 1993.

——. *Mark Twain's Letters to Mary.* Ed. Lewis Leary. New York: Columbia University Press, 1961.

——. *Mark Twain's Letters to Will Bowen.* Ed. Theodore Hornberger. Austin: University of Texas Press, 1941.

——. *Mark Twain's Notebook.* [1935]. Ed. Albert Bigelow Paine. New York: Harper and Row, 1971.

——. *Mark Twain's Notebooks and Journals.* Ed. Frederick Anderson. Vol. 3. Berkeley: University of California Press, 1979.

——. *Mark Twain's Satires and Burlesques.* Ed. Franklin R. Rogers. Berkeley: University of California Press, 1967.

——. *Mark Twain's Travels with Mr. Brown.* Ed. Franklin Walker and B. Ezra Dane. New York: Russell & Russell, 1971.

——. "Memorial to Olivia Susan Clemens." MTP.

——. *My Dear Bro: A Letter from Samuel Clemens to His Brother Orion.* Berkeley, Calif.: The Berkeley Albion, 1961.

——. *Personal Recollections of Joan of Arc.* [1896]. San Francisco, Calif.: Ignatius Press, 1989.

——. *Roughing It.* [1872]. Berkeley: University of California Press, 1972.

——. *The Unabridged Mark Twain.* Ed. Lawrence Teacher. Philadelphia: Running Press, 1976.

Waterbury, Maria. *Seven Years Among the Freedmen.* Chicago, 1891.

Webster Interview with Isabel Lyon, January 5, 1950, ts. MTP.

Secondary Works Cited

Aldrich, [Lilian] Mrs. Thomas Bailey. *Crowding Memories.* Boston: Houghton Mifflin, 1920.

Aspiz, Harold. "Mark Twain and 'Doctor' Newton." *American Literature* 44 (1972): 130–36.

Baetzhold, Howard G. "Mark Twain's 'First Date' with Olivia Langdon." *Mark Twain Society Bulletin* 4.2 (1981): 5.

Baym, Nina. *Woman's Fiction: A Guide to Novels by and about Women in America, 1820–1870.* Ithaca, N.Y.: Cornell University Press, 1978.

Blair, Karen J. *The Clubwoman as Feminist.* New York: Holmes & Meier Publishers, 1980.

Bordin, Ruth. *Frances Willard: A Biography.* Chapel Hill: University of North Carolina Press, 1986.

——. *Women and Temperance: The Quest for Power and Liberty, 1873–1900.* Philadelphia: Temple University Press, 1981.

Boydston, Jeanne, Mary Kelley, and Anne Margolis, eds. *The Limits of Sisterhood.* Chapel Hill: University of North Carolina Press, 1988.

Branch, Edgar. *The Literary Apprenticeship of Mark Twain.* Urbana: University of Illinois Press, 1950.

Bray, Robert. "Mark Twain Biography. Entering a New Phase." *Midwest Quarterly* 15 (Spring 1974): 286–301.

Brooks, Van Wyck. *The Ordeal of Mark Twain.* New York: E.P. Dutton & Co., 1933.

Brumberg, Joan Jacobs. " 'Ruined' Girls: Changing Community Responses to Illegitimacy in Upstate New York, 1890–1920." *Journal of Social History* (1984): 247–72.

Budd, Louis. *Our Mark Twain: The Making of His Public Personality*. Philadelphia: University of Pennsylvania Press, 1983.

Bush, Robert. "Grace King and Mark Twain." *American Literature* 44 (March 1972): 31–51.

Byrne, Thomas. *Chemung County, New York, History, 1890–1975*. Elmira, N.Y.: Chemung County Historical Society, 1975.

Cardwell, Guy A. "The Bowdlerizing of Mark Twain." *ESQ/A Journal of the American Renaissance* 21 (1975): 179–93.

———. *The Man Who Was Mark Twain*. New Haven, Conn.: Yale University Press, 1991.

Carter, Paul. "The New Dynasty." *New England Quarterly* 30 (September 1957).

Cayleff, Susan. *Wash and Be Healed*. Philadelphia: Temple University Press, 1987.

Chester, Giraud. *Embattled Maiden: The Life of Anna Dickinson*. New York: Putnam, 1951.

Cooley, John, ed. *Mark Twain's Aquarium: The Samuel Clemens Angelfish Correspondence, 1905–1910*. Athens: University of Georgia Press, 1991.

Cotten, Michelle L., Herbert Wisbey Jr., and Robert D. Jerome. *Mark Twain's Elmira: 1870–1910*. Elmira, N.Y.: Chemung County Historical Society, 1985.

Coultrap-McQuin, Susan. *Doing Literary Business: American Women Writers in the Nineteenth Century*. Chapel Hill: University of North Carolina Press, 1990.

Cox, James M. *Mark Twain: The Fate of Humor*. Princeton, N.J.: Princeton University Press, 1966.

Crocker, Elizabeth L. *Yesterdays in and around Pomfret N.Y.* Vol. 3. Fredonia, N.Y., 1962.

DeVoto, Bernard. *Mark Twain at Work*. Cambridge, Mass.: Harvard University Press, 1942.

———. *Mark Twain's America*. Boston: Little, Brown and Co., 1932.

Douglas, Ann. *The Feminization of American Culture*. New York: Avon, 1977.

Emerson, Everett. *The Authentic Mark Twain: A Literary Biography of Samuel L. Clemens*. Philadelphia: University of Pennsylvania Press, 1984.

Endicott, Laura A. Letter to the author, December 18, 1991. University of Virginia Library. Special Collections Department.

Epstein, Cynthia Fuchs. *Deceptive Distinctions: Sex, Gender and the Social Order*. New Haven, Conn.: Yale University Press, 1989.

Faludi, Susan. *Backlash: The Undeclared War Against American Women*. New York: Crown Publishers, 1991.

Farrell, Grace. "Lillie Devereux Blake." Unpublished essay, 1993.

Foner, Philip S. *Mark Twain, Social Critic*. New York: International Publishers, 1966.

Fraiberg, Louis. "Van Wyck Brooks versus Mark Twain versus Samuel Clemens." *Psychoanalysis and American Literary Criticism*. Detroit, Mich.: Wayne State University Press, 1960.

Freedman, Estelle. *Their Sisters Keepers: Women's Prison Reform in America, 1830–1930*. Ann Arbor: University of Michigan Press, 1981.

Ganzel, Dewey. *Mark Twain Abroad: The Cruise of the Quaker City*. Chicago: University of Chicago Press, 1968.

Gerber, John C. "Mark Twain's Search for Identity." *Essays in American and English Literature*. Ed. Max Schulz. Athens: Ohio University Press, 1967.

Gilbert, Sandra M., and Susan Gubar. *The Madwoman in the Attic: Women Writers and the Nineteenth-Century Literary Imagination*. New Haven, Conn.: Yale University Press, 1979.

Gillman, Susan. *Dark Twins: Imposture and Identity in Mark Twain's America*. Chicago: University of Chicago Press, 1989.

Goad, Mary Ellen. "The Image and the Woman in the Life and Writings of Mark Twain." Master's thesis, Kansas State Teachers College, 1971.

Gratto, Michelle. "Elmira Industrial School." Unpublished essay, 1990. CCHS.

Gribben, Alan. "'I Did Wish Tom Sawyer Was There': Boy-Book Elements in Tom Sawyer and Huckleberry Finn." *One Hundred Years of Huckleberry Finn*. Ed. Robert Sattelmeyer and J. Donald Crowley. Columbia: University of Missouri Press, 1985.

——. "'It Is Unsatisfactory to Read to One's Self': Mark Twain's Informal Readings." *Quarterly Journal of Speech* 62 (1976): 49–56.

——. *Mark Twain's Library: A Reconstruction*. 2 vols. Boston: G.K. Hall, 1980.

Hardesty, Nancy A. *Women Called to Witness*. Nashville, Tenn.: Abingdon Press, 1984.

Hard-Mead, Kate Campbell. *Medical Women of America*. New York: Froben Press, 1933.

Harris, Susan K. "Mark Twain's Bad Women." *Studies in American Fiction* 13 (1985): 157–68.

——. *Mark Twain's Escape from Time: A Study of Patterns and Images*. Columbia: University of Missouri Press, 1982.

Henderson, Archibald. [1912]. *Mark Twain*. Philadelphia: Folcroft Press, Inc., 1969.

Hendler, Glenn. "The Limits of Sympathy: Louisa May Alcott and the Sentimental Novel." *American Literary History* 3 (Winter 1991): 685–706.

Hergesheimer, Joseph. "The Feminine Nuisance in American Literature." *Yale Review* 10 (July 1921): 716–25.

Hill, Hamlin. *Mark Twain and Elisha Bliss*. Columbia: University of Missouri Press, 1964.

——. *Mark Twain: God's Fool*. New York: Harper and Row, 1973.

Holmes, Clay. *The Elmira Prison Camp*. New York: Putnam, 1912.

Horigan, J. Michael. "Elmira Prison Camp — A Second Opinion." *Chemung Historical Journal* (March 1985): 3,449–57.

Howells, William Dean. *My Mark Twain: Reminiscences and Criticisms*. New York: Harper and Brothers Publishers, 1910.

James, Edward T., ed. *Notable American Women, 1607–1950: A Biographical Dictionary*. 3 vols. Cambridge, Mass.: Belknap Press of Harvard University Press, 1973.

Jerome, Robert D., and Herbert A. Wisbey, Jr., eds. *Mark Twain in Elmira*. Elmira, N.Y.: Mark Twain Society, 1977.

Kaplan, Justin. *Mr. Clemens and Mark Twain*. New York: Simon and Schuster, 1966.

Kelley, Howard A. *American Medical Biography*. Baltimore, Md.: Norman, Remington Company, 1920.

King, Grace. *Memories of a Southern Woman of Letters.* [1932]. New York: Books for Libraries Press, 1971.

Kirst, Sean. "Mark Twain's 'Honeymoon' with Fredonia Didn't Last Long." *Evening Observer,* March 30, 1981: 16.

Kiskis, Michael. "Susy Clemens as the Fire for Mark Twain's Autobiography." *Mid-Hudson Language Studies* 10 (1987): 43–50.

Krauth, Leland. "Mark Twain: The Victorian of Southwestern Humor." *American Literature* 54 (October 1982): 368–84.

Kubler-Ross, Elisabeth. *On Death and Dying.* New York: Macmillan, 1973.

Langdon, Ida. *Some Childhood Memories of Mr. and Mrs. Beecher in Their Later Years.* Private Printing. Elmira, N.Y.: Park Church, 1956.

Lanmon, Lorraine Welling. *Quarry Farm: A Study of the "Picturesque."* Elmira, N.Y.: Elmira College Center for Mark Twain Studies at Quarry Farm, 1991.

Lauter, Paul. *Canons and Contexts.* New York: Oxford University Press, 1991.

Lawton, Mary. *A Lifetime with Mark Twain.* New York: Haskell House, 1972.

Leary, Lewis, ed. *A Casebook on Mark Twain's Wound.* New York: Thomas Y. Crowell Company, 1962.

Lerner, Gerda. "The Challenge of Women's History." *The Majority Finds Its Past: Placing Women in History.* New York: Oxford University Press, 1979.

Long, E. Hudson, and J. R. LeMaster, eds. *The New Mark Twain Handbook.* New York: Garland Press, 1985.

Macnaughton, William R. *Mark Twain's Last Years as a Writer.* Columbia: University of Missouri Press, 1979.

Maik, Thomas A. *A Reexamination of Mark Twain's Joan of Arc.* New York: The Edwin Mellen Press, 1992.

Malone, Dumas, ed. *Dictionary of American Biography.* Vol. 8. New York: Scribner's, 1946.

Margolis, Anne Throne, ed. *The Isabella Beecher Hooker Project.* Hartford, Conn.: Stowe-Day Foundation, 1979.

Martin, Jay. "The Genie in the Bottle: Huckleberry Finn in Mark Twain's Life." *One Hundred Years of Huckleberry Finn.* Ed. Robert Sattelmeyer and J. Donald Crowley. Columbia: University of Missouri Press, 1985.

Melder, Keith. *Beginnings of Sisterhood.* New York: Schocken Books, 1977.

Meltzer, Gilbert. *The Beginnings of Elmira College.* Elmira, N.Y.: Commercial Press, 1941.

The Merck Manual of Diagnosis and Therapy. Rahway, N.J.: Merck, Sharp and Dohme Laboratories, 1987.

Myres, Sandra L. *Westering Women and the Frontier Experience, 1800–1915.* Albuquerque: University of New Mexico Press, 1982.

Neider, Charles, ed. *Papa: An Intimate Biography of Mark Twain.* New York: Doubleday, 1985.

Orcutt, William Dana. *Celebrities off Parade.* New York: Willett, Clark, 1935.

Paine, Albert Bigelow. *Mark Twain: A Biography.* 3 vols. New York: Harper and Brothers, 1912.

Peiss, Kathy. "Going Public: Women in Nineteenth-Century Cultural History." *American Literary History* 3 (Winter 1991): 817–28.

Quick, Dorothy. *Enchantment: A Little Girl's Friendship with Mark Twain*. Norman: University of Oklahoma Press, 1961.

Rather, Lois. *Bittersweet: Ambrose Bierce & Women*. Oakland, Calif.: Rather Press, 1975.

Rice, Dr. Clarence C. "What Mark Twain's Doctor Remembers/The Missouri Writer's Humor and Philosophy as Related in the Anecdotes of a Friend/Incidents in a Long Friendship with the Missouri Author and Humorist." *Twainian* 33 (July–August 1974): 1–3.

Roy, Thomas M. "Pott's Disease in Kentucky: Diagnosis and Treatment." *Journal of the Kentucky Medical Association* 86 (September 1988): 499–502.

Schwartz, Richard W. *John Harvey Kellogg, M.D.* Nashville, Tenn.: Southern Publishing Association, 1970.

Scott, Anne Firor. *Natural Allies: Women's Associations in American History*. Chicago: University of Illinois Press, 1991.

Sedden, Herbert J. "The Choice of Treatment in Pott's Disease." *Journal of Bone and Joint Surgery* 58-B, no. 4 (November 1976): 395–97.

Shands, Alfred R., M.D. "Charles Fayette Taylor and His Times — 1827 to 1899." *Surgery, Gynecology and Obstetrics* 143 (November 1976): 811–13.

Sharlow, Gretchen. "The Cranes of Quarry Farm." Unpublished ms., Elmira College, 1990.

Sharlow, Gretchen, ed. *Glimpses: Elmira and Mark Twain*. Elmira, N.Y.: Elmira College, 1988.

Showalter, Elaine. *A Literature of Their Own*. Princeton, N.J.: Princeton University Press, 1977.

Simpson, Alan, and Mary Simpson. *Jean Webster, Storyteller*. Tymor Associates, 1984.

Skandera, Laura. "Letters from Hollywood." *Mark Twain Circular* 1, no. 2 (1987): 1–3.

Sklar, Kathryn Kish. "All Hail to Pure Cold Water." In *Women and Health in America*. Ed. Judith Walzer Leavitt. Madison: University of Wisconsin Press, 1984.

Sorin, Gretchen Sullivan. "The Black Community in Elmira." *A Heritage Uncovered: The Black Experience in Upstate New York, 1800–1925*. Ed. Cara Sutherland. Elmira, N.Y.: Chemung County Historical Society, 1988.

Stowe, Lyman Beecher. *Saints, Sinners and Beechers*. Indianapolis, Ind.: Bobbs-Merrill Company, 1934.

Swanbrow, Diane. "The Lost Legacy of Mark Twain." *Los Angeles Times Magazine* 10 (May 1987): 16–19, 32.

Taylor, Barbara Wiggans. "Education in the Life of Olivia Langdon Clemens to 1870." Master's thesis, Elmira College, 1991.

Taylor, Eva, and Frances Myers. *A History of Park Church: 1846–1981*. Private Printing, 1981.

Taylor, Helen. *Gender, Race, and Region in the Writings of Grace King, Ruth McEnery Stuart, and Kate Chopin*. Baton Rouge: Louisiana State University Press, 1989.

Trumble, Hugh C. "Tuberculosis of the Spine: Early Diagnosis and Treatment." *The Medical Journal of Australia* (August 21, 1926): 238–44.

Wagenknecht, Edward. *Mark Twain: The Man and His Work*. 3rd ed. Norman: University of Oklahoma Press, 1971.

Warren, Joyce W. "Old Ladies and Little Girls." *The American Narcissus: Individualism and Women in Nineteenth-Century American Fiction*. New Brunswick, N.J.: Rutgers University Press, 1984.

Waterbury, Maria. *Seven Years Among the Freedmen*. Chicago, 1891.

Webster, Samuel Charles. *Mark Twain, Business Man*. Boston: Little, Brown and Co., 1946.

Wecter, Dixon. *Sam Clemens of Hannibal*. Boston: Houghton Mifflin, 1952.

Weiss, Harry B. *The Great American Water-Cure Craze*. Trenton, N.J.: The Past Times Press, 1967.

White, Barbara A. "Lillie Devereux Blake." *American Women Writers: A Critical Reference Guide from Colonial Times to the Present*. 2 vols. Ed. Langdon Lynne Faust. New York: Frederick Ungar Publishing Co., 1983.

Willis, Resa. *Mark and Livy: The Love Story of Mark Twain and the Woman Who Almost Tamed Him*. New York: Atheneum, 1992.

———. "'Quietly and Steadily': Olivia Langdon Clemens's Commonplace Book." *Mark Twain Journal* 24, no. 1 (1986): 17–20.

Wisbey, Herbert. "Olivia Clemens Studied at Elmira College." *Mark Twain Society Bulletin* 2, no. 2 (1979): 7–8.

———. "One Hundred Years Ago: Mark Twain in Elmira in 1893." *Mark Twain Society Bulletin* 16, no. 2 (1993): 6–7.

Young, James Harvey. "Anna Dickinson, Mark Twain, and Bret Harte." *The Pennsylvania Magazine of History and Biography* 76 (January 1952): 39–46.

Index

This book has been set in Linotron Galliard. Galliard was designed for Mergenthaler in 1978 by Matthew Carter. Galliard retains many of the features of a sixteenth-century typeface cut by Robert Granjon but has some modifications that give it a more contemporary look.

Printed on acid-free paper.